ISBN 0-8373-3882-4

C-3882   **CAREER EXAMINATION SERIES**

*This is your
PASSBOOK® for...*

Building Permits Examiner

Test Preparation Study Guide

Questions & Answers

EAST NORTHPORT PUBLIC LIBRARY
EAST NORTHPORT, NEW YORK

NLC

NATIONAL LEARNING CORPORATION

Copyright © 2016 by

National Learning Corporation

212 Michael Drive, Syosset, New York 11791

All rights reserved, including the right of reproduction in whole or in part, in any form or by any means, electronic or mechanical, including photocopying, recording, or by any information storage and retrieval system, without permission in writing from the Publisher.

(516) 921-8888
(800) 645-6337
FAX: (516) 921-8743
www.passbooks.com
sales @ passbooks.com
info @ passbooks.com

PRINTED IN THE UNITED STATES OF AMERICA

PASSBOOK®
NOTICE

This book is SOLELY intended for, is sold ONLY to, and its use is RESTRICTED to *individual*, bona fide applicants or candidates who qualify by virtue of having seriously filed applications for appropriate license, certificate, professional and/or promotional advancement, higher school matriculation, scholarship, or other legitimate requirements of educational and/or governmental authorities.

This book is NOT intended for use, class instruction, tutoring, training, duplication, copying, reprinting, excerption, or adaptation, etc., by:

(1) Other publishers

(2) Proprietors and/or Instructors of "Coaching" and/or Preparatory Courses

(3) Personnel and/or Training Divisions of commercial, industrial, and governmental organizations

(4) Schools, colleges, or universities and/or their departments and staffs, including teachers and other personnel

(5) Testing Agencies or Bureaus

(6) Study groups which seek by the purchase of a single volume to copy and/or duplicate and/or adapt this material for use by the group as a whole without having purchased individual volumes for each of the members of the group

(7) Et al.

Such persons would be in violation of appropriate Federal and State statutes.

PROVISION OF LICENSING AGREEMENTS. — Recognized educational commercial, industrial, and governmental institutions and organizations, and others legitimately engaged in educational pursuits, including training, testing, and measurement activities, may address a request for a licensing agreement to the copyright owners, who will determine whether, and under what conditions, including fees and charges, the materials in this book may be used by them. In other words, a licensing facility exists for the legitimate use of the material in this book on other than an individual basis. However, it is asseverated and affirmed here that the material in this book *CANNOT* be used without the receipt of the express permission of such a licensing agreement from the Publishers.

NATIONAL LEARNING CORPORATION
212 Michael Drive
Syosset, New York 11791

Inquiries re licensing agreements should be addressed to:
The President
National Learning Corporation
212 Michael Drive
Syosset, New York 11791

PASSBOOK® SERIES

THE *PASSBOOK® SERIES* has been created to prepare applicants and candidates for the ultimate academic battlefield – the examination room.

At some time in our lives, each and every one of us may be required to take an examination – for validation, matriculation, admission, qualification, registration, certification, or licensure.

Based on the assumption that every applicant or candidate has met the basic formal educational standards, has taken the required number of courses, and read the necessary texts, the *PASSBOOK® SERIES* furnishes the one special preparation which may assure passing with confidence, instead of failing with insecurity. Examination questions – together with answers – are furnished as the basic vehicle for study so that the mysteries of the examination and its compounding difficulties may be eliminated or diminished by a sure method.

This book is meant to help you pass your examination provided that you qualify and are serious in your objective.

The entire field is reviewed through the huge store of content information which is succinctly presented through a provocative and challenging approach – the question-and-answer method.

A climate of success is established by furnishing the correct answers at the end of each test.

You soon learn to recognize types of questions, forms of questions, and patterns of questioning. You may even begin to anticipate expected outcomes.

You perceive that many questions are repeated or adapted so that you can gain acute insights, which may enable you to score many sure points.

You learn how to confront new questions, or types of questions, and to attack them confidently and work out the correct answers.

You note objectives and emphases, and recognize pitfalls and dangers, so that you may make positive educational adjustments.

Moreover, you are kept fully informed in relation to new concepts, methods, practices, and directions in the field.

You discover that you are actually taking the examination all the time: you are preparing for the examination by "taking" an examination, not by reading extraneous and/or supererogatory textbooks.

In short, this PASSBOOK®, used directedly, should be an important factor in helping you to pass your test.

BUILDING PERMITS EXAMINER

DUTIES
An employee in this class reviews, approves and issues building permits for a municipality. The incumbent serves as a liaison with other governmental agencies which review permits and develop regulations that may affect the use of property. Responsibility is included for issuing permits after ensuring that application material is complete, or for disapproving applications with specific references to the non-conforming usage. Performs related work as required.

SCOPE OF THE EXAMINATION
The written test will be designed to test for knowledge, skills, and/or abilities in such areas as:
1. Understanding and interpreting building plans and requirements;
2. Principles of zoning inspection, site plan interpretation and related laws and codes;
3. Principles of site and landscape design, including sidewalks, parking, soils, plantings and other related materials;
4. Organizing data into tables and records; and
5. Understanding and interpreting written material.

HOW TO TAKE A TEST

I. YOU MUST PASS AN EXAMINATION

A. WHAT EVERY CANDIDATE SHOULD KNOW

Examination applicants often ask us for help in preparing for the written test. What can I study in advance? What kinds of questions will be asked? How will the test be given? How will the papers be graded?

As an applicant for a civil service examination, you may be wondering about some of these things. Our purpose here is to suggest effective methods of advance study and to describe civil service examinations.

Your chances for success on this examination can be increased if you know how to prepare. Those "pre-examination jitters" can be reduced if you know what to expect. You can even experience an adventure in good citizenship if you know why civil service exams are given.

B. WHY ARE CIVIL SERVICE EXAMINATIONS GIVEN?

Civil service examinations are important to you in two ways. As a citizen, you want public jobs filled by employees who know how to do their work. As a job seeker, you want a fair chance to compete for that job on an equal footing with other candidates. The best-known means of accomplishing this two-fold goal is the competitive examination.

Exams are widely publicized throughout the nation. They may be administered for jobs in federal, state, city, municipal, town or village governments or agencies.

Any citizen may apply, with some limitations, such as the age or residence of applicants. Your experience and education may be reviewed to see whether you meet the requirements for the particular examination. When these requirements exist, they are reasonable and applied consistently to all applicants. Thus, a competitive examination may cause you some uneasiness now, but it is your privilege and safeguard.

C. HOW ARE CIVIL SERVICE EXAMS DEVELOPED?

Examinations are carefully written by trained technicians who are specialists in the field known as "psychological measurement," in consultation with recognized authorities in the field of work that the test will cover. These experts recommend the subject matter areas or skills to be tested; only those knowledges or skills important to your success on the job are included. The most reliable books and source materials available are used as references. Together, the experts and technicians judge the difficulty level of the questions.

Test technicians know how to phrase questions so that the problem is clearly stated. Their ethics do not permit "trick" or "catch" questions. Questions may have been tried out on sample groups, or subjected to statistical analysis, to determine their usefulness.

Written tests are often used in combination with performance tests, ratings of training and experience, and oral interviews. All of these measures combine to form the best-known means of finding the right person for the right job.

II. HOW TO PASS THE WRITTEN TEST

A. NATURE OF THE EXAMINATION

To prepare intelligently for civil service examinations, you should know how they differ from school examinations you have taken. In school you were assigned certain definite pages to read or subjects to cover. The examination questions were quite detailed and usually emphasized memory. Civil service exams, on the other hand, try to discover your present ability to perform the duties of a position, plus your potentiality to learn these duties. In other words, a civil service exam attempts to predict how successful you will be. Questions cover such a broad area that they cannot be as minute and detailed as school exam questions.

In the public service similar kinds of work, or positions, are grouped together in one "class." This process is known as *position-classification*. All the positions in a class are paid according to the salary range for that class. One class title covers all of these positions, and they are all tested by the same examination.

B. FOUR BASIC STEPS

1) Study the announcement

How, then, can you know what subjects to study? Our best answer is: "Learn as much as possible about the class of positions for which you've applied." The exam will test the knowledge, skills and abilities needed to do the work.

Your most valuable source of information about the position you want is the official exam announcement. This announcement lists the training and experience qualifications. Check these standards and apply only if you come reasonably close to meeting them.

The brief description of the position in the examination announcement offers some clues to the subjects which will be tested. Think about the job itself. Review the duties in your mind. Can you perform them, or are there some in which you are rusty? Fill in the blank spots in your preparation.

Many jurisdictions preview the written test in the exam announcement by including a section called "Knowledge and Abilities Required," "Scope of the Examination," or some similar heading. Here you will find out specifically what fields will be tested.

2) Review your own background

Once you learn in general what the position is all about, and what you need to know to do the work, ask yourself which subjects you already know fairly well and which need improvement. You may wonder whether to concentrate on improving your strong areas or on building some background in your fields of weakness. When the announcement has specified "some knowledge" or "considerable knowledge," or has used adjectives like "beginning principles of…" or "advanced … methods," you can get a clue as to the number and difficulty of questions to be asked in any given field. More questions, and hence broader coverage, would be included for those subjects which are more important in the work. Now weigh your strengths and weaknesses against the job requirements and prepare accordingly.

3) Determine the level of the position

Another way to tell how intensively you should prepare is to understand the level of the job for which you are applying. Is it the entering level? In other words, is this the position in which beginners in a field of work are hired? Or is it an intermediate or advanced level? Sometimes this is indicated by such words as "Junior" or "Senior" in the class title. Other jurisdictions use Roman numerals to designate the level – Clerk I, Clerk II, for example. The word "Supervisor" sometimes appears in the title. If the level is not indicated by the title, check the description of duties. Will you be working under very close supervision, or will you have responsibility for independent decisions in this work?

4) Choose appropriate study materials

Now that you know the subjects to be examined and the relative amount of each subject to be covered, you can choose suitable study materials. For beginning level jobs, or even advanced ones, if you have a pronounced weakness in some aspect of your training, read a modern, standard textbook in that field. Be sure it is up to date and has general coverage. Such books are normally available at your library, and the librarian will be glad to help you locate one. For entry-level positions, questions of appropriate difficulty are chosen – neither highly advanced questions, nor those too simple. Such questions require careful thought but not advanced training.

If the position for which you are applying is technical or advanced, you will read more advanced, specialized material. If you are already familiar with the basic principles of your field, elementary textbooks would waste your time. Concentrate on advanced textbooks and technical periodicals. Think through the concepts and review difficult problems in your field.

These are all general sources. You can get more ideas on your own initiative, following these leads. For example, training manuals and publications of the government agency which employs workers in your field can be useful, particularly for technical and professional positions. A letter or visit to the government department involved may result in more specific study suggestions, and certainly will provide you with a more definite idea of the exact nature of the position you are seeking.

III. KINDS OF TESTS

Tests are used for purposes other than measuring knowledge and ability to perform specified duties. For some positions, it is equally important to test ability to make adjustments to new situations or to profit from training. In others, basic mental abilities not dependent on information are essential. Questions which test these things may not appear as pertinent to the duties of the position as those which test for knowledge and information. Yet they are often highly important parts of a fair examination. For very general questions, it is almost impossible to help you direct your study efforts. What we can do is to point out some of the more common of these general abilities needed in public service positions and describe some typical questions.

1) General information

Broad, general information has been found useful for predicting job success in some kinds of work. This is tested in a variety of ways, from vocabulary lists to questions about current events. Basic background in some field of work, such as sociology or economics, may be sampled in a group of questions. Often these are principles which have become familiar to most persons through exposure rather than through formal training. It is difficult to advise you how to study for these questions; being alert to the world around you is our best suggestion.

2) Verbal ability

An example of an ability needed in many positions is verbal or language ability. Verbal ability is, in brief, the ability to use and understand words. Vocabulary and grammar tests are typical measures of this ability. Reading comprehension or paragraph interpretation questions are common in many kinds of civil service tests. You are given a paragraph of written material and asked to find its central meaning.

3) Numerical ability

Number skills can be tested by the familiar arithmetic problem, by checking paired lists of numbers to see which are alike and which are different, or by interpreting charts and graphs. In the latter test, a graph may be printed in the test booklet which you are asked to use as the basis for answering questions.

4) Observation

A popular test for law-enforcement positions is the observation test. A picture is shown to you for several minutes, then taken away. Questions about the picture test your ability to observe both details and larger elements.

5) Following directions

In many positions in the public service, the employee must be able to carry out written instructions dependably and accurately. You may be given a chart with several columns, each column listing a variety of information. The questions require you to carry out directions involving the information given in the chart.

6) Skills and aptitudes

Performance tests effectively measure some manual skills and aptitudes. When the skill is one in which you are trained, such as typing or shorthand, you can practice. These tests are often very much like those given in business school or high school courses. For many of the other skills and aptitudes, however, no short-time preparation can be made. Skills and abilities natural to you or that you have developed throughout your lifetime are being tested.

Many of the general questions just described provide all the data needed to answer the questions and ask you to use your reasoning ability to find the answers. Your best preparation for these tests, as well as for tests of facts and ideas, is to be at your physical and mental best. You, no doubt, have your own methods of getting into an exam-taking mood and keeping "in shape." The next section lists some ideas on this subject.

IV. KINDS OF QUESTIONS

Only rarely is the "essay" question, which you answer in narrative form, used in civil service tests. Civil service tests are usually of the short-answer type. Full instructions for answering these questions will be given to you at the examination. But in case this is your first experience with short-answer questions and separate answer sheets, here is what you need to know:

1) Multiple-choice Questions

Most popular of the short-answer questions is the "multiple choice" or "best answer" question. It can be used, for example, to test for factual knowledge, ability to solve problems or judgment in meeting situations found at work.

A multiple-choice question is normally one of three types—
- It can begin with an incomplete statement followed by several possible endings. You are to find the one ending which *best* completes the statement, although some of the others may not be entirely wrong.
- It can also be a complete statement in the form of a question which is answered by choosing one of the statements listed.

- It can be in the form of a problem – again you select the best answer.

Here is an example of a multiple-choice question with a discussion which should give you some clues as to the method for choosing the right answer:

When an employee has a complaint about his assignment, the action which will *best* help him overcome his difficulty is to
- A. discuss his difficulty with his coworkers
- B. take the problem to the head of the organization
- C. take the problem to the person who gave him the assignment
- D. say nothing to anyone about his complaint

In answering this question, you should study each of the choices to find which is best. Consider choice "A" – Certainly an employee may discuss his complaint with fellow employees, but no change or improvement can result, and the complaint remains unresolved. Choice "B" is a poor choice since the head of the organization probably does not know what assignment you have been given, and taking your problem to him is known as "going over the head" of the supervisor. The supervisor, or person who made the assignment, is the person who can clarify it or correct any injustice. Choice "C" is, therefore, correct. To say nothing, as in choice "D," is unwise. Supervisors have and interest in knowing the problems employees are facing, and the employee is seeking a solution to his problem.

2) True/False Questions

The "true/false" or "right/wrong" form of question is sometimes used. Here a complete statement is given. Your job is to decide whether the statement is right or wrong.

SAMPLE: A roaming cell-phone call to a nearby city costs less than a non-roaming call to a distant city.

This statement is wrong, or false, since roaming calls are more expensive.
This is not a complete list of all possible question forms, although most of the others are variations of these common types. You will always get complete directions for answering questions. Be sure you understand *how* to mark your answers – ask questions until you do.

V. RECORDING YOUR ANSWERS

Computer terminals are used more and more today for many different kinds of exams.
For an examination with very few applicants, you may be told to record your answers in the test booklet itself. Separate answer sheets are much more common. If this separate answer sheet is to be scored by machine – and this is often the case – it is highly important that you mark your answers correctly in order to get credit.
An electronic scoring machine is often used in civil service offices because of the speed with which papers can be scored. Machine-scored answer sheets must be marked with a pencil, which will be given to you. This pencil has a high graphite content which responds to the electronic scoring machine. As a matter of fact, stray dots may register as answers, so do not let your pencil rest on the answer sheet while you are pondering the correct answer. Also, if your pencil lead breaks or is otherwise defective, ask for another.

Since the answer sheet will be dropped in a slot in the scoring machine, be careful not to bend the corners or get the paper crumpled.

The answer sheet normally has five vertical columns of numbers, with 30 numbers to a column. These numbers correspond to the question numbers in your test booklet. After each number, going across the page are four or five pairs of dotted lines. These short dotted lines have small letters or numbers above them. The first two pairs may also have a "T" or "F" above the letters. This indicates that the first two pairs only are to be used if the questions are of the true-false type. If the questions are multiple choice, disregard the "T" and "F" and pay attention only to the small letters or numbers.

Answer your questions in the manner of the sample that follows:

32. The largest city in the United States is
    A. Washington, D.C.
    B. New York City
    C. Chicago
    D. Detroit
    E. San Francisco

1) Choose the answer you think is best. (New York City is the largest, so "B" is correct.)
2) Find the row of dotted lines numbered the same as the question you are answering. (Find row number 32)
3) Find the pair of dotted lines corresponding to the answer. (Find the pair of lines under the mark "B.")
4) Make a solid black mark between the dotted lines.

VI. BEFORE THE TEST

Common sense will help you find procedures to follow to get ready for an examination. Too many of us, however, overlook these sensible measures. Indeed, nervousness and fatigue have been found to be the most serious reasons why applicants fail to do their best on civil service tests. Here is a list of reminders:

- Begin your preparation early – Don't wait until the last minute to go scurrying around for books and materials or to find out what the position is all about.
- Prepare continuously – An hour a night for a week is better than an all-night cram session. This has been definitely established. What is more, a night a week for a month will return better dividends than crowding your study into a shorter period of time.
- Locate the place of the exam – You have been sent a notice telling you when and where to report for the examination. If the location is in a different town or otherwise unfamiliar to you, it would be well to inquire the best route and learn something about the building.
- Relax the night before the test – Allow your mind to rest. Do not study at all that night. Plan some mild recreation or diversion; then go to bed early and get a good night's sleep.
- Get up early enough to make a leisurely trip to the place for the test – This way unforeseen events, traffic snarls, unfamiliar buildings, etc. will not upset you.
- Dress comfortably – A written test is not a fashion show. You will be known by number and not by name, so wear something comfortable.

- Leave excess paraphernalia at home – Shopping bags and odd bundles will get in your way. You need bring only the items mentioned in the official notice you received; usually everything you need is provided. Do not bring reference books to the exam. They will only confuse those last minutes and be taken away from you when in the test room.
- Arrive somewhat ahead of time – If because of transportation schedules you must get there very early, bring a newspaper or magazine to take your mind off yourself while waiting.
- Locate the examination room – When you have found the proper room, you will be directed to the seat or part of the room where you will sit. Sometimes you are given a sheet of instructions to read while you are waiting. Do not fill out any forms until you are told to do so; just read them and be prepared.
- Relax and prepare to listen to the instructions
- If you have any physical problem that may keep you from doing your best, be sure to tell the test administrator. If you are sick or in poor health, you really cannot do your best on the exam. You can come back and take the test some other time.

VII. AT THE TEST

The day of the test is here and you have the test booklet in your hand. The temptation to get going is very strong. Caution! There is more to success than knowing the right answers. You must know how to identify your papers and understand variations in the type of short-answer question used in this particular examination. Follow these suggestions for maximum results from your efforts:

1) Cooperate with the monitor
The test administrator has a duty to create a situation in which you can be as much at ease as possible. He will give instructions, tell you when to begin, check to see that you are marking your answer sheet correctly, and so on. He is not there to guard you, although he will see that your competitors do not take unfair advantage. He wants to help you do your best.

2) Listen to all instructions
Don't jump the gun! Wait until you understand all directions. In most civil service tests you get more time than you need to answer the questions. So don't be in a hurry. Read each word of instructions until you clearly understand the meaning. Study the examples, listen to all announcements and follow directions. Ask questions if you do not understand what to do.

3) Identify your papers
Civil service exams are usually identified by number only. You will be assigned a number; you must not put your name on your test papers. Be sure to copy your number correctly. Since more than one exam may be given, copy your exact examination title.

4) Plan your time
Unless you are told that a test is a "speed" or "rate of work" test, speed itself is usually not important. Time enough to answer all the questions will be provided, but this does not mean that you have all day. An overall time limit has been set. Divide the total time (in minutes) by the number of questions to determine the approximate time you have for each question.

5) Do not linger over difficult questions

If you come across a difficult question, mark it with a paper clip (useful to have along) and come back to it when you have been through the booklet. One caution if you do this – be sure to skip a number on your answer sheet as well. Check often to be sure that you have not lost your place and that you are marking in the row numbered the same as the question you are answering.

6) Read the questions

Be sure you know what the question asks! Many capable people are unsuccessful because they failed to *read* the questions correctly.

7) Answer all questions

Unless you have been instructed that a penalty will be deducted for incorrect answers, it is better to guess than to omit a question.

8) Speed tests

It is often better NOT to guess on speed tests. It has been found that on timed tests people are tempted to spend the last few seconds before time is called in marking answers at random – without even reading them – in the hope of picking up a few extra points. To discourage this practice, the instructions may warn you that your score will be "corrected" for guessing. That is, a penalty will be applied. The incorrect answers will be deducted from the correct ones, or some other penalty formula will be used.

9) Review your answers

If you finish before time is called, go back to the questions you guessed or omitted to give them further thought. Review other answers if you have time.

10) Return your test materials

If you are ready to leave before others have finished or time is called, take ALL your materials to the monitor and leave quietly. Never take any test material with you. The monitor can discover whose papers are not complete, and taking a test booklet may be grounds for disqualification.

VIII. EXAMINATION TECHNIQUES

1) Read the general instructions carefully. These are usually printed on the first page of the exam booklet. As a rule, these instructions refer to the timing of the examination; the fact that you should not start work until the signal and must stop work at a signal, etc. If there are any *special* instructions, such as a choice of questions to be answered, make sure that you note this instruction carefully.

2) When you are ready to start work on the examination, that is as soon as the signal has been given, read the instructions to each question booklet, underline any key words or phrases, such as *least*, *best*, *outline*, *describe* and the like. In this way you will tend to answer as requested rather than discover on reviewing your paper that you *listed without describing*, that you selected the *worst* choice rather than the *best* choice, etc.

3) If the examination is of the objective or multiple-choice type – that is, each question will also give a series of possible answers: A, B, C or D, and you are called upon to select the best answer and write the letter next to that answer on your answer paper – it is advisable to start answering each question in turn. There may be anywhere from 50 to 100 such questions in the three or four hours allotted and you can see how much time would be taken if you read through all the questions before beginning to answer any. Furthermore, if you come across a question or group of questions which you know would be difficult to answer, it would undoubtedly affect your handling of all the other questions.

4) If the examination is of the essay type and contains but a few questions, it is a moot point as to whether you should read all the questions before starting to answer any one. Of course, if you are given a choice – say five out of seven and the like – then it is essential to read all the questions so you can eliminate the two that are most difficult. If, however, you are asked to answer all the questions, there may be danger in trying to answer the easiest one first because you may find that you will spend too much time on it. The best technique is to answer the first question, then proceed to the second, etc.

5) Time your answers. Before the exam begins, write down the time it started, then add the time allowed for the examination and write down the time it must be completed, then divide the time available somewhat as follows:
   - If 3-1/2 hours are allowed, that would be 210 minutes. If you have 80 objective-type questions, that would be an average of 2-1/2 minutes per question. Allow yourself no more than 2 minutes per question, or a total of 160 minutes, which will permit about 50 minutes to review.
   - If for the time allotment of 210 minutes there are 7 essay questions to answer, that would average about 30 minutes a question. Give yourself only 25 minutes per question so that you have about 35 minutes to review.

6) The most important instruction is to *read each question* and make sure you know what is wanted. The second most important instruction is to *time yourself properly* so that you answer every question. The third most important instruction is to *answer every question*. Guess if you have to but include something for each question. Remember that you will receive no credit for a blank and will probably receive some credit if you write something in answer to an essay question. If you guess a letter – say "B" for a multiple-choice question – you may have guessed right. If you leave a blank as an answer to a multiple-choice question, the examiners may respect your feelings but it will not add a point to your score. Some exams may penalize you for wrong answers, so in such cases *only*, you may not want to guess unless you have some basis for your answer.

7) Suggestions
   a. Objective-type questions
      1. Examine the question booklet for proper sequence of pages and questions
      2. Read all instructions carefully
      3. Skip any question which seems too difficult; return to it after all other questions have been answered
      4. Apportion your time properly; do not spend too much time on any single question or group of questions

5. Note and underline key words – *all, most, fewest, least, best, worst, same, opposite,* etc.
6. Pay particular attention to negatives
7. Note unusual option, e.g., unduly long, short, complex, different or similar in content to the body of the question
8. Observe the use of "hedging" words – *probably, may, most likely,* etc.
9. Make sure that your answer is put next to the same number as the question
10. Do not second-guess unless you have good reason to believe the second answer is definitely more correct
11. Cross out original answer if you decide another answer is more accurate; do not erase until you are ready to hand your paper in
12. Answer all questions; guess unless instructed otherwise
13. Leave time for review

b. Essay questions
1. Read each question carefully
2. Determine exactly what is wanted. Underline key words or phrases.
3. Decide on outline or paragraph answer
4. Include many different points and elements unless asked to develop any one or two points or elements
5. Show impartiality by giving pros and cons unless directed to select one side only
6. Make and write down any assumptions you find necessary to answer the questions
7. Watch your English, grammar, punctuation and choice of words
8. Time your answers; don't crowd material

8) Answering the essay question

Most essay questions can be answered by framing the specific response around several key words or ideas. Here are a few such key words or ideas:

M's: manpower, materials, methods, money, management
P's: purpose, program, policy, plan, procedure, practice, problems, pitfalls, personnel, public relations

a. Six basic steps in handling problems:
1. Preliminary plan and background development
2. Collect information, data and facts
3. Analyze and interpret information, data and facts
4. Analyze and develop solutions as well as make recommendations
5. Prepare report and sell recommendations
6. Install recommendations and follow up effectiveness

b. Pitfalls to avoid
1. *Taking things for granted* – A statement of the situation does not necessarily imply that each of the elements is necessarily true; for example, a complaint may be invalid and biased so that all that can be taken for granted is that a complaint has been registered

2. *Considering only one side of a situation* – Wherever possible, indicate several alternatives and then point out the reasons you selected the best one
3. *Failing to indicate follow up* – Whenever your answer indicates action on your part, make certain that you will take proper follow-up action to see how successful your recommendations, procedures or actions turn out to be
4. *Taking too long in answering any single question* – Remember to time your answers properly

IX. AFTER THE TEST

Scoring procedures differ in detail among civil service jurisdictions although the general principles are the same. Whether the papers are hand-scored or graded by machine we have described, they are nearly always graded by number. That is, the person who marks the paper knows only the number – never the name – of the applicant. Not until all the papers have been graded will they be matched with names. If other tests, such as training and experience or oral interview ratings have been given, scores will be combined. Different parts of the examination usually have different weights. For example, the written test might count 60 percent of the final grade, and a rating of training and experience 40 percent. In many jurisdictions, veterans will have a certain number of points added to their grades.

After the final grade has been determined, the names are placed in grade order and an eligible list is established. There are various methods for resolving ties between those who get the same final grade – probably the most common is to place first the name of the person whose application was received first. Job offers are made from the eligible list in the order the names appear on it. You will be notified of your grade and your rank as soon as all these computations have been made. This will be done as rapidly as possible.

People who are found to meet the requirements in the announcement are called "eligibles." Their names are put on a list of eligible candidates. An eligible's chances of getting a job depend on how high he stands on this list and how fast agencies are filling jobs from the list.

When a job is to be filled from a list of eligibles, the agency asks for the names of people on the list of eligibles for that job. When the civil service commission receives this request, it sends to the agency the names of the three people highest on this list. Or, if the job to be filled has specialized requirements, the office sends the agency the names of the top three persons who meet these requirements from the general list.

The appointing officer makes a choice from among the three people whose names were sent to him. If the selected person accepts the appointment, the names of the others are put back on the list to be considered for future openings.

That is the rule in hiring from all kinds of eligible lists, whether they are for typist, carpenter, chemist, or something else. For every vacancy, the appointing officer has his choice of any one of the top three eligibles on the list. This explains why the person whose name is on top of the list sometimes does not get an appointment when some of the persons lower on the list do. If the appointing officer chooses the second or third eligible, the No. 1 eligible does not get a job at once, but stays on the list until he is appointed or the list is terminated.

X. HOW TO PASS THE INTERVIEW TEST

The examination for which you applied requires an oral interview test. You have already taken the written test and you are now being called for the interview test – the final part of the formal examination.

You may think that it is not possible to prepare for an interview test and that there are no procedures to follow during an interview. Our purpose is to point out some things you can do in advance that will help you and some good rules to follow and pitfalls to avoid while you are being interviewed.

What is an interview supposed to test?

The written examination is designed to test the technical knowledge and competence of the candidate; the oral is designed to evaluate intangible qualities, not readily measured otherwise, and to establish a list showing the relative fitness of each candidate – as measured against his competitors – for the position sought. Scoring is not on the basis of "right" and "wrong," but on a sliding scale of values ranging from "not passable" to "outstanding." As a matter of fact, it is possible to achieve a relatively low score without a single "incorrect" answer because of evident weakness in the qualities being measured.

Occasionally, an examination may consist entirely of an oral test – either an individual or a group oral. In such cases, information is sought concerning the technical knowledges and abilities of the candidate, since there has been no written examination for this purpose. More commonly, however, an oral test is used to supplement a written examination.

Who conducts interviews?

The composition of oral boards varies among different jurisdictions. In nearly all, a representative of the personnel department serves as chairman. One of the members of the board may be a representative of the department in which the candidate would work. In some cases, "outside experts" are used, and, frequently, a businessman or some other representative of the general public is asked to serve. Labor and management or other special groups may be represented. The aim is to secure the services of experts in the appropriate field.

However the board is composed, it is a good idea (and not at all improper or unethical) to ascertain in advance of the interview who the members are and what groups they represent. When you are introduced to them, you will have some idea of their backgrounds and interests, and at least you will not stutter and stammer over their names.

What should be done before the interview?

While knowledge about the board members is useful and takes some of the surprise element out of the interview, there is other preparation which is more substantive. It *is* possible to prepare for an oral interview – in several ways:

1) Keep a copy of your application and review it carefully before the interview

This may be the only document before the oral board, and the starting point of the interview. Know what education and experience you have listed there, and the sequence and dates of all of it. Sometimes the board will ask you to review the highlights of your experience for them; you should not have to hem and haw doing it.

2) Study the class specification and the examination announcement

Usually, the oral board has one or both of these to guide them. The qualities, characteristics or knowledges required by the position sought are stated in these documents. They offer valuable clues as to the nature of the oral interview. For example, if the job involves supervisory responsibilities, the announcement will usually indicate that knowledge of modern supervisory methods and the qualifications of the candidate as a supervisor will be tested. If so, you can expect such questions, frequently in the form of a hypothetical situation which you are expected to solve. NEVER go into an oral without knowledge of the duties and responsibilities of the job you seek.

3) **Think through each qualification required**
Try to visualize the kind of questions you would ask if you were a board member. How well could you answer them? Try especially to appraise your own knowledge and background in each area, *measured against the job sought*, and identify any areas in which you are weak. Be critical and realistic – do not flatter yourself.

4) **Do some general reading in areas in which you feel you may be weak**
For example, if the job involves supervision and your past experience has NOT, some general reading in supervisory methods and practices, particularly in the field of human relations, might be useful. Do NOT study agency procedures or detailed manuals. The oral board will be testing your understanding and capacity, not your memory.

5) **Get a good night's sleep and watch your general health and mental attitude**
You will want a clear head at the interview. Take care of a cold or any other minor ailment, and of course, no hangovers.

What should be done on the day of the interview?
Now comes the day of the interview itself. Give yourself plenty of time to get there. Plan to arrive somewhat ahead of the scheduled time, particularly if your appointment is in the fore part of the day. If a previous candidate fails to appear, the board might be ready for you a bit early. By early afternoon an oral board is almost invariably behind schedule if there are many candidates, and you may have to wait. Take along a book or magazine to read, or your application to review, but leave any extraneous material in the waiting room when you go in for your interview. In any event, relax and compose yourself.

The matter of dress is important. The board is forming impressions about you – from your experience, your manners, your attitude, and your appearance. Give your personal appearance careful attention. Dress your best, but not your flashiest. Choose conservative, appropriate clothing, and be sure it is immaculate. This is a business interview, and your appearance should indicate that you regard it as such. Besides, being well groomed and properly dressed will help boost your confidence.

Sooner or later, someone will call your name and escort you into the interview room. *This is it.* From here on you are on your own. It is too late for any more preparation. But remember, you asked for this opportunity to prove your fitness, and you are here because your request was granted.

What happens when you go in?
The usual sequence of events will be as follows: The clerk (who is often the board stenographer) will introduce you to the chairman of the oral board, who will introduce you to the other members of the board. Acknowledge the introductions before you sit down. Do not be surprised if you find a microphone facing you or a stenotypist sitting by. Oral interviews are usually recorded in the event of an appeal or other review.

Usually the chairman of the board will open the interview by reviewing the highlights of your education and work experience from your application – primarily for the benefit of the other members of the board, as well as to get the material into the record. Do not interrupt or comment unless there is an error or significant misinterpretation; if that is the case, do not hesitate. But do not quibble about insignificant matters. Also, he will usually ask you some question about your education, experience or your present job – partly to get you to start talking and to establish the interviewing "rapport." He may start the actual questioning, or turn it over to one of the other members. Frequently, each member undertakes the questioning on a particular area, one in which he is perhaps most competent, so you can expect each member to participate in the examination. Because time is limited, you may also expect some rather abrupt switches in the direction the questioning takes, so do not be upset by it. Normally, a board member will not pursue a single line of questioning unless he discovers a particular strength or weakness.

After each member has participated, the chairman will usually ask whether any member has any further questions, then will ask you if you have anything you wish to add. Unless you are expecting this question, it may floor you. Worse, it may start you off on an extended, extemporaneous speech. The board is not usually seeking more information. The question is principally to offer you a last opportunity to present further qualifications or to indicate that you have nothing to add. So, if you feel that a significant qualification or characteristic has been overlooked, it is proper to point it out in a sentence or so. Do not compliment the board on the thoroughness of their examination – they have been sketchy, and you know it. If you wish, merely say, "No thank you, I have nothing further to add." This is a point where you can "talk yourself out" of a good impression or fail to present an important bit of information. Remember, *you close the interview yourself.*

The chairman will then say, "That is all, Mr. _____, thank you." Do not be startled; the interview is over, and quicker than you think. Thank him, gather your belongings and take your leave. Save your sigh of relief for the other side of the door.

How to put your best foot forward

Throughout this entire process, you may feel that the board individually and collectively is trying to pierce your defenses, seek out your hidden weaknesses and embarrass and confuse you. Actually, this is not true. They are obliged to make an appraisal of your qualifications for the job you are seeking, and they want to see you in your best light. Remember, they must interview all candidates and a non-cooperative candidate may become a failure in spite of their best efforts to bring out his qualifications. Here are 15 suggestions that will help you:

1) Be natural – Keep your attitude confident, not cocky

If you are not confident that you can do the job, do not expect the board to be. Do not apologize for your weaknesses, try to bring out your strong points. The board is interested in a positive, not negative, presentation. Cockiness will antagonize any board member and make him wonder if you are covering up a weakness by a false show of strength.

2) Get comfortable, but don't lounge or sprawl

Sit erectly but not stiffly. A careless posture may lead the board to conclude that you are careless in other things, or at least that you are not impressed by the importance of the occasion. Either conclusion is natural, even if incorrect. Do not fuss with your clothing, a pencil or an ashtray. Your hands may occasionally be useful to emphasize a point; do not let them become a point of distraction.

3) Do not wisecrack or make small talk

This is a serious situation, and your attitude should show that you consider it as such. Further, the time of the board is limited – they do not want to waste it, and neither should you.

4) Do not exaggerate your experience or abilities

In the first place, from information in the application or other interviews and sources, the board may know more about you than you think. Secondly, you probably will not get away with it. An experienced board is rather adept at spotting such a situation, so do not take the chance.

5) If you know a board member, do not make a point of it, yet do not hide it

Certainly you are not fooling him, and probably not the other members of the board. Do not try to take advantage of your acquaintanceship – it will probably do you little good.

6) Do not dominate the interview

Let the board do that. They will give you the clues – do not assume that you have to do all the talking. Realize that the board has a number of questions to ask you, and do not try to take up all the interview time by showing off your extensive knowledge of the answer to the first one.

7) Be attentive

You only have 20 minutes or so, and you should keep your attention at its sharpest throughout. When a member is addressing a problem or question to you, give him your undivided attention. Address your reply principally to him, but do not exclude the other board members.

8) Do not interrupt

A board member may be stating a problem for you to analyze. He will ask you a question when the time comes. Let him state the problem, and wait for the question.

9) Make sure you understand the question

Do not try to answer until you are sure what the question is. If it is not clear, restate it in your own words or ask the board member to clarify it for you. However, do not haggle about minor elements.

10) Reply promptly but not hastily

A common entry on oral board rating sheets is "candidate responded readily," or "candidate hesitated in replies." Respond as promptly and quickly as you can, but do not jump to a hasty, ill-considered answer.

11) Do not be peremptory in your answers

A brief answer is proper – but do not fire your answer back. That is a losing game from your point of view. The board member can probably ask questions much faster than you can answer them.

12) Do not try to create the answer you think the board member wants

He is interested in what kind of mind you have and how it works – not in playing games. Furthermore, he can usually spot this practice and will actually grade you down on it.

13) Do not switch sides in your reply merely to agree with a board member

Frequently, a member will take a contrary position merely to draw you out and to see if you are willing and able to defend your point of view. Do not start a debate, yet do not surrender a good position. If a position is worth taking, it is worth defending.

14) Do not be afraid to admit an error in judgment if you are shown to be wrong

The board knows that you are forced to reply without any opportunity for careful consideration. Your answer may be demonstrably wrong. If so, admit it and get on with the interview.

15) Do not dwell at length on your present job

The opening question may relate to your present assignment. Answer the question but do not go into an extended discussion. You are being examined for a *new* job, not your present one. As a matter of fact, try to phrase ALL your answers in terms of the job for which you are being examined.

Basis of Rating

Probably you will forget most of these "do's" and "don'ts" when you walk into the oral interview room. Even remembering them all will not ensure you a passing grade. Perhaps you did not have the qualifications in the first place. But remembering them will help you to put your best foot forward, without treading on the toes of the board members.

Rumor and popular opinion to the contrary notwithstanding, an oral board wants you to make the best appearance possible. They know you are under pressure – but they also want to see how you respond to it as a guide to what your reaction would be under the pressures of the job you seek. They will be influenced by the degree of poise you display, the personal traits you show and the manner in which you respond.

ABOUT THIS BOOK

This book contains tests divided into Examination Sections. Go through each test, answering every question in the margin. We have also attached a sample answer sheet at the back of the book that can be removed and used. At the end of each test look at the answer key and check your answers. On the ones you got wrong, look at the right answer choice and learn. Do not fill in the answers first. Do not memorize the questions and answers, but understand the answer and principles involved. On your test, the questions will likely be different from the samples. Questions are changed and new ones added. If you understand these past questions you should have success with any changes that arise. Tests may consist of several types of questions. We have additional books on each subject should more study be advisable or necessary for you. Finally, the more you study, the better prepared you will be. This book is intended to be the last thing you study before you walk into the examination room. Prior study of relevant texts is also recommended. NLC publishes some of these in our Fundamental Series. Knowledge and good sense are important factors in passing your exam. Good luck also helps. So now study this Passbook, absorb the material contained within and take that knowledge into the examination. Then do your best to pass that exam.

EXAMINATION SECTION

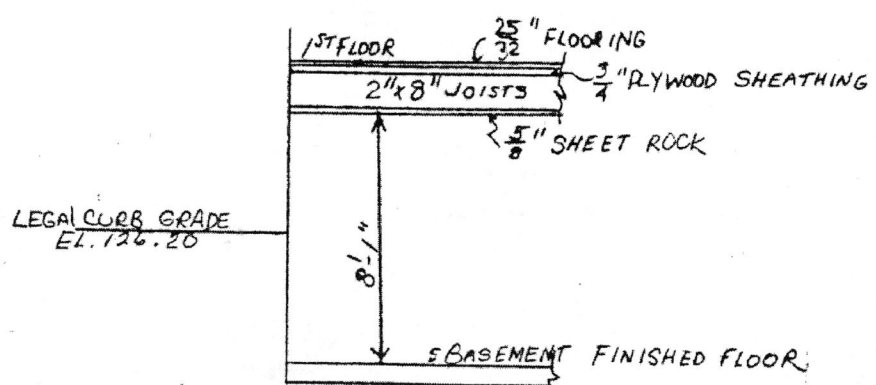

EXAMINATION SECTION
TEST 1

DIRECTIONS: Each question or incomplete statement is followed by several suggested answers or completions. Select the one that BEST answers the question or completes the statement. *PRINT THE LETTER OF THE CORRECT ANSWER IN THE SPACE AT THE RIGHT.*

1. Assume that a two story building measures 21'6" x 53'7". It is in a district that calls for an open space ratio of .80. The required open space on this lot must be *most nearly* square feet.

    A. 922   B. 1152   C. 1843   D. 2880

    1.____

2. Assume that the elevation at the back of a lot is 127.36 ft. and the elevation at the front of the same lot is 125.49 ft.
   The difference in elevation between front and back of the lot is *most nearly*

    A. 1'10 1/8"   B. 1'10 1/4"   C. 1'10 3/8"   D. 1'10 1/2"

    2.____

3. The sketch below represents the lowest story of a new building. In order for this story to be considered a basement, the elevation of the first floor must be AT LEAST

    A. 131.09   B. 131.14   C. 131.19   D. 131.24

    3.____

4. The MOST important requirement of a good report is that it should be

    A. properly addressed   B. clear and concise
    C. verbose   D. spelled correctly

    4.____

5. Of the following, in determining whether a violation should be referred for court action, the MOST important item that should be considered is

    A. the amount of available time you have to process the case
    B. the availability of the inspector
    C. whether or not the owner has indicated a desire to cooperate with the department
    D. whether or not the case is important enough to warrant court action

    5.____

2 (#1)

6. In the Zoning Resolution, the size of required side yards would be found in the chapters on

   A. Use Groups
   B. Bulk Regulations
   C. Area Districts
   D. District Boundaries

   6.___

7. According to the Zoning Resolution, the one of the following that is NOT considered part of the floor area of a building is a(n)

   A. basement
   B. stairwell at floor level
   C. penthouse
   D. attached garage on 1st floor

   7.___

8. The one of the following that is permitted by the Zoning Resolution as a home occupation is

   A. veterinary medicine
   B. real estate broker
   C. teaching of music
   D. public relations agency

   8.___

9. For the purpose of determining the number of rooms in a dwelling unit, the Zoning Resolution adds an arbitrary number to the number of *living rooms*.
   Where there are six or less living rooms, this arbitrary number is

   A. 1/2
   B. 1
   C. 1 1/2
   D. 2

   9.___

10. Assuming the following signs are all 10 square feet in area, the one that is NOT subject to the provisions of the Zoning Resolution is one indicating

    A. a freight entrance to a building
    B. a fund drive for a civic organization
    C. vacancies in an apartment building
    D. a parking area at the rear of a structure

    10.___

11. On a plan, the symbol ⟨symbol⟩ represents

    A. earth
    B. wood
    C. metal lath
    D. marble

    11.___

12. On a plan, ⟨symbol⟩ the symbol represents

    A. cinder
    B. brick
    C. plywood
    D. rock lath and plaster

    12.___

13. On a plan, the symbol ⟨symbol⟩ represents

    A. glass
    B. asphalt shingles
    C. concrete
    D. porcelain enamel

    13.___

14. A corbel is a form of

    A. cricket
    B. crown molding
    C. cantilever
    D. curtain wall

15. In balloon type framing, the second floor joists rest on a

    A. sole plate
    B. ribband
    C. header
    D. sill

16. Condensation of moisture in inadequately ventilated attics or roof spaces is usually GREATEST in

    A. summer B. autumn C. winter D. spring

17. Of the following combinations of tread and riser, the one that would be acceptable for required stairs in either a new office building or a multiple dwelling is

    A. 9 1/4", 7 1/2"
    B. 9 1/2", 7 1/4"
    C. 9 1/2", 7 3/4"
    D. 10", 8"

18. A meeting rail is a common part of a

    A. door frame
    B. window sash
    C. stairwell
    D. bulkhead

19. If doors in an old building do not close, it is MOST probably an indication that the

    A. frames have shrunk
    B. building has settled
    C. hinges were not set properly
    D. wood used for the doors are of inferior grade

20. Cracks in concrete are not necessarily caused by settlement of a structure. Sometimes they are caused by

    A. shrinkage
    B. curing
    C. hydration
    D. over-troweling

KEY (CORRECT ANSWERS)

1. C
2. D
3. A
4. B
5. C

6. B
7. D
8. C
9. C
10. B

11. A
12. B
13. A
14. C
15. B

16. C
17. C
18. B
19. B
20. A

TEST 2

DIRECTIONS: Each question or incomplete statement is followed by several suggested answers or completions. Select the one that BEST answers the question or completes the statement. *PRINT THE LETTER OF THE CORRECT ANSWER IN THE SPACE AT THE RIGHT.*

1. Required exit doors from a room must open in the direction of egress when the room is occupied by more than _____ persons.   1._____
   A. 15   B. 25   C. 35   D. 50

2. A window in a masonry wall on a lot line   2._____
   A. is not permitted
   B. must have a fire resistive rating of 3/4 hour
   C. must have a fire resistive rating of 1 hour
   D. must have a fire resistive rating of 1 1/2 hours

3. Air entrained concrete is required in all cases for   3._____
   A. garage floors   B. footings
   C. grade beams   D. columns

4. A parapet wall or railing would be required on new non-residential structures where the height of the structure is greater than (give lowest height specified by law) _____ feet.   4._____
   A. 15   B. 19   C. 22   D. 25

5. Of the following statements, the one that is CORRECT is that wood joists may   5._____
   A. not be supported on a fire wall
   B. be supported on a fire wall only if fireproofed wall is used
   C. be supported on a fire wall only if they are separated from each other by at least 4 inches of solid masonry
   D. be supported on a fire wall only if they are separated from each other by at least 12 inches of solid masonry

6. A foundation wall below grade may be of hollow block only if the building   6._____
   A. is a residence
   B. is no more than one story high
   C. is of frame construction
   D. has no cellar or basement

7. The Building Code specifies that lintels are required to be fire-proofed when the opening is more than _____ feet.   7._____
   A. 3   B. 4   C. 5   D. 6

8. In a 12-inch brick wall, the MAXIMUM permitted depth of a chase is   8._____
   A. none   B. 4"   C. 6"   D. 8"

9. Wood joists should clear flues and chimneys by at least   9._____
   A. 1"   B. 2"   C. 3"   D. 4"

10. Fire retarding or enclosure in shafts of all vent ducts are required when they

    A. go through more than one floor
    B. are used for intake as well as exhaust
    C. are more than 144 square inches in area
    D. are in rooms subdivided with wood partitions

11. Assume a builder is unable to complete the pour for a continuous concrete floor slab. The slab is supported by beams and girders.
    The construction joint should be made at a point

    A. over a beam
    B. one quarter of the span length from the beam
    C. one third of the span length from the beam
    D. midway between beams

12. Under required stairs in a Class 3 building,

    A. it is unlawful to locate a closet
    B. a closet is permitted provided that the stringers are fire retarded
    C. a closet is permitted provided that the closet is completely lined with incombustible material
    D. a closet is permitted provided that fireproof wood is used to frame out the closet

13. In New York City, the exit provisions of the State Labor Law apply

    A. only to factories
    B. to factories and warehouses
    C. to factories, warehouses, and restaurants
    D. to all types of uses

14. A Class 3 building, two stories high, may have required stairs enclosed with stud partitions fire retarded with gypsum boards unless the building is used for a

    A. factory
    B. storage warehouse
    C. bowling alley
    D. department store

15. The one of the following rooms in a *place of assembly* that is required to be sprinklered is a

    A. performer's dressing room
    B. kitchen
    C. service pantry
    D. waiting room

16. Of the following, the FIRST operation in the demolition of a building is the

    A. shoring of the adjoining buildings
    B. erection of railings around stairwells
    C. removal of windows
    D. venting of the roof

17. As used in the Building Code, *consistency* of concrete refers to

    A. composition
    B. water-cement ratio
    C. relative plasticity
    D. proportion of aggregates

18. One condition that is required for a building to be considered a *Special Occupancy Structure* is that the building is used for   18.____

    A. a theater
    B. a church
    C. a restaurant
    D. motor vehicle repairs

19. A wire glass vision panel on a door opening into a fire tower is   19.____

    A. not permitted
    B. permitted if the panel has a fire rating of 3/4 hour
    C. permitted if the panel has a fire rating of 3/4 hour and is less than 100 square inches in area
    D. permitted if the panel has a fire rating of 3/4 hour, is less than 100 square inches in area, and is glazed with two thicknesses of wire glass with an air space between

20. One of the requirements that must be met before untreated wood can be used as a subdividing partition in a Class 1 building is that the partition   20.____

    A. be no more than 8 feet high
    B. enclose an area less than 200 square feet in size
    C. enclose office space only
    D. be made of a single thickness of wood

KEY (CORRECT ANSWERS)

1.	D	11.	D
2.	B	12.	C
3.	A	13.	A
4.	C	14.	C
5.	C	15.	A
6.	D	16.	C
7.	B	17.	C
8.	B	18.	A
9.	D	19.	A
10.	A	20.	D

TEST 3

DIRECTIONS: Each question or incomplete statement is followed by several suggested answers or completions. Select the one that BEST answers the question or completes the statement. *PRINT THE LETTER OF THE CORRECT ANSWER IN THE SPACE AT THE RIGHT.*

1. There are two criteria required for determining whether a multiple dwelling shall be classified as a *converted dwelling*.
   The FIRST is the number of families originally occupying the dwelling, and the second is the

   A. conjunctive uses
   B. date of erection of the building
   C. classification, whether Class A or B
   D. number of families now occupying the dwelling

2. According to the Multiple Dwelling Law, a *dinette* is NOT considered a living room if its area is _____ sq. ft. or less.

   A. 50   B. 55   C. 59   D. 64

3. Where a building faces only one street, the curb level used for measuring the height of the building is the

   A. lowest curb level in front of the building
   B. highest curb level in front of the building
   C. level of the curb at the center of the front of the building
   D. average of the levels of the lowest and highest curb level in front of the building

4. According to the Multiple Dwelling Code, one of the living rooms in each apartment of a newly created multiple dwelling shall have a MINIMUM floor area of _____ square feet.

   A. 59   B. 110   C. 150   D. 175

5. It is proposed to alter an old law tenement so as to increase the number of apartments. Of the following, the one that MOST completely gives the requirements to be met before the alteration can be approved is: Each new apartment must be provided a

   A. water closet
   B. water closet and a wash basin
   C. water closet, a wash basin, and a bath or shower
   D. water closet, a wash basin, a bath or shower, and centrally supplied heat

6. Gas fueled space heaters may be permitted in lieu of centrally supplied heat.
   One of the following conditions required before the use of space heaters can be permitted is that

   A. each apartment has no more than two living rooms
   B. the building is a Class A multiple dwelling
   C. all apartments are used for single room occupancy
   D. D, the gas line supplying the heater be connected directly to the main so that the tenant cannot control the flow of gas

7. An incinerator is required in all multiple

   A. dwellings
   B. dwellings four or more stories in height
   C. dwellings four or more stories in height and occupied by more than twelve families
   D. dwellings four or more stories in height occupied by more than twelve families and erected after October 1, 1951

8. Tests of required sprinkler systems in a single room occupancy building must be made

   A. monthly
   B. quarterly
   C. semi-annually
   D. annually

9. An additional apartment may be created on the first floor of a Class A frame converted dwelling provided that no more than two families will occupy this floor and

   A. the entrance hall is sprinklered
   B. the building is brick veneered
   C. there is no basement occupancy
   D. all stairs are enclosed in one hour fire partitions

10. The MAIN feature differentiating a *five tower* from a *fire stair* is the

    A. fire rating of the enclosure walls
    B. use to which the fire tower is put
    C. method of entering the fire tower from the building
    D. height of the fire tower

11. A new elevator shaft is to be built into a non-fireproof multiple dwelling. Of the following materials, the one that has the lowest fire resistance that would be acceptable for the enclosure walls of this shaft is

    A. 3" solid gypsum block
    B. 2" x 4" studs with 5/8" fire code 60 each side
    C. steel studs, wire mesh and 3/4" P.C. plaster
    D. 4" hollow concrete blocks, plastered both sides

12. Of the following statements, the one that is MOST complete and accurate is that a frame extension 70 sq. ft. in area added to a frame multiple dwelling is

    A. not permitted
    B. permitted only if the walls of the extension are brick filled
    C. permitted only if the walls of the extension are brick filled and the extension is to be used solely for bathrooms
    D. permitted only if the walls of the extension are brick filled, the extension is to be used solely for bathrooms and the walls are at least 3 ft. from the side lot lines

13. Assume it is proposed to extend a business use in a non-fireproof multiple dwelling by erecting an extension at the rear of the building.
    The roof the extension is required to be fireproof

    A. in all cases
    B. when the business use requires a combustible occupancy permit
    C. when there are fire escapes above the extension
    D. if the business use is a factory

14. In a Class A dwelling, two water closets may

    A. be placed in one compartment only in old law tenements
    B. be placed in one compartment in either old law or new law tenements
    C. be placed in one compartment in all types of apartment houses
    D. not be placed in one compartment

15. According to the Multiple Dwelling Law, a janitor is NOT required when the maximum number of families occupying the dwelling is

    A. 6   B. 9   C. 12   D. 15

16. The first floor above the lowest cellar in a non-fireproof multiple dwelling does NOT have to be fireproof if

    A. the cellar is used only for incombustible storage
    B. there are two means of egress from the cellar
    C. the building is no more than three stories in height
    D. the dwelling is occupied by no more than nine families

17. In a converted multiple dwelling, ventilation of a room on the top story may be obtained by

    A. a skylight
    B. a duct with a wind blown hood
    C. a duct with an electrically operated fan
    D. by a window only and no other method is acceptable

18. It is proposed to build a closet under the stairs leading to the second floor in a non-fireproof *new law* tenement. This is

    A. not permitted
    B. permitted only if the entire closet is built of non-combustible materials
    C. permitted only if the closet is used for non-combustible storage
    D. permitted if the closet is built of fire-retarded partitions and the soffit of the stairs is also fire-retarded

19. For multiple dwellings erected after April 18, 1929, a ladder from a fire escape to a roof is NOT required when

    A. the building is three stories or less in height
    B. the roof is built of incombustible material
    C. the fire escape is on the front of the building
    D. there is no safe access from the roof to another building

20. It is proposed to convert a Class B multiple dwelling used for summer resort occupancy to year-round Class B use. This conversion is

    A. illegal
    B. legal provided the exits comply with the requirements for Class B use
    C. legal provided the exits and toilet facilities comply with the requirements for Class B use
    D. legal provided the exits, toilet facilities, and ventilation requirements comply with the requirements for Class B use

KEY (CORRECT ANSWERS)

1.	B		11.	A
2.	B		12.	A
3.	C		13.	C
4.	C		14.	A
5.	D		15.	C
6.	B		16.	C
7.	D		17.	A
8.	D		18.	A
9.	B		19.	C
10.	C		20.	A

EXAMINATION SECTION
TEST 1

DIRECTIONS: Each question or incomplete statement is followed by several suggested answers or completions. Select the one that BEST answers the question or completes the statement. *PRINT THE LETTER OF THE CORRECT ANSWER IN THE SPACE AT THE RIGHT.*

1. The basis of differentiating between a *Class A* and a *Class B* multiple dwelling is   1._____

   A. the date when the building was erected
   B. the size of the building
   C. whether residents are permanent or transient
   D. the number of families living in the building

2. The basis of differentiating between a *cellar* and a *basement* is   2._____

   A. whether or not there are windows
   B. the relationship of its height to curb level
   C. the ventilation available
   D. the number of exists provided

3. The MINIMUM horizontal dimension permitted for a living room in an apartment house erected after 1929 is   3._____

   A. 8'0"   B. 8'6"   C. 9'0"   D. 9'6"

4. It is proposed to build a garage for two cars for use by the tenants in a three-family dwelling. The garage will be on the same lot as the dwelling.   4._____
   Of the following, the statement that MOST completely gives the type or types of construction that would be permitted for the garage is _____ with concrete roof.

   A. frame or block walls with flat wood roof or block walls with wood peak roof, or block walls
   B. block walls with flat wood roof or block walls with wood peak roof or block walls
   C. block walls with wood peak roof or block walls
   D. block walls

5. A restaurant is permitted in a hotel of non-fireproof construction providing that   5._____

   A. there are automatic sprinkler heads in the kitchen
   B. there are two means of egress from the kitchen
   C. the kitchen has windows opening to a required yard
   D. the walls of the kitchen have one hour fire rating

6. The one of the following that is considered a *living room* is a   6._____

   A. bathroom   B. foyer
   C. public room   D. kitchen

7. In certain types of occupancies, gas-fueled space heaters may be used instead of a central heating system. One of the requirements that MUST be met in order that space heaters be permitted in an apartment is that the   7._____

A. building be of fireproof construction
B. apartment must consist of two or more living rooms
C. building is not a tenement
D. apartment has two means of egress

8. Where a parapet wall is required, the MINIMUM height permitted is

   A. 3'0" B. 3'6" C. 4'0" D. 4'6"

9. Ceilings over boilers in converted dwellings MUST be fire-retarded with

   A. two layers of 3/8" sheet rock
   B. wire lath and 3/4" cement mortar
   C. 3/8" rock lath and 1/2" gypsum mortar
   D. 3/8" sheet rock with #26 U.S. gage stamped metal

10. A fire alarm signal is required in all multiple dwellings which have the following type of occupancy:

    A. tenement   B. hotel
    C. converted dwelling D. single room

11. The multiple dwelling law requires that every living room be ventilated by windows having an area of at least 10% of the floor surface of the room. Assume that a certain living room is 10'6" long by 9'6" wide.
    Of the following, the MINIMUM window size that would be acceptable is

    A. 3'2" x 3'6"   B. 3'4" x 3'6"
    C. 3'4" x 3'8"   D. 3'6" x 3'8"

12. The multiple dwelling law specifies the minimum area and height of living rooms. The PRINCIPAL reason for this is to

    A. insure adequate light and air
    B. make inspections easier
    C. reduce possibility of serious fires
    D. control the number of occupants

13. The one of the following that is considered a multiple dwelling when located in a building separate from other buildings is a

    A. jail   B. monastery
    C. nurses' residence D. asylum

14. When any part of a building is to be fire-retarded, that part of the building MUST be protected by materials having a fire rating of at least _____ hour(s).

    A. 1 B. 2 C. 3 D. 4

15. A *fire damper* is necessary to

    A. adjust the draft in a chimney
    B. wet down combustible material in case of fire
    C. prevent the passage of heat and smoke through an air duct
    D. control the flame in an incinerator

Questions 16-18.

DIRECTIONS: Questions 16 through 18 must be answered in accordance with the following paragraph.

When constructed within a multiple dwelling, such storage space shall be equipped with a sprinkler system and also with a system of mechanical ventilation in no way connected with any other ventilating system. Such storage space shall have no opening into any other part of the dwelling except through a fireproof vestibule. Any such vestibule shall have a minimum superficial floor area of fifty square feet and its maximum area shall not exceed seventy-five square feet. It shall be enclosed with incombustible partitions having a fire-resistive rating of three hours. The floor and ceiling of such vestibule shall also be of incombustible material having a fire-resistive rating of at least three hours. There shall be two doors to provide access from the dwelling to the car storage space. Each such door shall have a fire-resistive rating of one and one-half hours and shall be provided with a device to prevent the opening of one door until the other door is entirely closed.

16. According to the above paragraph, the one of the following that is REQUIRED in order for cars to be permitted to be stored in a multiple dwelling is a(n)   16._____

    A. fireproof vestibule
    B. elevator from the garage
    C. approved heating system
    D. sprinkler system

17. According to the above paragraph, the one of the following materials that would NOT be acceptable for the walls of a vestibule connecting a garage to the dwelling portion of a building is   17._____

    A. 3" solid gypsum blocks
    B. 4" brick
    C. 4" hollow gypsum blocks, plastered both sides
    D. 6" solid cinder concrete blocks

18. According to the above paragraph, the one of the following that would be ACCEPTABLE for the width and length of a vestibule connecting a garage that is within a multiple dwelling to the dwelling portion of the building is   18._____

    A. 3'8" x 13'0"   B. 4'6" x 18'6"
    C. 4'9" x 14'6"   D. 4'3" x 19'3"

Questions 19-20.

DIRECTIONS: Questions 19 and 20 must be answered in accordance with the following paragraph.

It shall be unlawful to place, use, or to maintain in a condition intended, arranged or designed for use, any gas-fired cooking appliance, laundry stove, heating stove, range or water heater or combination of such appliances in any room or space used for living or sleeping in any new or existing multiple dwelling unless such room or space has a window opening to the outer air or such gas appliance is vented to the outer air. All automatically operated gas appliances shall be equipped with a device which shall shut off automatically the gas supply to the main burners when the pilot light in such appliance is extinguished. A gas range or the cooking portion of a gas appliance incorporating a room heater shall not be deemed an automatically operated gas appliance. However, burners in gas ovens and broilers which can be turned on and off or ignited by non-manual means shall be equipped with a device which shall shut off automatically the gas supply to those burners when the operation of such non-manual means fails.

19. According to the above paragraph, an automatic shut-off device is NOT required on a gas

    A. hot water heater
    B. laundry drier
    C. space heater
    D. range

20. According to the above paragraph, a gas-fired water heater is permitted

    A. only in kitchens
    B. only in bathrooms
    C. only in living rooms
    D. in any type of room

21. A tenant tells an inspector that the spring on the entrance door to his apartment is broken and the door remains open.
    Of the following, the BEST action for the inspector to take, after verifying the facts, is to

    A. tell the tenant to get the janitor to fix it
    B. tell the janitor to get it fixed
    C. tell the landlord to hire someone to fix it
    D. report it as a violation and tell the janitor to get it fixed

22. An owner of a two-family house tells you, an inspector, that he wants to convert his house to a three-family dwelling. He asks you for your advice as to the requirements that must be met for this change.
    You should

    A. inspect the building so that you can give him all the necessary information
    B. refer him to your supervisor for fuller advice
    C. tell him to consult a competent architect
    D. tell him you can't give him the information unless he gives you the plans of the building to check

23. An inspector receiving a complaint from a tenant should consider it as

    A. most likely the result of a quarrel with the landlord
    B. usually an exaggerated statement of the facts
    C. a matter which should be investigated
    D. something to be checked after all other work has been completed

24. In a dispute about a matter covered by the multiple dwelling law, an inspector should carefully AVOID

    A. taking the attitude that the landlord is always wrong
    B. sounding out both the landlord and the tenant when both sides disagree
    C. investigating the basis of the disagreement
    D. getting involved in the matter until both the landlord and the tenant agree on the facts

25. If an inspector does not clearly understand one of the provisions of the multiple dwelling law, he should

    A. interpret it as best he can
    B. get his superior to explain it to him
    C. avoid having to enforce this provision
    D. consider this provision unimportant

25.____

26. If a tenant continues to ask an inspector a great many questions, the inspector should

    A. tell the tenant not to ask so many questions because the inspector has too many other things to do
    B. pretend he does not hear the tenant unless the tenant persists
    C. tell the tenant that all questions should be referred to the main office
    D. answer the questions as briefly as he can without creating the impression he is trying to *brush off* the tenant

26.____

27. If an inspector is dissatisfied with his assignment, he should

    A. demand that he be re-assigned to another task
    B. slow down his work so that his superior knows he is dissatisfied
    C. continue doing his work as well as he can but request a reassignment at the earliest opportunity
    D. make sure his fellow inspectors know his feelings

27.____

28. The MAIN reason why an inspector should know the value of his work is that

    A. he will have more of an incentive to do a better job
    B. he can better explain his job to the public
    C. it will be easier for him to get a promotion
    D. he will be able to ignore minor inspections

28.____

29. A landlord has made an unjustified complaint about an inspector to the inspector's superiors.
In future contacts with this landlord, the inspector should be

    A. cool and distant to avoid more trouble
    B. smiling and friendly to ease matters
    C. courteous and fair in enforcing the law
    D. strict so that the landlord knows he must comply with his orders

29.____

30. Assume that an inspector believes that one of the provisions of the multiple dwelling law is unfair.
The inspector should

    A. refuse to enforce this provision because it is unfair
    B. enforce this provision because it does not matter whether the law is fair or not
    C. refuse to enforce this provision because it is impossible to make the public comply with this provision
    D. enforce the provision because it is the law

30.____

31. In wood frame construction, mortise and tenon joints may be illegal. The basis for determining whether or not such a joint is legal is

   A. type of wood
   B. size of members
   C. load carried by the members
   D. age of wood

32. Of the following terms, the one LEAST related to the others is

   A. scuttle   B. buttress   C. bulkhead   D. parapet

33. Of the following terms, the one LEAST related to the others is

   A. egress
   B. fire tower
   C. fire wall
   D. fire escape

34. A deformed bar would MOST likely be used in

   A. masonry work
   B. steel construction
   C. wood construction
   D. reinforced concrete construction

35. A party wall is a(n)

   A. wall serving two structures
   B. interior wall
   C. retaining wall
   D. wall without openings

36. Of the following types of walls, the one LEAST related to the others is

   A. faced   B. spandrel   C. apron   D. panel

37. A bar bending table would MOST likely be used in the following type of construction:

   A. steel
   B. reinforced concrete
   C. wood
   D. masonry

38. Of the following terms, the one which is LEAST related to the others is

   A. down-spout
   B. ground seat
   C. gutter
   D. leader

39. Of the following terms, the one which is LEAST related to the others is

   A. ball-peen
   B. doublecut flat
   C. file card
   D. rat tail

40. Of the following, the one which is LEAST related to the others is

   A. chase   B. footing   C. pier   D. pile

Questions 41-45.

DIRECTIONS: Questions 41 through 45 are to be answered in accordance with the floor plan of one floor of a converted dwelling shown on the last page of this test.

41. The depth of the linen closet, indicated by the letter S, is 41.____

    A. 1'4"   B. 1'5"   C. 1'6"   D. 1'7"

42. The door that should have a fire rating is indicated by the letter 42.____

    A. G   B. H   C. J   D. K

43. The walls of the building are of 43.____

    A. frame construction   B. solid brick
    C. brick and block   D. solid block

44. Of the following types of steel sections, the one that MOST closely resembles, in appearance, the steel beams used to support the floor joists is 44.____

    A. ⎵   B. ST   C. L   D. W

45. The grade of lumber indicated for joists FORMERLY was called # 45.____

    A. 1 common   B. 1 select   C. 2 common   D. 2 select

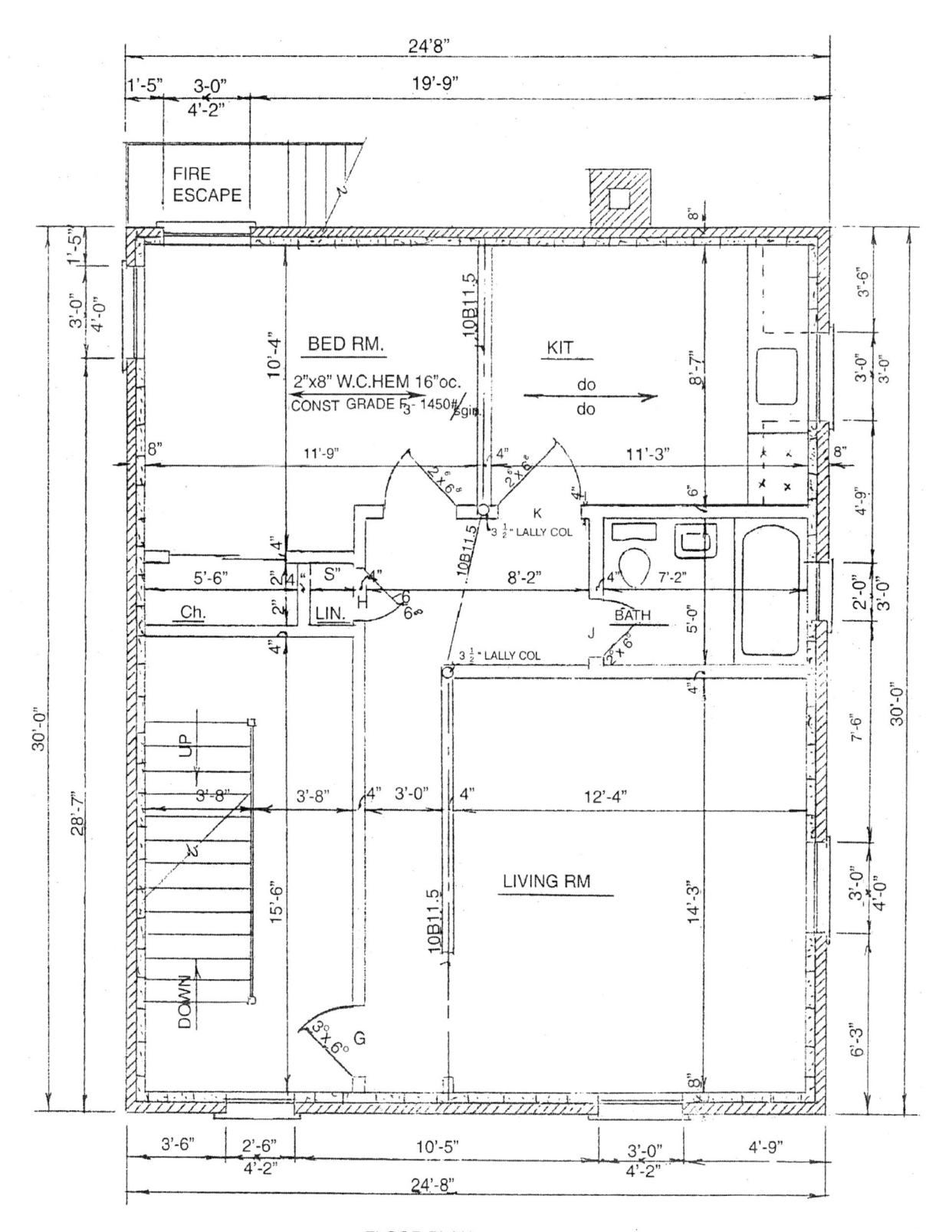

FLOOR PLAN

KEY (CORRECT ANSWERS)

1. C	11. A	21. D	31. B	41. C
2. B	12. A	22. C	32. B	42. A
3. A	13. C	23. C	33. C	43. C
4. D	14. A	24. A	34. D	44. D
5. A	15. C	25. B	35. A	45. A
6. D	16. D	26. D	36. A	
7. B	17. B	27. C	37. B	
8. B	18. C	28. A	38. B	
9. B	19. D	29. C	39. A	
10. D	20. D	30. D	40. A	

EXAMINATION SECTION
TEST 1

DIRECTIONS: Each question or incomplete statement is followed by several suggested answers or completions. Select the one that BEST answers the question or completes the statement. *PRINT THE LETTER OF THE CORRECT ANSWER IN THE SPACE AT THE RIGHT.*

1. A kitchenette is defined as a cooking space having a floor area of LESS than _____ square feet.

    A. 57   B. 58   C. 59   D. 60

    1._____

2. The one of the following that is classed as a converted dwelling is a(n)

    A. apartment house erected prior to 1929, now used as a hotel
    B. lodging house erected prior to 1913, now used as a multiple dwelling
    C. one-family house erected prior to 1929, now used as a multiple dwelling
    D. rooming house erected prior to 1913, now used as a hotel

    2._____

3. A *fire-retarded* partition must have a fire-resistive rating of AT LEAST _____ hour(s).

    A. 1   B. 2   C. 3   D. 4

    3._____

4. The multiple dwelling law states that the total window area of a room must be at least one-tenth of the floor surface area of the room.
The one of the following types of rooms that is exempted from this provision is a

    A. bedroom   B. kitchen
    C. recreation room   D. bathroom

    4._____

5. In a non-fireproof multiple dwelling, the HIGHEST story in which a factory may be operated is the

    A. 1st   B. 2nd   C. 3rd   D. 4th

    5._____

6. In a multiple dwelling under construction, the MINIMUM required width of an entrance hall, from the entrance to the first stair, is

    A. 3'4"   B. 3'8"   C. 4'0"   D. 4'4"

    6._____

7. Access to a required fire escape, used as a legal second means of egress from an apartment, may be from a

    A. public hall   B. kitchen
    C. bathroom   D. closet

    7._____

8. The basis for differentiating between a *tenement* and any other *Class A multiple dwelling* is

    A. the year in which it was built
    B. the number of families now residing therein
    C. whether residents are permanent or transient
    D. classification of construction

    8._____

9. In a 6-story multiple dwelling under construction, wood floor joists would NOT be used for

   A. apartments
   B. recreation rooms
   C. toilets
   D. public halls

10. If plans were to be filed now for a change of occupancy, the type of occupancy for which a fire escape is NOT acceptable as a second means of egress is

    A. club house
    B. single room
    C. tenement
    D. garden type maisonette

11. The multiple dwelling law requires self-closing doors between apartments and halls in all Class A multiple dwellings.
    The PRINCIPAL reason for this is to

    A. insure privacy of the tenants
    B. protect other tenants from excessive noise
    C. reduce heat loss
    D. prevent the spread of fire

12. The multiple dwelling law prohibits the erection of a building the height of which is in excess of one and one-half times the width of the widest street on which it faces.
    The MAIN reason for this prohibition is to

    A. insure that tenants will not have to travel too far to the street in case of fire
    B. provide adequate light and air
    C. prevent excessive loadings on the footings
    D. provide adequate water pressure on the top floor

13. The multiple dwelling law requires that the walls of all interior courts shall be built with a light-colored brick. The PRINCIPAL reason for this is that

    A. light-colored brick is easier to clean
    B. more light will be reflected into the apartments
    C. light-colored brick is usually stronger
    D. rain will not penetrate light-colored brick readily

14. The multiple dwelling law requires that every fire escape constructed of material subject to rusting shall be painted with two or more coats of paint of contrasting colors.
    The reason that each coat is required to be of a different color is that

    A. the different pigments in the two coats will better protect the steel from rust
    B. when two colors are used, the sun will not bleach the top color as rapidly as when only one color is used
    C. the contrasting colors make inspection easier
    D. a better bond is obtained between paint of different color

15. The multiple dwelling law requires that every fire escape at the top story of a building shall be provided with a stairway or ladder to the roof, except where the roof is a peak roof with a pitch in excess of twenty degrees. The reason that access to the roof from the fire escape is NOT required where the pitch of the roof is in excess of twenty degrees is that

    A. it would be difficult to walk on a roof with such a slope
    B. a steep roof would tend to catch fire quicker, so people should not be on the roof

C. sparks from a fire would tend to roll down the roof toward any person climbing up the ladder
D. it is almost impossible to anchor a ladder to a steep roof

16. The multiple dwelling law states that for stairs, each tread shall be not less than nine and one-half inches wide; each riser shall not exceed seven and three-quarters inches in height; and the product of the number of inches in the width of the tread and the number of inches in the height of the riser shall be at least seventy and at most seventy-five. The one of the following sets of dimensions that is acceptable for the stairs of a multiple dwelling is tread _____, riser _____.

   A. 9 3/4"; 7 1/8"
   B. 9 1/4"; 8"
   C. 10 1/4"; 7 1/8"
   D. 10 1/2"; 7 1/2"

17. The multiple dwelling law prohibits construction of a frame multiple dwelling.
    The PRINCIPAL reason for this is that

    A. frame buildings are more susceptible to vermin infection
    B. the heavier loads occurring in multiple dwellings can not be supported in frame buildings
    C. frame buildings, used as multiple dwellings, tend to become slums
    D. fire in a frame building is more dangerous than in other types of buildings

18. The multiple dwelling law states that no radio or other wires shall be attached to any vent line extending above the roof.
    The PRINCIPAL reason for this prohibition is that

    A. vent lines are relatively weak structures
    B. wires increase the danger of electric shock due to lightning
    C. low wires are a safety hazard
    D. ventilation will be blocked

19. In a non-fireproof building, the multiple dwelling law requires that certain partitions shall be fire-stopped. This means that

    A. fireproof doors must be used
    B. the partitions must be constructed of incombustible material
    C. the covering of the studs must be of incombustible material
    D. the spaces between the top of a partition and the ceiling and floors above must be filled with incombustible material

20. The building code states that the floor of a multiple dwelling shall be designed for a live load of 40 pounds per square foot.
    Live load means weight of

    A. floor joists, beams, and girders
    B. tenants only
    C. tenants and their furniture
    D. floor joists, beams, girders, tenants, and furniture

21. An anonymous complaint is made to the Department of Buildings. 21.____
This complaint should be

    A. ignored because it is not signed
    B. investigated because it may be valid
    C. filed to see if further complaints of a like nature are made
    D. ignored because only troublemakers make anonymous complaints

22. In order to make certain emergency repairs to an occupied multiple dwelling, a fire 22.____
escape must be removed. The owner asks you, an inspector, for permission to do this.
You should

    A. grant the request, since the only way to make the repair is to remove the fire escape
    B. tell the owner to find another method of making the repair since a fire escape may not be removed
    C. refer the owner to your superiors, since you do not have the authority to grant the request
    D. grant the request only if fire extinguishers are provided to prevent danger of fire

23. The cellar ceiling of a converted multiple dwelling is to be fire-retarded by applying two 23.____
layers of 1/2" plaster boards to the existing ceiling. The owner tells you that the existing
lath is too weak to support the weight of the additional plaster boards.
You should

    A. insist that the plaster boards shall be applied on the existing ceiling
    B. tell the owner that the plaster boards will not be necessary since their application would be dangerous
    C. permit installation of only one layer of plaster boards in order to reduce the load on the lath
    D. require that the lath be strengthened first and then that the two layers of plaster boards be applied

24. A tenant has made a complaint that water leaking from a pipe in the apartment above 24.____
has damaged the ceiling of the tenant's apartment. While the premises are being
inspected, the tenant mentions other complaints to you. You should

    A. tell the tenant you are there to inspect the original complaint only
    B. listen courteously to the tenant, but discourage further complaints
    C. check each of the complaints to determine their validity
    D. place a violation on the landlord for all the complaints

25. The public halls of a multiple dwelling were painted two months ago. A tenant has filed a 25.____
complaint stating that the walls are now peeling and are in a dirty, deteriorated condition.
When investigating this complaint, you find that it is justified.
You should

    A. test the paint to find out why it peeled so rapidly
    B. notify the landlord to repaint the walls properly
    C. tell the tenant that since the walls were painted within three years, nothing further can be done
    D. refer the complaint to the legal department so that court action may be taken

26. A multiple dwelling is being erected with one wall on a lot line. On the adjoining lot is a two-family house. The owner of this house complaints that the new building is cutting off light and ventilation from the two-family house.
You should

   A. tell the small home owner that nothing can be done since the law permits such construction
   B. tell the small home owner that nothing can be done since two-family houses are not within your jurisdiction
   C. stop construction of the multiple dwelling since it is illegal to block ventilation of another house
   D. tell the small home owner to sue the city for the decrease in the value of his property

27. The approved plans for a converted multiple dwelling call for fireproofing the stair enclosure with metal lath and cement plaster. The contractor would like to substitute two layers of 1/2 inch plaster board since this has the same fire-resistive rating as the lath and plaster.
The inspector should

   A. permit this, since the fire ratings are the same
   B. deny this, since the structural strengths may not be the same
   C. permit this only if an amended plan showing the substitution is approved
   D. permit this only if the structural strengths and the fire-resistive ratings are the same

28. During a routine inspection of a multiple dwelling, an inspector discovers that a fire door has been blocked open.
The FIRST action of the inspector should be to

   A. order the owner or his representative to remove the blocking immediately
   B. notify the owner in writing that a violation of the law exists on the premises
   C. warn the tenants that a fire hazard exists
   D. remove the blocking himself

29. When writing a report of an investigation of a tenant's complaint, the item that you should consider LEAST important for inclusion in the report is the

   A. name of tenant   B. apartment number
   C. age of building   D. location of building

30. A tenant asks you about the procedures the Department of Buildings uses in processing a violation complaint.
You should

   A. refer the tenant to your superiors since they are the only ones permitted to give official information
   B. tell the tenant that such information is none of his business
   C. give the tenant the information in as concise a manner as possible
   D. explain completely and in detail all the ramifications of departmental procedure

31. In investigating the adequacy of the exits of a multiple dwelling, the LEAST important item to check is the

    A. location of exits
    B. width of stairs
    C. size of stair platforms
    D. number of treads and risers

32. In a 8-story fireproof multiple dwelling of skeleton steel construction, the one of the following members that would be LEAST likely to have a fire-resistive enclosure is a

    A. beam   B. column   C. joist   D. lintel

33. The one of the following that is LEAST related to the others is

    A. pile   B. footing   C. caisson   D. pilaster

34. A pit at the low point of a cellar floor is known as a(n)

    A. sump
    C. accumulator
    B. well
    D. drain

35. The structure above the roof of a building that encloses a stairway is called a

    A. bulkhead
    C. mezzanine
    B. penthouse
    D. stairwell

36. To prevent flying sparks, incinerator chimneys in multiple dwellings are frequently covered with

    A. cement copings
    C. goosenecks
    B. draft hoods
    D. wire mesh

37. A valve used to prevent boiler explosions due to excessive pressure is a _____ valve.

    A. check   B. gate   C. relief   D. fuller

38. The one of the following that is acceptable according to the building code for a 3-hour fire partition is 6"

    A. solid brick
    B. solid stone concrete blocks
    C. solid cinder concrete blocks
    D. plain concrete

39. A fire tower is a

    A. means of egress from a building
    B. water tank on the roof of a building
    C. piece of Fire Department equipment
    D. draft space through which fire will spread

Questions 40-45.

7 (#1)

DIRECTIONS: Questions 40 through 45, inclusive, refer to the sketch of an apartment building shown on the last page. All questions are to be answered on the basis of this sketch.

40. The dimension of the bedroom indicated by the letter Y is 40._____

    A. 9'1 5/16"   B. 9'1 13/16"
    C. 9'2 3/16"   D. 9'2 11/16"

41. Following is an abstract of the multiple dwelling law: 41._____
    1. Every living room (including bedrooms) shall contain at least 80 square feet of floor space.
    2. Every living room shall be at least eight feet in least horizontal dimension except that any number of bedrooms up to one-half the total number in any apartment containing three or more bedrooms may have a least horizontal dimension of seven feet or more.
    In order to increase the width of the hall, it is necessary to decrease the width of the bedroom indicated by the letter Y.
    The one of the following that is the smallest acceptable width of this room is

    A. 7'0"   B. 7'6"   C. 8'0"   D. 8'6"

42. The columns shown are 42._____

    A. wood posts   B. concrete filled pipes
    C. I beams   D. built up channels

43. The letter indicating the partition that is MOST likely to be a bearing partition is 43._____

    A. M
    B. W
    C. X
    D. There are no bearing partitions

44. The exit door 44._____

    A. does not swing in the direction of egress
    B. is too large
    C. will block the stairs
    D. is not fireproof

45. The one of the following general notes that is MOST likely to appear in connection with this plan is: 45._____

    A. Masonry walls shall be braced horizontally at maximum intervals of twenty times the wall thickness
    B. Buttresses shall be bonded into the wall by masonry in the same manner as employed in the construction of the wall
    C. Masonry walls shall be anchored at maximum intervals of four feet, to each tier of joists bearing on such walls, by metal anchors
    D. Openings in the masonry wall shall be spanned by a lintel or arch of incombustible materia

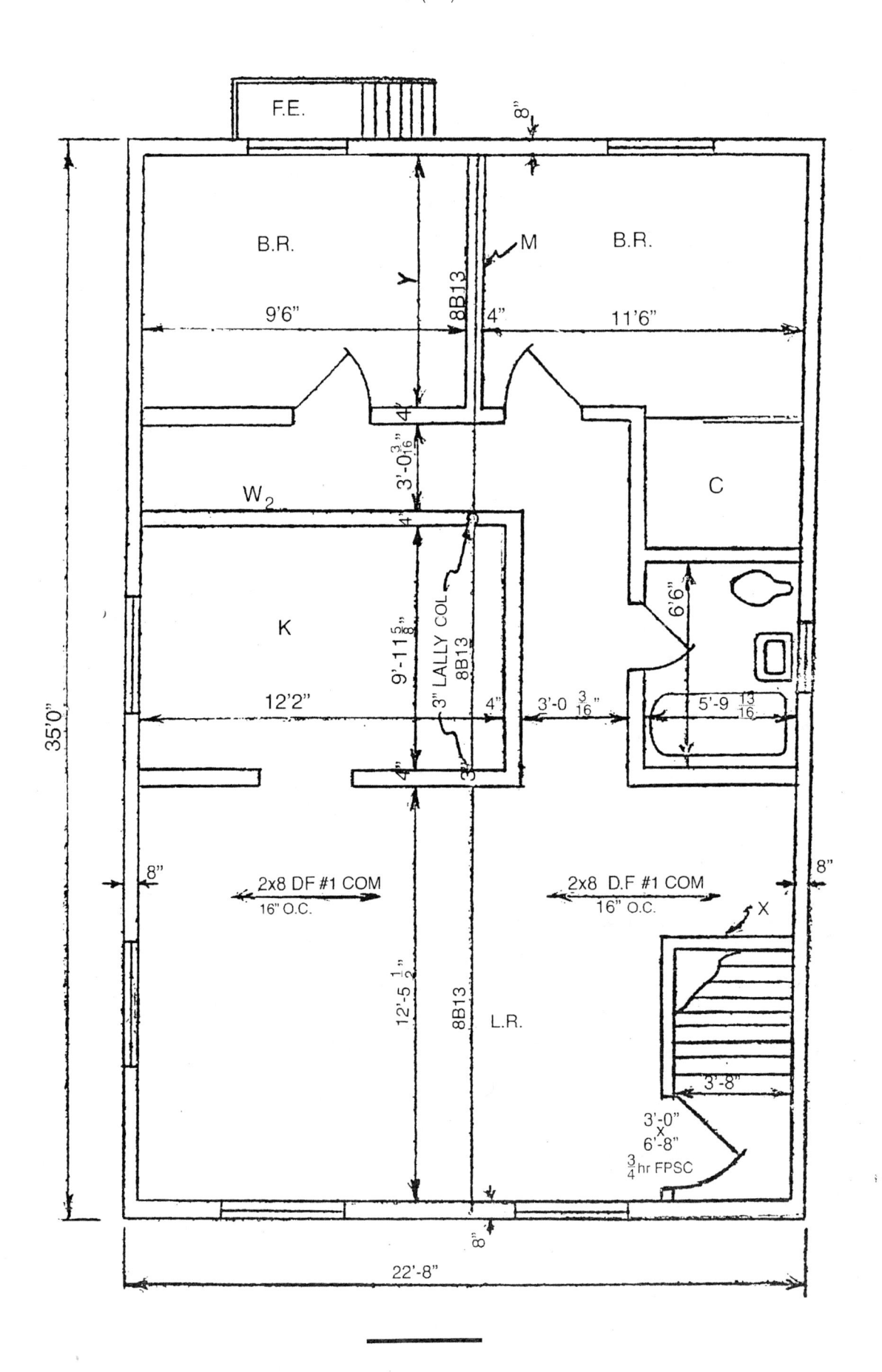

8 (#1)

KEY (CORRECT ANSWERS)

1. C	11. D	21. B	31. D	41. D
2. C	12. B	22. C	32. D	42. B
3. A	13. B	23. D	33. D	43. D
4. D	14. C	24. C	34. A	44. C
5. B	15. A	25. B	35. A	45. C
6. C	16. C	26. A	36. D	
7. B	17. D	27. C	37. C	
8. A	18. A	28. A	38. C	
9. D	19. D	29. C	39. A	
10. B	20. C	30. C	40. D	

EXAMINATION SECTION
TEST 1

DIRECTIONS: Each question consists of a statement You are to indicate whether the statement is TRUE (T) or FALSE (F). *PRINT THE LETTER OF THE CORRECT ANSWER IN THE SPACE AT THE RIGHT.*

1. In 1916, New York City adopted the first comprehensive zoning ordinance in this country.   1.____

2. Since that time, American cities, with numerous exceptions, have adopted zoning ordinances so that now over 1,100 cities with populations in excess of 10,000 are zoned.   2.____

3. It is purely academic for the broker or salesman to be knowledgeable of planning, zoning, restrictive covenants, and other land use controls.   3.____

4. The purchaser, when he signs the usual form of purchase contract, agrees to take the land subject to restrictions of record, zoning, and other ordinances.   4.____

5. To the purchaser, use limitations are NOT usually so important as technical flaws on title that may be uncovered by examination of the abstract of title.   5.____

6. False information, intentionally or negligently given about land use restrictions, may be grounds for setting the sale aside.   6.____

7. Covenants that *run with the land* may be binding on those who inherit, buy or otherwise acquire the land after the owner of the land.   7.____

8. Restrictions imposed by subdivision developers are few in number and uniform in purpose.   8.____

9. Great care should be taken NOT to burden the land unduly because once on the land, they are hard to eliminate.   9.____

10. Many people, when the phrase *restrictive covenant* is used, think ONLY of racial or religious restrictions on land use.   10.____

11. Easements are SELDOM used by developers to implement their private plans.   11.____

12. *Conservation easements,* like privately imposed easements, will become increasingly important encumbrances on more and more tracts of land.   12.____

13. An existing filling station in a district zoned residential is an example of a non-conforming use.   13.____

14. For practical political reasons and in order to protect the zoning from attack on constitutional grounds, zoning ordinances uniformly permit the continuance of non-conforming uses.   14.____

15. An illegal use is one established before enactment of a zoning ordinance and in violation of it.   15.____

16. A method of bringing zoning into line with the prospective buyer's wishes is through the so-called zoning *variance.*   16.____

17. The zoning exception or special use permit is a method to meet the objectives of a prospective seller in appropriate cases. 17.____

18. It is a fact that the subdivider lays down an indelible land use pattern which will enhance or blight the community for generations to come. 18.____

19. The object of the official map is to preserve the land needed for future streets or for street-widening at bare land prices. 19.____

20. The restrictive covenant is the PRINCIPAL legal tool for the accomplishment of private land use planning goals. 20.____

21. Because land is rural, it is NOT zoned. 21.____

22. Zoning deals PRINCIPALLY with so-called bulk and density controls. 22.____

23. Land use planning may be both private and public. 23.____

24. In the absence of legal restraints, landowners exercising their broad common-law privileges of use may so use their land as to defeat both private or public planners goals and expectations. 24.____

25. Where a landowner stopped a non-conforming use some time ago and is now offering his premises for sale, the right to resume the use may have been lost by abandonment. 25.____

KEY (CORRECT ANSWERS)

1.	T		11.	F
2.	F		12.	T
3.	F		13.	T
4.	T		14.	T
5.	F		15.	F
6.	T		16.	T
7.	T		17.	F
8.	F		18.	T
9.	T		19.	T
10.	T		20.	T

21. F
22. F
23. T
24. T
25. T

TEST 2

DIRECTIONS: Each question consists of a statement. You are to indicate whether the statement is TRUE (T) or FALSE (F). *PRINT THE LETTER OF THE CORRECT ANSWER IN THE SPACE AT THE RIGHT.*

1. The real estate business in the United States is largely concerned with the land and buildings in highly concentrated areas of population which we call cities, metropolitan areas, or urban communities. 1.____

2. Zoning may retard value decline but it CANNOT prevent it. 2.____

3. There is little consistency in zoning symbols and descriptions in the political subdivisions of state government. 3.____

4. Government is involved in the real estate business at the federal level but NOT at the state and local levels. 4.____

5. The subdivision laws are designed primarily to protect the seller from misrepresentation, deceit, and fraud in the sale of new subdivisions by disclosing to the prospective purchaser the pertinent facts concerning the project. 5.____

6. Where one lot in a subdivision is made security for the payment of a trust, deed, note, or other lien or encumbrance to be satisfied with the payment of money, this is called a *blanket encumbrance*. 6.____

7. The power of eminent domain is the same as the *police power*. 7.____

8. The MAIN issue in almost all condemnation or eminent domain cases is the amount of *just compensation* required to be paid to the attorneys. 8.____

9. A defined channel is any natural watercourse even though dry during a good portion of the year. 9.____

10. If water is flowing in a defined channel, a landowner may obstruct or direct such water. 10.____

11. Waters overflowing a defined channel are considered *floodwaters,* and any landowner may protect himself from them by reasonable methods even though this might result in the floodwaters entering another man's land. 11.____

12. A purchaser of a condominium owns the air space in which his particular unit is situated in fee simple, has a deed thereto, gets a separate tax assessment, and may apply for and acquire a title insurance policy on his property. 12.____

13. Land development generally means the creation of a *subdivision.* 13.____

14. Before starting a land development program, the prudent developer will first contact the county surveyor. 14.____

15. *Subdivision* does NOT include certain types of multi-family structures. 15.____

16. A person may sell or offer for sale a lot or parcel of land in a subdivision pending final approval from the proper authorities. 16.____

17. The approval of the tentative map of the subdivision submitted to the planning commission constitutes a final approval of the plat for recording. 17.____

18. The survey and plat of the subdivision may be made by a surveyor who is NOT a registered engineer or a licensed land surveyor. 18.____

19. The plat of the subdivision must be of such a scale that survey and mathematical information and other details can be easily obtained from it. 19.____

20. Before a plat is approved, all taxes and assessments MUST be paid. 20.____

21. Before any sales can be made of subdivided lands, certain documents and instruments must be placed in escrow with a legal escrow depository. 21.____

22. The law prohibits any person selling or offering to sell lots or parcels in a subdivision from issuing, circulating, or publishing any prospectus. 22.____

23. The law prohibits any person selling or offering to sell lots or parcels in a subdivision from making any statement or representation UNLESS he declares that the real estate subdivision has been approved or indorsed by the commission. 23.____

24. The law prohibits any person selling or offering to sell lots or parcels in a subdivision from issuing, circulating, or publishing any advertising matter UNLESS he does so anonymously. 24.____

25. The real estate commission or commissioner is generally given authority to issue a *cease or desist* order whenever he finds a subdivider violating any provisions of the subdivision act. 25.____

KEY (CORRECT ANSWERS)

1. T
2. T
3. T
4. F
5. F

6. F
7. F
8. F
9. T
10. F

11. T
12. T
13. T
14. T
15. F

16. F
17. F
18. F
19. T
20. T

21. T
22. F
23. F
24. F
25. T

TEST 3

DIRECTIONS: Each question consists of a statement. You are to indicate whether the statement is TRUE (T) or FALSE (F). *PRINT THE LETTER OF THE CORRECT ANSWER IN THE SPACE AT THE RIGHT.*

1. The purchaser, when he signs the USUAL form of purchase contract, agrees to take the land exempt from restrictions of record, zoning, and other municipal ordinances. 1.____

2. False information, intentionally or negligently given about land use restrictions, MAY be grounds for setting the sale aside. 2.____

3. Standing silently by when you know the prospect is intending to use the land for a purpose forbidden by public or private restrictions will NOT endanger the sale unless the prospect is intentionally led astray. 3.____

4. It is important for the broker or salesman to know the ways in which zoning restrictions can be changed and whether or not a change in the zoning restrictions on a certain piece of property is possible to enhance the possibilities of a sale. 4.____

5. In the absence of legal restraints, land owners exercising their broad common law privileges of use may so use their land as to defeat both private or public planners' goals and expectations. 5.____

6. The easement is the PRINCIPAL legal tool for the accomplishment of private land use planning goals. 6.____

7. It is possible through covenants to set up virtually a private municipal government by creating a neighborhood association, giving it power to police the residential and other use restrictions, maintain streets, provide water, or render other services and assess charges against the benefited lots so as to raise the money needed to finance the services. 7.____

8. A covenant restriction is USUALLY of a very minor nature. 8.____

9. Covenants may NOT be recorded. 9.____

10. Once a covenant is in effect, it is binding and can NEVER be removed. 10.____

11. No state may act through its courts or otherwise to enforce racial or religious land use restrictive covenants. 11.____

12. Set-back, side yard, and back yard requirements are common restrictions imposed by covenants. 12.____

13. Presence of a covenant based on religion or race will bar Federal Housing Administration mortgage insurance and Veterans Administration financing. 13.____

14. Sometimes set-backs from the street take the form of easements established by declaration or grant. 14.____

15. Brokers and salesmen have an obligation to know about the existence of both publicly purchased and privately imposed easements as well as about restrictive covenants so that prospective buyers can be informed. 15.____

16. Zoning consists of dividing the land within a given governmental unit into districts and then specifying what uses are permitted and which ones prohibited in each district. 16.____

17. Zoning does NOT deal with the placement and height of buildings on the land and with bulk and density controls. 17.____

18. There are ONLY three types of zones: residential, commercial, and industrial. 18.____

19. In modern zoning plans, industry is barred from residential areas, but residences may be built in industrial areas. 19.____

20. It is safe to assume that rural land is unzoned. 20.____

21. A non-conforming use is one which was in existence when zoning went into effect and which is inconsistent with zoning purposes. 21.____

22. Zoning ordinances uniformly PROHIBIT the continuance of non-conforming uses in zoning ordinances. 22.____

23. There is USUALLY a prohibition against the expansion of non-conforming uses in zoning ordinances. 23.____

24. Once a non-conforming use has been abandoned, it can ALWAYS be re-established. 24.____

25. A landowner whose use is non-conforming may NOT sell his land and pass on the right to continue the use to the buyer. 25.____

KEY (CORRECT ANSWERS)

1.	F	11.	T
2.	T	12.	T
3.	F	13.	T
4.	T	14.	T
5.	T	15.	T
6.	F	16.	T
7.	T	17.	F
8.	F	18.	F
9.	F	19.	F
10.	F	20.	F

21. T
22. F
23. T
24. T
25. F

TEST 4

DIRECTIONS: Each question consists of a statement. You are to indicate whether the statement is TRUE (T) or FALSE (F). *PRINT THE LETTER OF THE CORRECT ANSWER IN THE SPACE AT THE RIGHT.*

1. Where a buyer is purchasing a non-conforming structure, the broker should warn him that in case of substantial destruction by fire or otherwise, zoning may bar rebuilding. 1._____

2. Where a landowner stopped the non-conforming use some time ago and now is offering his premises for sale, the right to resume the use may have been lost by abandonment. 2._____

3. There is no difference between a variance and a special use permit. 3._____

4. Wherever federal law is applicable, it is paramount. 4._____

5. Ordinarily, the basis of federal law is interstate commerce. 5._____

6. This is true of the U.S. Supreme Court case Jones v. Mayer and Title VIII of the Civil Rights Act of 1968. 6._____

7. Title VIII applies even to the MOST local transactions. 7._____

8. What discrimination state laws do NOT prohibit, federal law now does. 8._____

9. While no one may refuse to sell, lease, or rent to another because of race or color, a real estate licensee may do so when acting under his principal's directions. 9._____

10. Should a principal seek to restrict a listing according to race or color, the licensee MUST refuse to accept the listing. 10._____

11. Title VIII prohibits denial of membership or participation in a real estate board or multiple listing service to a person because of race, color, religion, or national origin, or discrimination against him in terms or conditions of membership. 11._____

12. Real estate licensees must not discriminate but they may accept restrictive listings. 12._____

Questions 13-22.

DIRECTIONS: In each of the following questions, a blank space indicates that a word or phrase has been omitted. Supply the missing word or phrase that will complete the statement correctly.

13. Before subdivided land can be sold or leased, a notice of _____ MUST be filed with the commissioner. 13._____

14. In MOST cases, the owner and subdivider are the same, but sometimes the owner will turn over the land to someone else to develop and assume necessary authority to offer it for sale. This person is commonly known as a _____. 14._____

15. The _____ type of subdivision is the kind MOST frequently developed. 15._____

16. A _____ is an estate in real property consisting of an undivided interest in common in a portion of a parcel of real property together with a separate interest in space in a residential, industrial, or commercial building on such real property, such as an apartment, office, or store, and may include, in addition, a separate interest in other portions of such property. 16._____

17. The power of eminent domain is _____ the *police power*. 17._____

18. The power of eminent domain involves a _____ and the payment of compensation to the property owner. 18._____

19. The use of the power of eminent domain is often referred to as _____. 19._____

20. The MAIN issue in almost all eminent domain cases is the amount of _____ required to be paid to the property owner. 20._____

21. _____ is a general principle underlying a vast body of detailed water law. 21._____

22. Waters overflowing a defined channel are considered _____. 22._____

Questions 23-25.

DIRECTIONS: In continuous discourse, briefly and concisely answer the following questions.

23. What is a stock cooperative? 23._____
24. What is meant by a blanket encumbrance. 24._____
25. What is meant by *fair market value*? 25._____

KEY (CORRECT ANSWERS)

1. T
2. T
3. F
4. T
5. T
6. F
7. T
8. T
9. F
10. T
11. T
12. F
13. intention
14. subdivider
15. standard
16. condominium

17. different from
18. taking
19. condemnation
20. just compensation
21. Conservation
22. floodwaters
23. A stock cooperative is a corporation which is formed or availed of primarily for the purpose of holding title to, either in fee simple or for a term of years, improved real property, if all or substantially all of the stockholders of such corporation receive a right of exclusive occupancy in a portion of the real property, title to which is held by the corporation, which right of occupancy is transferrable only concurrently with the transfer of the share or shares of stock in the corporation held by the person having such right of occupancy.
24. A blanket encumbrance is where more than one lot in a subdivision is made security for the payment of a trust deed note or other lien or encumbrance to be satisfied with the payment of money.
25. Fair market value is the highest price land would bring if exposed for sale in the open market with reasonable time allowed to find a purchaser with knowledge of all uses and purposes to which the land is adapted, the seller not being required to sell or the purchaser required to purchase.

EXAMINATION SECTION
TEST 1

DIRECTIONS: Each question or incomplete statement is followed by several suggested answers or completions. Select the one that BEST answers the question or completes the statement. *PRINT THE LETTER OF THE CORRECT ANSWER IN THE SPACE AT THE RIGHT.*

1. What is represented by the architectural symbol shown at the right?

    A. Stone concrete
    B. Cinder concrete
    C. Gravel
    D. Plaster

    1.____

2. Poured installation of fiberglass or mineral wool insulation material will typically occur at a rate of _____ cubic feet per day.

    A. 20 B. 80 C. 120 D. 180

    2.____

3. What is the MOST effective method for backfilling excavated material?

    A. Sheepfoot roller
    B. Bulldozer
    C. Shoveling
    D. Pneumatic tamper

    3.____

4. Approximately how many square feet of unfinished plank flooring can be installed in an average work day?

    A. 50 B. 150 C. 225 D. 300

    4.____

5. Studs for concrete basement forms are typically spaced _____ apart.

    A. 18 inches B. 2 feet C. 4 feet D. 8 feet

    5.____

6. Most construction stone is calculated and purchased by the

    A. square foot
    B. linear foot
    C. cubic yard
    D. ton

    6.____

7. When earth backfill is replaced at a site, it is required to be compacted to within _____% of the original density.

    A. 65-75 B. 75-90 C. 85-95 D. 80-100

    7.____

8. What type of brick masonry unit is represented by the drawing shown at the right?
    A. Norman
    B. Norwegian
    C. Corner
    D. Skippy

    8.____

9. A laborer on a plain gable roof will typically install approximately _____ bundles of straight shingles in an average work day.

    A. 3-5 B. 6-9 C. 10-15 D. 17-20

    9.____

10. What material is applied behind wall support mesh to reduce plaster waste?
    A. Mastic
    B. Gypsum board
    C. Chicken wire
    D. Asphalt-saturated felt

11. A _____ line is represented by the mechanical _____ symbol shown at the right.
    A. fuel oil
    B. vent
    C. cold water
    D. hot water

12. Approximately how many square feet of exterior surface can be prepared for paint or stain in one hour?
    A. 50
    B. 100
    C. 150
    D. 250

13. What tool is used to rough level concrete when it is still plastic?
    A. Drum
    B. Header
    C. Float
    D. Screed

14. Most stains that are applied to heavy timber can cover about _____ square feet per gallon.
    A. 100
    B. 250
    C. 350
    D. 550

15. Which of the following is NOT one of the three standard methods for installing glazed tile?
    A. Furan resin grout
    B. Full mortar beds
    C. Organic adhesives
    D. Dry-set thin cement

16. Generally, the cost for a buildings's heating/air conditioning make up about _____% of the total construction cost.
    A. 1-3
    B. 4-8
    C. 5-10
    D. 8-12

17. What is represented by the electrical symbol shown at the right?
    A. Lock or key switch
    B. Two-way switch
    C. Switch with duplex receptacle
    D. Triplex receptacle

18. Most structural lumber is considered *yard dry* at a MAXIMUM of about _____% moisture content.
    A. 5
    B. 10
    C. 20
    D. 30

19. What is the term for a wood or metal edge applied to the wall and used as a guide to determine the depth of plaster?
    A. Rake
    B. Float
    C. Screed
    D. Stud

20. Approximately how many single rolls of wall covering can be hung by one worker in a typical work day?
    A. 12
    B. 20
    C. 30
    D. 45

21. What is represented by the architectural symbol shown at the right?

    A. Structural tile
    B. Concrete block
    C. Fire brick
    D. Brick

22. Approximately how many square feet of interior wall space can one painter, using a roller, cover in an hour?

    A. 25-50   B. 100   C. 175-200   D. 250

23. Cement plaster scratch coat for tile installation can typically be applied at a rate of _____ square yards per work day.

    A. 150   B. 300   C. 500   D. 750

24. MOST gas lines are made of

    A. black iron
    B. copper
    C. galvanized steel
    D. plastic

25. For most types of resilient flooring installation, approximately how many hours of labor will be required to install 100 square feet?

    A. 1/2   B. 1   C. 3   D. 4 1/2

KEY (CORRECT ANSWERS)

1. C
2. A
3. B
4. B
5. C

6. D
7. C
8. A
9. C
10. D

11. C
12. B
13. C
14. B
15. A

16. B
17. C
18. C
19. C
20. C

21. C
22. C
23. B
24. A
25. C

TEST 2

DIRECTIONS: Each question or incomplete statement is followed by several suggested answers or completions. Select the one that BEST answers the question or completes the Statement. *PRINT THE LETTER OF THE CORRECT ANSWER IN THE SPACE AT THE RIGHT.*

1. Approximately how much labor will be required for the testing of a single unit of installed water or sewer line?

    A. 30 minutes
    B. 1 hour
    C. 2 hours
    D. 3 hours

2. Concrete reinforcing bars are sized according to _____ inch increments.

    A. 1/16   B. 1/8   C. 1/4   D. 1/2

3. Approximately how many square feet of 4 1/4" x 4 1/4" glazed wall tile, set in mortar, can be applied in an average work day?

    A. 60   B. 130   C. 175   D. 220

4. In residential work, what type of estimate is MOST likely to be used to estimate the cost of excavation work?

    A. Quantity survey
    B. Lump-sum amount
    C. Cost-per-square-foot estimate
    D. Unit cost estimate

5. What type of brick masonry unit is represented by the drawing shown at the right?
    A. Trough
    B. Economy
    C. King Norman
    D. Engineer

6. Which of the following types of windows would be MOST expensive to install?

    A. Aluminum, single-hung vertical
    B. Wood, double-hung
    C. Steel, projected vent
    D. Aluminum, projected vent

7. For estimating the labor cost of the installation of tile base and cap units, the typical tile labor time should be multiplied by

    A. 1/2   B. 2   C. 3   D. 4

8. What is represented by the architectural symbol shown at the right?

    A. Plywood
    B. Vertical paneling
    C. Brick
    D. Rough lumber

9. Approximately how long should it take a 2-person crew to install 100 linear feet of 4" x 6" girder?

   A. 30 minutes
   B. 1 hour
   C. 3 hours
   D. 1 work day

10. Each of the following is considered a fixed overhead cost EXCEPT

    A. office rent
    B. job site utilities
    C. assembly space
    D. stationery

11. How many square feet of solid plywood roof sheathing should two carpenters be able to install in a typical work day?

    A. 400
    B. 800
    C. 1,000
    D. 1,400

12. What type of concrete masonry unit is represented by the drawing shown at the right?

    A. Floor
    B. Bull nose
    C. Trough
    D. Jamb

13. Which type of paving material will generally take LONGEST to install?

    A. Asphalt
    B. Gravel base course
    C. Concrete curb/gutter
    D. Concrete sidewalk

14. If a roof needs to be framed for locations such as dormers, hips, or valleys, an estimator should calculate a reduction in output of _____%.

    A. 5
    B. 10
    C. 20
    D. 30

15. What is represented by the architectural symbol shown at the right?

    A. Stone concrete
    B. Cinder concrete
    C. Gravel
    D. Rock

16. Which of the following types of tile for resilient flooring would be MOST expensive?

    A. Pure vinyl
    B. Cork
    C. Vinyl asbestos
    D. Rubberized marbleized

17. Installation of tempered or insulated glass will cost approximately _____% more than the installation of 1/4" polished plate glass.

    A. 20
    B. 50
    C. 75
    D. 100

18. Most concrete is considered to be completely cured after a period of

    A. 1 1/2 weeks
    B. 28 days
    C. 45 days
    D. 4 months

19. What type of window is hinged at the top so that it may be opened outward at the bottom?

    A. Storm
    B. Casement
    C. Sash
    D. Awning

20. What is the usual thickness, in inches, for the finish coat in MOST plastering projects?   20.___

    A. 1/16   B. 1/8   C. 1/4   D. 1/2

21. Due to the *swell factor* involved in excavation, 1 cubic yard of excavated sand or gravel may measure _____% more as waste or backfill.   21.___

    A. 10   B. 20   C. 30   D. 50

22. What is represented by the electrical symbol shown at the right?   22.___
    A. Blanked outlet
    B. Signal push button
    C. Special purpose outlet
    D. Gauge

23. What type of nails are typically used for installing rafters?   23.___

    A. 4d   B. 8d   C. 12d   D. 16d

24. Most flat interior paint averages a coverage of about _____ square feet per gallon.   24.___

    A. 100-150   B. 200-250   C. 300-400   D. 450-550

25. Which of the following types of doors would be MOST expensive?   25.___

    A. Hollow core, birch-veneer face
    B. Solid core, walnut-faced
    C. Hollow core, hardboard-faced
    D. Solid core, birch-veneer face

KEY (CORRECT ANSWERS)

1.	C	11.	D
2.	B	12.	D
3.	A	13.	C
4.	D	14.	B
5.	D	15.	A
6.	B	16.	A
7.	B	17.	D
8.	D	18.	B
9.	C	19.	D
10.	B	20.	B

21.	B
22.	C
23.	D
24.	C
25.	B

TEST 3

DIRECTIONS: Each question or incomplete statement is followed by several suggested answers or completions. Select the one that BEST answers the question or completes the statement. *PRINT THE LETTER OF THE CORRECT ANSWER IN THE SPACE AT THE RIGHT.*

1. Most tubs, toilets, sinks, and lavatories require an average of _____ hours labor for the installation of finish plumbing. 1.____

    A. 3 B. 5 C. 7 D. 9

2. What size is most wire used for ranges and other heavy-draw equipment? 2.____

    A. 2-4 B. 5-7 C. 8-10 D. 12-16

3. A 4-man crew using hand application will typically be able to apply _____ square yards of gypsum plaster in one work day. 3.____

    A. 35-40 B. 45-60 C. 75-80 D. 85-100

4. A _____ is represented by the mechanical symbol shown at the right. 4.____

    A. lock and shield valve B. strainer
    C. pressure reducing valve D. drain line

5. What type of drywall surface is used for ceramic tile installation? 5.____

    A. Plain manila paper B. Chemically-treated paper
    C. Aluminum foil D. Greenboard

6. Which of the following steps in a grading-quantity estimation would be performed LAST? 6.____

    A. Determine approximate finish grade
    B. Calculate difference between cut and fill
    C. Estimate elevation of grid corners from contours
    D. Average the elevation of each grid square

7. In order to give desired rigidity to a wall, the top plates must overlap AT LEAST _____ inches at each joint along the wall. 7.____

    A. 12 B. 24 C. 48 D. 60

8. The horizontal framing member above window and door openings is called the 8.____

    A. molding B. footer C. chord D. lintel

9. Which of the following waterproofing materials is MOST expensive? 9.____

    A. 30-lb. asphalt paper with elastic adhesive
    B. Elastomeric waterproofing (1/32")
    C. Asphalt-coated protective board, installed in mastic
    D. Sprayed-on bituminous coating

10. If a site lawn is seeded, for how long will a contractor typically assume the responsibility for maintaining the lawn? 10.____

    A. 3 weeks B. 1 month C. 3 months D. 6 months

11. What is represented by the architectural symbol shown at the right?

    A. Brick
    B. Vertical paneling
    C. Ceramic tile
    D. Concrete block

12. In an average work day, approximately how many square feet of brick (on sand bed) paving can be laid down?

    A. 80-100   B. 600   C. 1800   D. 3000-4000

13. In lumber take-off and ordering, costs are kept separate and calculated for each of the following specifications EXCEPT

    A. size   B. grade   C. length   D. species

14. The excavation of sand will require an angle of repose (slope) of 1 ft. vertical to _____ ft. horizontal.

    A. 3/4   B. 1   C. 1 1/2   D. 2

15. Concrete sidewalks are typically poured to a depth of _____ inches.

    A. 2   B. 4   C. 6   D. 8

16. What type of concrete masonry unit is represented by the drawing shown at the right?
    A. Stretcher
    B. Pier
    C. Jamb
    D. Beam

17. Each of the following is a factor in estimating the total cost according to a quantity survey EXCEPT

    A. quantity of each material
    B. square foot area of building
    C. cost of labor for each unit of material
    D. profit

18. Approximately how many hours will it take carpentry labor to install 100 square feet of wall space, without openings?

    A. 1   B. 3   C. 5   D. 7

19. Each of the following is included in a site plan EXCEPT

    A. size of property
    B. legal description
    C. number of external doors
    D. driveways

20. What is represented by the electrical symbol shown at the right? 20.____

    A. Street light and bracket
    B. Call system
    C. Wall bracket light fixture
    D. Sound system

21. Normally, horizontal reinforcements for masonry walls are spaced about _____ inches apart. 21.____

    A. 18   B. 36   C. 48   D. 60

22. Which of the following paving materials is generally LEAST expensive? 22.____

    A. Brick on sand bed   B. Random flagstone
    C. Asphalt   D. Concrete

23. What type of nails are typically used for installing shingles? 23.____

    A. 4d   B. 8d   C. 12d   D. 16d

24. A miter joint is cut at a _____ ° angle. 24.____

    A. 30   B. 45   C. 60   D. 90

25. Generally, ceiling joists must be braced if the distance between supports is greater than 25.____

    A. 18 inches   B. 24 inches   C. 4 feet   D. 8 feet

KEY (CORRECT ANSWERS)

1. A
2. C
3. C
4. A
5. B
6. B
7. C
8. D
9. C
10. C
11. B
12. A
13. C
14. D
15. B
16. B
17. B
18. B
19. C
20. A
21. C
22. C
23. A
24. B
25. D

EXAMINATION SECTION
TEST 1

DIRECTIONS: Each question or incomplete statement is followed by several suggested answers or completions. Select the one that BEST answers the question or completes the statement. *PRINT THE LETTER OF THE CORRECT ANSWER IN THE SPACE AT THE RIGHT.*

1. What is the term for the single wood member laid on top of the foundation wall? 1.____
   A. Soffit   B. Primer   C. Jack   D. Sill

2. What is represented by the mechanical symbol shown at the right? 2.____
   A. Gauge
   C. Shower head
   B. 45° elbow
   D. Lavatory or sink

3. What is generally considered to be the MINIMUM roof pitch allowable for the use of shingles and shakes? ____ in 12. 3.____
   A. 1   B. 2   C. 3   D. 4

4. Approximately how many square feet of drywall can be hung by a single installer in an average work day? 4.____
   A. 200   B. 450   C. 800   D. 1150

5. Normally, the length of a nail is designated as 5.____
   A. casing   B. gauge   C. chase   D. penny

6. Approximately how many pounds of prepared drywall taping compound, or *mud*, will be required for 1000 square feet of area? 6.____
   A. 25   B. 50   C. 75   D. 100

7. What is represented by the architectural symbol shown at the right? 7.____
   A. Stone concrete
   C. Gravel
   B. Cinder concrete
   D. Rock

8. Which of the following constructions is NOT typically found in kitchen sinks? 8.____
   A. Enameled pressed steel
   C. Cast ceramic
   B. Enameled cast iron
   D. Stainless steel

9. The Uniform System separates construction specifications into ____ divisions. 9.____
   A. 4   B. 7   C. 11   D. 16

10. Which of the following structures typically requires lumber that has been pressure-treated? 10.____
    A. Mud sill   B. Joist   C. Stud   D. Rafter

11. If boards, rather than plywood, are used as the contact surface for foundation forms, how much of the board material should be calculated as waste?

    A. 5%   B. 15%   C. 25%   D. 40%

12. What is the term for the lateral bracing of floor joists?

    A. Crippling   B. Coursing   C. Fitting   D. Bridging

13. Approximately how many pounds of 8d nails will be required to install 1,000 board-feet of roof sheathing?

    A. 10   B. 25   C. 40   D. 65

14. What is represented by the electrical symbol shown at the right?

    A. Wiring in floor
    B. Circuit breaker
    C. Conduit with wires
    D. Switch and pilot light

15. Approximately how long will it take a two-person team to install a 10' length of 4" plastic soil line?

    A. 15 minutes
    B. 30 minutes
    C. 1 hour
    D. 1 1/2 hours

16. If forms are to be used for a foundation, the exterior face of the excavation should be made _____ inches beyond the wall line of the foundation.

    A. 6   B. 12   C. 18   D. 32

17. What is the MOST commonly used type of roll roofing material?

    A. Smooth
    B. Saturated felt
    C. Selvage edged
    D. Mineral surfaced

18. Approximately how many pounds of oakum are required per joint in one sewer line lead-and-oakum seal?

    A. 1/4   B. 1/2   C. 1 1/2   D. 3

19. What is the term for the construction beneath a foundation, usually of concrete, which helps distribute the imposed loads?

    A. Gasket
    B. Footing
    C. Escutcheon
    D. Sill

20. Approximately how many hours of labor are required for the installation of a single check valve in a length of water pipe?

    A. 1/4-1/2   B. 3/4-1 1/2   C. 1-3   D. 2-4

21. In an average work day, how many cubic yards of earth can be excavated by means of a backhoe?

    A. 10   B. 75   C. 125   D. 350

2 (#1)

22. A _____ line is represented by the mechanical symbol shown at the right? — — — —   22.____

    A. compressed air
    B. sprinkler main
    C. cold water
    D. vent

23. How many floor joists would be required for a 20-foot-long span of flooring? 23.____

    A. 10   B. 15   C. 16   D. 20

24. Of the following, bathroom tubs are MOST commonly made of 24.____

    A. enameled cast iron
    B. enameled pressed steel
    C. glazed cast ceramic
    D. enameled stainless steel

25. When calculating the air conditioning needs for a building, a loss factor of _____ should be used for the exposure of walls to the exterior on all sides. 25.____

    A. 2.0   B. 3.5   C. 6.0   D. 7.5

KEY (CORRECT ANSWERS)

1.	D	11.	B
2.	A	12.	D
3.	C	13.	C
4.	C	14.	B
5.	D	15.	C
6.	C	16.	C
7.	D	17.	D
8.	C	18.	A
9.	D	19.	B
10.	A	20.	B

21. B
22. D
23. C
24. A
25. C

TEST 2

DIRECTIONS: Each question or incomplete statement is followed by several suggested answers or completions. Select the one that BEST answers the question or completes the statement. *PRINT THE LETTER OF THE CORRECT ANSWER IN THE SPACE AT THE RIGHT.*

1. Which of the following are typically drawn to a larger scale than architectural plans? 1.___

   A. Diagrams   B. Sections   C. Details   D. Elevations

2. About how many door/window openings should a workman be able to caulk or seal in an average work day? 2.___

   A. 10   B. 20   C. 30   D. 40

3. The typical residential air conditioning requirement per 1 square foot of space is about _____ British Thermal Units (BTU's). 3.___

   A. 20   B. 30   C. 40   D. 50

4. What is represented by the mechanical symbol shown at the right? 4.___
   A. Automatic expansion valve
   B. Gauge
   C. Compressor
   D. Water closet, tank type

5. In an average work day, approximately how many cubic yards of earth can be excavated by means of crew hand shoveling and truck loading? 5.___

   A. 3-7   B. 8-10   C. 12-27   D. 18-32

6. The labor for installation of bath accessories should be calculated as 6.___

   A. plumbing   B. tile
   C. common labor   D. carpentry

7. Which of the following materials, purchased for gutters, would be LEAST expensive? 7.___

   A. Zinc alloy   B. Galvanized steel
   C. Copper   D. Zinc

8. Which of the following is NOT classified as *rough* electrical work? 8.___

   A. Conduit and wiring
   B. Installation of service equipment
   C. Switch and outlet boxes
   D. Connections to motors and fans

9. Approximately how many square feet of interior acoustic duct lining can be installed in an average work day? 9.___

   A. 25-50   B. 50-75   C. 75-120   D. 100-125

10. The *R-value* of insulation material is a function of each of the following characteristics EXCEPT

   A. thickness B. height
   C. vapor barrier D. air space

11. Generally, finishing hardware costs will be a MINIMUM of _____% of the total job cost.

   A. .5 B. 1 C. 3 D. 7

12. Due to the *swell factor* involved in excavation, 1 cubic yard of excavated rock may measure _____% more as waste or backfill.

   A. 10 B. 20 C. 30 D. 50

13. What type of concrete masonry unit is represented by the drawing shown at the right?
   A. Partition
   B. Floor
   C. Trough
   D. Frogged brick

14. Which of the following wood floor materials would be LEAST expensive to install?

   A. Unfinished plank B. Walnut parquet
   C. Maple strip D. Oak parquet

15. What is generally considered to be the MAXIMUM roof pitch allowable for the use of mineral-surfaced roll roofing? _____ in 12.

   A. 1 B. 2 C. 3 D. 4

16. Most stains that are applied to interior wood finish can cover about _____ square feet per gallon.

   A. 100 B. 250 C. 350 D. 550

17. The exposed finishing hardware on windows is USUALLY made of

   A. steel B. aluminum C. wood D. bronze

18. What would the calculated BM (board measure) be for a length of lumber measuring 2" x 12" x 10"?

   A. 10 B. 20 C. 48 D. 240

19. Which of the following materials, purchased as sheet metal flashing for roofing, would be LEAST expensive?

   A. Aluminum B. Galvanized steel
   C. Copper D. Zinc

20. Approximately how long will it take one worker to complete the lathing work for 100 square feet of a non-bearing wall?

   A. 30 minutes B. 1 hour
   C. 90 minutes D. Two hours

21. Sewer pipe is MOST often made of 21.____

   A. plastic B. copper
   C. galvanized steel D. cast iron

22. In an average work day, approximately how many cubic yards of earth can be backfilled by means of a man-operated pneumatic tamper? 22.____

   A. 8-10 B. 12-20 C. 30-40 D. 75

23. A _____ is used to calculate the total cost of electrical work. 23.____

   A. quantity survey
   B. lump-sum amount
   C. cost-per-square-foot estimate
   D. unit cost estimate

24. What is represented by the architectural symbol shown at the right? 24.____

   A. Plywood B. Wood finish
   C. Rough lumber D. Vertical paneling

25. For how many hours should a *C label* fire door be able to withstand continuous fire exposure? 25.____

   A. 3/4 B. 1 C. 1 1/2 D. 3

KEY (CORRECT ANSWERS)

1.	B	11.	A
2.	C	12.	D
3.	A	13.	D
4.	C	14.	C
5.	B	15.	A
6.	D	16.	D
7.	B	17.	D
8.	D	18.	B
9.	D	19.	A
10.	B	20.	D

21. D
22. C
23. A
24. A
25. A

TEST 3

DIRECTIONS: Each question or incomplete statement is followed by several suggested answers or completions. Select the one that BEST answers the question or completes the statement. *PRINT THE LETTER OF THE CORRECT ANSWER IN THE SPACE AT THE RIGHT.*

1. Exterior paints are commonly made from all of the following materials EXCEPT   1.____

   A. alkyd resin B. oleoresin
   C. full latex   D. oil latex

2. Due to the *swell factor* involved in excavation, 1 cubic yard of excavated *normal* earth may measure _____% more as waste or backfill.   2.____

   A. 10   B. 20   C. 30   D. 50

3. According to established finish-designation standards, which of the following finish materials would be ranked at the LOWEST grade?   3.____

   A. White bronze   B. Bright bronze
   C. Sanded dull black D. Cadmium-plated

4. Which plumbing component takes waste from a building to the municipal sewer?   4.____

   A. Drain line   B. Soil line
   C. Clean-out   D. Trap

5. Approximately how many pounds of 6d nails will be required to install 1000 square feet of siding?   5.____

   A. 10-12   B. 15-17   C. 35-40   D. 45-50

6. Calculations for paving amounts are typically made in units of   6.____

   A. surface square feet   B. surface linear feet
   C. cubic feet   D. weight

7. Which of the following types of glass will be MOST expensive?   7.____

   A. 1/4" clear plate
   B. 1/8" patterned *obscure* glass
   C. 1/4" tempered plate
   D. 1/4" wire glass

8. What type of brick masonry unit is represented by the drawing shown at the right?   8.____
   A. Modular
   B. Norwegian
   C. Roman
   D. Engineer

9. Approximately how many pounds of flooring nails are required for the installation of 1000 square feet of wood strip flooring?   9.____

   A. 10   B. 25   C. 35   D. 50

10. The cost for masonry work is typically estimated in terms of

    A. surface square feet   B. surface linear feet
    C. cubic feet   D. weight

11. In most newer buildings, vent piping is made of

    A. galvanized steel   B. lead
    C. cast iron   D. plastic

12. If 2" x 10" ceiling joists are installed with 16" of space between them, approximately how many hours of labor will it take to install joists for 100 square feet of ceiling area?

    A. 1 1/2   B. 3 1/2   C. 5 1/2   D. 7 1/2

13. What type of labor will usually be responsible for the installation of fiberglass batten insulation?

    A. Finish   B. Roofing
    C. Common labor   D. Carpentry

14. What is generally considered to be the MINIMUM allowable pitch of a roof that will be furnished with standing seam?
    _____ in 12.

    A. 2   B. 3   C. 4   D. 5

15. A _____ valve is represented by the mechanical symbol shown at the right?

    A. diaphragm   B. lock and shield
    C. gate   D. check

16. Approximately how many linear feet of galvanized steel pipe can be installed in a typical work day?

    A. 35-40   B. 50-60   C. 65-75   D. 85-100

17. Reinforcement anchor bolts are typically spaced around a building at _____ intervals.

    A. 4"-6"   B. 8"-12"   C. 1'-4'   D. 4'-6'

18. Which of the following types of wall constructions will have the GREATEST sound-dampening effect?

    A. Single-stud gypsum board
    B. Metal-stud plaster on lath
    C. Single-stud plaster on gypsum board
    D. Staggered-stud gypsum board

19. For accurate painting estimates for wall openings, such as doors and windows, the general practice is to add _____ to all height and width figures associated with the openings.

    A. 6 inches   B. 1 foot   C. 2 feet   D. 4 feet

20. In an average work day, approximately how many square feet of rock or gravel base course for paving can be laid down?

A. 80-100   B. 600   C. 1800   D. 3000-4000

21. Each of the following is a factor in the estimation of door costs EXCEPT   21._____

    A. size   B. lockset   C. type   D. finish

22. What is represented by the mechanical symbol shown at the right?   22._____
    A. Automatic expansion valve
    B. Ceiling air outlet
    C. Floor drain
    D. Reducer

23. Concrete for on-grade floor installations should typically have a compressive strength of AT LEAST _____ psi.   23._____

    A. 500   B. 1000   C. 1500   D. 2000

24. Bathroom toilets are MOST commonly made of   24._____

    A. enameled cast iron
    B. enameled pressed steel
    C. glazed cast ceramic
    D. enameled stainless steel

25. Which of the following types of windows would be LEAST expensive to install?   25._____

    A. Aluminum, horizontal sliding
    B. Wood, casement
    C. Steel, double-hung
    D. Aluminum, projected vent

KEY (CORRECT ANSWERS)

1.	B	11.	D
2.	C	12.	B
3.	D	13.	D
4.	B	14.	B
5.	A	15.	D
6.	A	16.	C
7.	C	17.	D
8.	C	18.	D
9.	D	19.	C
10.	A	20.	D

21. B
22. A
23. D
24. C
25. A

EXAMINATION SECTION
TEST 1

DIRECTIONS: Each question or incomplete statement is followed by several suggested answers or completions. Select the one that BEST answers the question or completes the statement. *PRINT THE LETTER OF THE CORRECT ANSWER IN THE SPACE AT THE RIGHT.*

1. Concrete with a slump of 2 inches would *most likely* be used for

    A. floors
    B. thin wall sections
    C. columns
    D. deep beams

    1._____

2. The structure above the roof of a building which encloses a stairway is called a

    A. scuttle
    B. bulkhead
    C. penthouse
    D. shaft

    2._____

3. A #4 reinforcing bar has a diameter, in inches, of *approximately*

    A. 1/4   B. 3/8   C. 1/2   D. 5/8

    3._____

4. A spandrel beam will usually be found

    A. at the wall
    B. around stairs
    C. at the peak of a roof
    D. underneath a column

    4._____

5. Oil is applied to the inside surfaces of concrete forms to

    A. prevent loss of water from the concrete
    B. obtain smoother concrete surfaces
    C. make stripping easier
    D. prevent honeycombing

    5._____

6. A retaining wall is built with a batter.
   Of the following conditions, the one which *most likely* applies to the wall is

    A. it is out of plumb
    B. it is thinner at top than at bottom
    C. neither surface is vertical
    D. both surfaces are vertical

    6._____

7. Two cubic yards of sand and four cubic yards of broken stone are to be used to make 1:2:4 concrete.
   If all the aggregate is used, the number of bags of cement that would be required is

    A. 1   B. 9   C. 18   D. 27

    7._____

8. A rectangular plot is 30 feet wide by 60 feet long. The length of the diagonal, in feet, is *most nearly*

    A. 68   B. 67   C. 66   D. 65

    8._____

9. Wood floor joists are supported on masonry walls which have a clear spacing of 17'0". The number of rows of cross-bridging required is

    A. 4   B. 3   C. 2   D. 1

    9._____

10. When painting wood, the puttying of nail holes and cracks should be done

   A. *after* the priming coat is dry
   B. *before* the priming coat is applied
   C. *while* the priming coat is still wet
   D. *after* the finish coat is applied

11. The material that would normally be used to make a corbel in a brick wall is

   A. brick   B. wood   C. steel   D. concrete

12. Headers and trimmers are used in the construction of

   A. footings   B. walls   C. floors   D. arches

13. In the design of stairs, the designer should consider

   A. maximum height of riser only
   B. minimum width of tread only
   C. product of riser height by tread width only
   D. all of the above

14. A reduction in the required number of columns in a building can be made by using one of the following types of beam. Which one?

   A. floor   B. girder   C. cantilever   D. jack

15. Doors sheathed in metal are known as _____ doors.

   A. kalamein   B. tin-clad   C. bethlehem   D. flemish

16. A coat of plaster which is scratched deliberately would *most likely* be

   A. used in two-coat work only
   B. the first coat placed
   C. the second coat placed
   D. condemned by the inspector

17. A concealed draft opening is

   A. *good* because it improves the appearance of a room
   B. *bad* because it might be accidentally blocked up
   C. *good* because it can be used to regulate the flow of fresh air
   D. *bad* because it is a fire hazard

18. A groove is cut in the underside of a stone sill. This is done to

   A. keep rain water from running down the wall
   B. allow the insertion of dowels
   C. improve the mortar bond
   D. reduce the weight of the sill

19. Of the following, the one which would LEAST likely be used in conjunction with the others is 19._____

　　A. rafter　　　　　　　　　　B. collar beam
　　C. ridgeboard　　　　　　　　D. tail beam

20. The dimensions of a 2 x 4 when dressed are, *most nearly,* 20._____

　　A. 2 x 4　　　　　　　　　　B. 1 1/2 x 3 1/2
　　C. 1 5/8 x 3 5/8　　　　　　D. 1 3/4 x 3 1/2

21. The story heights of a building could be MOST readily determined from 21._____

　　A. a plan view
　　B. an elevation view
　　C. a plot map
　　D. all of the above

22. Honeycombing in concrete is *most likely* to occur 22._____

　　A. if the forms are vibrated
　　B. near the top of the forms
　　C. if the mix is stiff
　　D. if the concrete is well-spaded

23. A weather joint in brick work is one in which the mortar is 23._____

　　A. flush with the face of the lower brick and slopes inward
　　B. flush with the face of the upper brick and slopes inward
　　C. recessed a fixed distance behind the face of the brick
　　D. flush with the face of upper and lower brick but curves inward between the two bricks

24. A 12 inch brick wall is constructed using stretchers only.
The PRINCIPAL objection to such a wall is with 24._____

　　A. appearance　　　　　　　　B. construction difficulties
　　C. bond　　　　　　　　　　　D. dimensional problems

25. To prevent sagging joists from damaging a brick wall in the event of a fire, it is BEST to 25._____

　　A. anchor the joists firmly in the wall
　　B. make a bevel cut on the end of the joists
　　C. use bridal irons to support the joists
　　D. box out the wall for the joists

26. Flashing would *most likely* be found in a 26._____

　　A. footing　　　B. floor　　　C. ceiling　　　D. parapet

27. Vermiculite is used in plaster to 27._____

　　A. reduce weight
　　B. permit easier cleaning
　　C. give architectural effects
　　D. reduce the mixing water required

28. The volume in cubic feet of a room 8'6" wide by 10'6" long by 8'8" high is *most nearly*

    A. 770   B. 774   C. 778   D. 782

29. A slab of concrete is 2'0" by 3'0" by 8" thick.
    The weight of the slab is, in pounds, *most nearly*

    A. 450   B. 500   C. 550   D. 600

30. Wainscoting is USUALLY found on

    A. floors   B. walls   C. ceilings   D. roofs

31. A piece of wood covering the plaster below the stool of a window is called a(n)

    A. apron   B. sill   C. coping   D. trimmer

32. English bond is used in

    A. plastering   B. papering   C. roofing   D. bricklaying

33. In plastering, coves would *most likely* be found where

    A. wall meets ceiling   B. one wall meets another
    C. wall meets floor   D. wall meets column

34. Fire stopping is usually accomplished by

    A. installing self-closing doors
    B. bricking up the space between furring at floors
    C. installing wire glass
    D. using fire resistive materials throughout the building

35. A Class 1 (fireproof structure) building has floor sleepers of wood. This is

    A. *not permitted*
    B. *permitted*
    C. *permitted* if the space between sleepers is filled with incombustible material
    D. *permitted* if a wearing surface similar to asphalt tile is applied to the wooden flooring

KEY (CORRECT ANSWERS)

1.	A		16.	B
2.	B		17.	D
3.	C		18.	A
4.	A		19.	D
5.	C		20.	C
6.	B		21.	B
7.	D		22.	C
8.	B		23.	A
9.	C		24.	C
10.	A		25.	B
11.	A		26.	D
12.	C		27.	A
13.	D		28.	B
14.	C		29.	D
15.	A		30.	B

31.	A
32.	D
33.	A
34.	B
35.	C

TEST 2

DIRECTIONS: Each question or incomplete statement is followed by several suggested answers or completions. Select the one that BEST answers the question or completes the statement. *PRINT THE LETTER OF THE CORRECT ANSWER IN THE SPACE AT THE RIGHT.*

1. Joints on interior surfaces of brick walls are usually flush joints EXCEPT when the walls are to be

    A. painted
    B. plastered
    C. waterproofed
    D. dampproofed

    1.____

2. The headers in a brick veneer wall serve

    A. both a structural and an architectural purpose
    B. a structural purpose only
    C. an architectural purpose only
    D. NO structural or architectural purpose

    2.____

3. Of the following, the one which is NOT usually classified as interior wood trim is

    A. apron   B. ribbon   C. jamb   D. base mold

    3.____

4. Single-strength glass would *most likely* be found in

    A. single light sash
    B. doors in fire walls
    C. doors in fire partitions
    D. multi-light sash

    4.____

5. The one of the following items that is LEAST related to the others is

    A. newel   B. riser   C. nosing   D. sill

    5.____

6. In a plastered room, grounds for plaster are LEAST likely to be used

    A. at baseboards
    B. around windows
    C. around doors
    D. at the top of wainscoting

    6.____

7. Of the following types of walls, the type which is *most likely* an interior wall is _____ wall.

    A. curtain   B. faced   C. panel   D. fire

    7.____

8. *Boxing* is *most likely* to be performed by a

    A. mason
    B. plasterer
    C. plumber
    D. painter

    8.____

9. Linseed oil is classified as a

    A. vehicle
    B. thinner
    C. drying oil
    D. pigment

    9.____

10. Curing of concrete would be MOST critical when the temperature and humidity are, respectively,

   A. 75° and 80%
   B. 80° and 90%
   C. 85° and 10%
   D. 90° and 95%

11. Of the following items, the item which is LEAST related to the others is

   A. putty
   B. sash weight
   C. glazier's points
   D. lights

12. Assume that a wood-frame house has studs of 2 x 4's.
    Placing the studs so that the wider dimension is parallel to the wall is

   A. *good* because it provides a wider nailing surface for sheathing and lathing
   B. *bad* because it reduces the open space available for windows
   C. *good* because it stiffens the frame
   D. *bad* because it reduces the load-carrying capacity of the studs

13. Government anchors are used in one of the following types of construction. Which one?

   A. Wood frame
   B. Steel beams supported on masonry bearing walls
   C. Wooden joists on masonry bearing walls
   D. Steel frame with steel joists

14. When rivet holes in structural steel fail to match up by an eighth of an inch, the BEST thing to do is

   A. ignore the mismatch and force the rivet into the hole
   B. enlarge the holes with a drift pin
   C. ream the holes to a larger diameter
   D. use a smaller sized rivet

15. The BEST way to use two angles to make a lintel is

16. A single channel section would *most likely* be used for a

   A. floor beam
   B. girder
   C. spandrel beam
   D. column

17. An oil-base paint is usually thinned with

   A. linseed oil
   B. turpentine
   C. a drying oil
   D. a resin

18. Red lead is often used as a pigment in metal priming paints PRIMARILY because it

   A. provides good coverage
   B. presents a good appearance
   C. makes painting easier
   D. is a rust inhibitor

19. Knots in wood that is to be painted

    A. require no special treatment
    B. should be painted with the priming paint before the priming paint is applied to the rest of the wood
    C. should be coated with linseed oil before any painting is done
    D. should be coated with shellac before any painting is done

20. A dove-tail anchor would *most likely* be used to bond brick veneer with a _____ wall.

    A. brick   B. concrete   C. wood frame   D. concrete block

21. A rafter is MOST similar in function to a

    A. joist   B. stud   C. sill   D. girder

22. In steel construction, it is usually MOST important to mill the ends of

    A. beams   B. girders   C. columns   D. lintels

23. Furring tile is usually set so that the air spaces in the tile are

    A. continuous in a vertical direction
    B. continuous in a horizontal direction
    C. closed off at the ends of each tile
    D. set at random

24. When plastering a wall surface of glazed tile, it is MOST important that the tile

    A. be wet   B. be dry
    C. be scored   D. joints be raked

25. In a peaked roof, the run of a rafter is

    A. less than the length of the rafter
    B. greater than the length of the rafter
    C. equal to the length of the rafter
    D. dependent upon the slope of the rafter

26. Construction of a dormer window does NOT usually involve

    A. cut rafters   B. rafter headers
    C. trimmer rafters   D. hip rafters

27. In a four-ply slag roof,

    A. there is no overlap of the roofing felt
    B. a uniform coating of pitch or asphalt is placed on top of the top layer of felt
    C. slag is placed between the layers of felt
    D. there is no need to use flashing

28. Copper wire basket strainers would *most likely* be used by a

    A. carpenter   B. plumber   C. painter   D. roofer

29. Splices of columns in steel construction are usually made

    A. at floor level
    B. two feet above floor level
    C. two feet below floor level
    D. midway between floors

30. In plumbing, a lead bend is usually used in the line from a

    A. slop sink   B. shower
    C. water closet   D. kitchen sink

31. The location of leaks in gas piping may be BEST detected by use of a

    A. match   B. heated filament
    C. soapy water solution D. guinea pig

32. The one of the following items that would be MOST useful in eliminating water hammer from a water system is a

    A. magnesium anode   B. surge tank
    C. clean out   D. quick-closing valve

33. The MAIN purpose of a fixture trap is to

    A. catch small articles that may have accidentally dropped in the fixture
    B. prevent back syphonage
    C. make it easier to repair the fixture
    D. block the passage of foul air

34. In a certain district, the area of a building may be no longer than 55% of the area of the lot on which it stands. On a rectangular lot 75 ft. by 125 ft., the maximum permissible area of building is, in square feet, *most nearly*

    A. 5148   B. 5152   C. 5156   D. 5160

35. The allowable tensile stress in steel is 18,000 pounds per square inch. The maximum permissible tensile load in a 1-inch diameter steel bar is, in pounds, *most nearly*

    A. 13,500   B. 13,800   C. 14,100   D. 14,400

KEY (CORRECT ANSWERS)

1.	B		16.	C
2.	C		17.	B
3.	B		18.	D
4.	D		19.	D
5.	D		20.	B
6.	D		21.	A
7.	D		22.	C
8.	D		23.	B
9.	A		24.	C
10.	C		25.	A
11.	B		26.	D
12.	D		27.	B
13.	B		28.	D
14.	C		29.	B
15.	A		30.	C

31.	C
32.	B
33.	D
34.	C
35.	C

TEST 3

DIRECTIONS: Each question or incomplete statement is followed by several suggested answers or completions. Select the one that BEST answers the question or completes the statement. *PRINT THE LETTER OF THE CORRECT ANSWER IN THE SPACE AT THE RIGHT.*

1. The ends of a joist in a brick building are cut to a bevel. This is done PRINCIPALLY to prevent damage to

    A. joist   B. floor   C. sill   D. wall

    1.____

2. Of the following, the wood that is MOST commonly used today for floor joists is

    A. long leaf yellow pine   B. douglas fir
    C. oak   D. birch

    2.____

3. Quarter sawed lumber is preferred for the best finished flooring PRINCIPALLY because it

    A. has the greatest strength
    B. shrinks the least
    C. is the easiest to nail
    D. is the easiest to handle

    3.____

4. Of the following, the MAXIMUM height that would be considered acceptable for a stair riser is

    A. 6 1/2"   B. 7 1/2"   C. 8 1/2"   D. 9 1/2"

    4.____

5. The part of a tree that will produce the DENSEST wood is the _____ wood.

    A. spring   B. summer   C. sap   D. heart

    5.____

6. Lumber in quantity is ordered by

    A. cubic feet   B. foot board measure
    C. lineal feet   D. weight and length

    6.____

7. A *chase* in a brick wall is a

    A. pilaster   B. waterstop   C. recess   D. corbel

    7.____

8. *Parging* refers to

    A. increasing the thickness of a brick wall
    B. plastering the back of face brickwork
    C. bonding face brick to backing blocks
    D. leveling each course of brick

    8.____

9. In brickwork, muriatic acid is commonly used to

    A. increase the strength of the mortar
    B. etch the brick
    C. waterproof the wall
    D. clean the wall

    9.____

10. Cement mortar can be made easier to work by the addition of a small quantity of

    A. lime   B. soda   C. litharge   D. plaster

11. Joints in brick walls are tooled

    A. immediately after each brick is laid
    B. after the mortar has had its initial set
    C. after the entire wall is completed
    D. 28 days after the wall has been built

12. If cement mortar has begun to set before it can be used in a wall, the BEST thing to do is to

    A. use the mortar immediately as is
    B. add a small quantity of lime
    C. add some water and mix thoroughly
    D. discard the mortar

13. The BEST flux to use when soldering galvanized iron is

    A. killed acid   B. sal-ammoniac
    C. muriatic acid   D. resin

14. The type of solder that would be used in *hard soldering* is _____ solder.

    A. bismuth   B. wiping   C. 50-50   D. silver

15. Roll roofing material is usually felt which has been impregnated with

    A. cement   B. mastic   C. tar   D. latex

16. The purpose of flashing on roofs is to

    A. secure roofing materials to the roof
    B. make it easier to lay the roofing
    C. prevent leaks through the roof
    D. insulate the roof from excessive heat

17. The type of chain used with sash weights is _____ link.

    A. flat   B. round
    C. figure-eight   D. basketweave

18. The material that would be used to seal around a window frame is

    A. oakum   B. litharge   C. grout   D. calking

19. The function of a window sill is *most nearly* the same as that of a

    A. jamb   B. coping   C. lintel   D. buck

20. Lightweight plaster would be made with

    A. sand   B. cinders   C. potash   D. vermiculite

21. The FIRST coat of plaster to be applied on a three-coat plaster job is the _____ coat.

    A. brown   B. scratch   C. white   D. keene

22. The FIRST coat of plaster over rock lath should be a _____ plaster.   22._____

    A. gypsum   B. lime
    C. Portland cement   D. pozzolan cement

23. The PRINCIPAL reason for covering a concrete sidewalk with straw or paper after the concrete has been poured is to   23._____

    A. prevent people from walking on the concrete while it is still wet
    B. impart a rough, non-slip surface to the concrete
    C. prevent excessive evaporation of water in the concrete
    D. shorten the length of time it would take for the concrete to harden

24. Concrete is *rubbed* with a(n)   24._____

    A. emery wheel   B. carborundum brick
    C. sandstone   D. alundum stick

25. To prevent concrete from sticking to forms, the forms should be painted with   25._____

    A. oil   B. kerosene   C. water   D. lime

26. One method of measuring the consistency of a concrete mix is by means of a _____ test.   26._____

    A. penetration   B. flow
    C. slump   D. weight

27. A chemical that is sometimes used to prevent the freezing of concrete in cold weather is   27._____

    A. alum   B. glycerine
    C. calcium chloride D. sodium nitrate

28. The one of the following that is LEAST commonly used for columns is   28._____

    A. wide flange beams   B. angles
    C. concrete-filled pipe D. "I" beams

29. Fire protection of steel floor beams is MOST frequently accomplished by the use of   29._____

    A. gypsum block   B. brick
    C. rock wool fill   D. vermiculite gypsum plaster

30. A *Pittsburgh lock* is a(n)   30._____

    A. emergency door lock   B. sheet metal joint
    C. elevator safety   D. boiler valve

31. Of the following items, the one which is NOT used in making fastenings to masonry or plaster walls is a(n)   31._____

    A. lead shield   B. expansion bolt
    C. rawl plug   D. steel bushing

32. The term *bell and spigot* USUALLY refers to   32._____

    A. refrigerator motors   B. cast iron pipes
    C. steam radiator outlets D. electrical receptacles

33. In plumbing work, a valve which allows water to flow in one direction only is commonly known as a _____ valve.

   A. check   B. globe   C. gate   D. stop

34. A pipe coupling is BEST used to connect two pieces of pipe of

   A. the same diameter in a straight line
   B. the same diameter at right angles to each other
   C. different diameters at a 45° angle
   D. different diameters in a 1/8th bend

35. One method of testing fuses is to connect a pair of test lamps in the circuit in such a manner that the test lamp will light up if the fuse is good and will remain dark if the fuse is bad. In the illustration, 1 and 2 are fuses. In order to test if fuse 1 is bad, test lamps should be connected between

   A. A and B   B. B and D   C. A and D   D. C and B

36. Operating an incandescent electric light bulb at less than its rated voltage will result in

   A. shorter life and brighter light
   B. longer life and dimmer light
   C. brighter light and longer life
   D. dimmer light and shorter life

37. In order to control a lamp from two different positions, it is necessary to use

   A. two single pole switches
   B. one single pole switch and one four-way switch
   C. two three-way switches
   D. one single pole switch and one four-way switch

38. The PRINCIPAL reason for the grounding of electrical equipment and circuits is to

   A. prevent short circuits   B. insure safety from shock
   C. save power   D. increase voltage

39. The ordinary single-pole flush wall type switch must be connected

   A. across the line
   B. in the "hot" conductor
   C. in the grounded conductor
   D. in the white conductor

40. A strike plate is MOST closely associated with a

   A. lock   B. sash   C. butt   D. tie rod

41. A room is 7'6" wide by 9'0" long, with a ceiling height of 8'0". One gallon of flat paint will cover approximately 400 square feet of wall.
The number of gallons of this paint required to paint the walls of this room, making no deductions for windows or doors, is *most nearly* _____ gallon.

   A. 1/4 B. 1/3 C. 3/4 D. 1

42. The cost of a certain job is broken down as follows:
   Materials $375
   Rental of equipment 120
   Labor   315
The percentage of the total cost of the job that can be charged to materials is *most nearly*

   A. 40% B. 42% C. 44% D. 46%

43. By trial, it is found that by using two cubic feet of sand, a 5 cubic foot batch of concrete is produced. Using the same proportions, the amount of sand required to produce 2 cubic yards of concrete is *most nearly* _____ cubic feet.

   A. 20 B. 22 C. 24 D. 26

44. It takes four men six days to do a certain job. Working at the same speed, the number of days it will take three men to do this job is

   A. 7 B. 8 C. 9 D. 10

45. The cost of rawl plugs is $2.75 per gross. The cost of 2,448 rawl plugs is

   A. $46.75 B. $47.25 C. $47.75 D. $48.25

KEY (CORRECT ANSWERS)

1. D	11. B	21. B	31. D	41. C
2. B	12. D	22. A	32. B	42. D
3. B	13. C	23. C	33. A	43. B
4. B	14. D	24. B	34. A	44. B
5. D	15. C	25. A	35. C	45. A
6. B	16. C	26. C	36. B	
7. C	17. A	27. C	37. C	
8. B	18. D	28. B	38. B	
9. D	19. B	29. D	39. B	
10. A	20. D	30. B	40. A	

EXAMINATION SECTION
TEST 1

DIRECTIONS: Each question or incomplete statement is followed by several suggested answers or completions. Select the one that BEST answers the question or completes the statement. *PRINT THE LETTER OF THE CORRECT ANSWER IN THE SPACE AT THE RIGHT.*

Questions 1-5.

DIRECTIONS: For Questions 1 through 5, inclusive, Column I lists frequently used construction terms. Column II lists some of the building trades. For each item listed in Column I, enter in the appropriate space at the right the capital letter in front of the trade listed in Column II that is MOST closely associated with the item. Each trade may be used more than once or not at all.

COLUMN I	COLUMN II	
1. Bed	A. Plumbing	1.____
2. Wiping	B. Plastering	2.____
3. Brown	C. Carpentry	3.____
4. Key	D. Masonry	4.____
5. Bridging	E. Painting	5.____
	F. Steelwork	
	G. Roofing	

6. A *cricket* would be found 6.____

    A. on a roof
    B. at a structural steel connection
    C. supporting reinforcing steel
    D. over a window

7. *Cutting in* is done when 7.____

    A. trimming a stud to size
    B. fitting a bat in a brick wall
    C. painting in tight corners
    D. trimming tallow for a wiped joint

8. *Corbeling* results in 8.____

    A. strengthening a concrete column
    B. waterproofing a foundation wall
    C. anchoring a steel girder to a bearing wall
    D. increasing the thickness of a brick wall

9. Solder used for copper gutters is MOST frequently

   A. 30-70   B. 40-60   C. 50-50   D. 60-40

10. A jack rafter runs from

    A. plate to ridge
    B. hip to ridge
    C. plate to hip
    D. plate to plate

11. The one of the following items that is LEAST related to the others is

    A. sill   B. joist   C. sole   D. newel

12. A *fire cut* is made on

    A. timber posts
    B. rafters
    C. floor joists
    D. lathing

13. The one of the following items that is LEAST related to the others is

    A. joist hanger
    B. pintle
    C. bridle iron
    D. stirrup

14. The PROPER order of nailing sub-flooring and bridging is

    A. top of bridging, bottom of bridging, sub-flooring
    B. bottom of bridging, sub-flooring, top of bridging
    C. top of bridging, sub-flooring, bottom of bridging
    D. bottom of bridging, top of bridging, sub-flooring

15. Sleepers would be found in

    A. walls   B. doors   C. footings   D. floors

16. The one of the following woods that is MOST commonly used for finish flooring is

    A. hemlock   B. cypress   C. larch   D. oak

17. Spacing of studs in a stud partition is MOST frequently _____" o.c.

    A. 12   B. 14   C. 16   D. 18

18. A hollow masonry wall should be used in preference to a solid masonry wall when the characteristic MOST desired is

    A. insulation
    B. strength
    C. beauty
    D. durability

19. The arrangement of headers and stretchers in brickwork is known as the

    A. bond   B. stringer   C. lacing   D. stile

20. Of the following, the reason that is LEAST likely to justify pointing brickwork is that pointing _____ the wall.

    A. improves the appearance of
    B. helps prevent cracking of
    C. increases the useful life of
    D. helps waterproof

3 (#1)

21. The purpose of flashing is to

   A. keep water out
   B. speed the set of mortar
   C. anchor a cornice
   D. cover exposed joists

22. The one of the following classes of wall that would LEAST likely be the outside wall of a building is a

   A. spandrel   B. fire   C. curtain   D. parapet

23. Lime is added to mortar USUALLY to

   A. increase the strength of the mortar
   B. make the mortar water resistant
   C. make it easier to apply the mortar
   D. improve the appearance of the mortar joint

24. Efflorescence on the face of a brick wall is BEST removed by scrubbing with a solution of

   A. muriatic acid
   B. sodium silicate
   C. oxalic acid
   D. calcium oxide

25. The one of the following that is NOT a defect in painting is

   A. chalking
   B. checking
   C. alligatoring
   D. waning

26. The one of the following ingredients of a paint that would be called the *vehicle* is

   A. white lead
   B. turpentine
   C. linseed oil
   D. pigment

27. The one of the following that is used as a rust preventative in the prime coat for painting steel is

   A. aluminum
   B. red lead
   C. titanium dioxide
   D. carbon black

28. *Boxing*, with reference to paint, means

   A. thinning   B. mixing   C. spreading   D. drying

29. When painting new wood, filling of nail holes and cracks with putty should be done

   A. 24 hours before priming
   B. immediately before priming
   C. after priming and before the second coat
   D. after the second coat and before the finish coat

30. The one of the following that is the size of a reinforcing rod MOST commonly used in reinforced concrete construction is

   A. 1 3/4" ϕ B. 18 gauge   C. #9   D. 2 ST3

31. Honeycombing in concrete is USUALLY caused by

   A. too plastic a mix
   B. high fall of concrete
   C. mixing too long
   D. inadequate vibration

32. A concrete mix is indicated as 1:2:3 1/2 mix. The number 2 refers to the proportion by volume of

　　A. water　　B. cement　　C. gravel　　D. sand

33. Specifications for concrete mixes frequently call for the use of dry sand. The reason for this is that the additional water in wet sand will

　　A. make it more difficult to place the concrete
　　B. decrease the strength of the concrete
　　C. cause the sand and stone to segregate
　　D. increase the cost of waterproofing

34. Curing of concrete serves PRIMARILY to

　　A. prevent freezing of the concrete
　　B. permit early removal of forms
　　C. delay setting of the concrete
　　D. prevent evaporation of moisture

35. The MAIN reason that forms for concrete work are oiled is to

　　A. *permit* easy removal of forms
　　B. *prevent* rust marks on the concrete
　　C. *prevent* bleeding of water
　　D. *permit* easier vibration of the concrete

36. The one of the following terms that is LEAST related to the others is

　　A. 5-ply　　　　　　　B. mastic
　　C. vapor barrier　　　D. flashing

37. Before quicklime can be used for plaster, it must be

　　A. slaked　　B. burned　　C. floated　　D. glazed

38. When a hard plaster is required, as in halls, the one of the following that would MOST likely be used is

　　A. lime　　　　　B. Keene's cement
　　C. stucco　　　　D. marbling

39. To give plaster a hard finish, hydrated lime is mixed with

　　A. white cement　　B. linseed oil putty
　　C. white lead　　　　D. plaster of paris

40. The purpose of a ground in plaster work is to

　　A. provide a key for the plaster
　　B. help the plasterer make an even wall
　　C. prevent the plasterer's scaffold from slipping
　　D. hold the loose plaster before it is placed

41. When a lightweight plaster is required, the one of the following fine aggregates that is MOST likely to be used is

   A. cinders
   B. sand
   C. talc
   D. vermiculite

42. Of the following fireproofing materials, the one which would be MOST frequently used to fireproof steel columns in a fireproof building is

   A. sheet rock
   B. vermiculite plaster
   C. brick
   D. rock lath

43. The one of the following items that is LEAST related to the others is

   A. rock wool
   B. wall board
   C. sheet rock
   D. rock lath

44. The first layer of plaster placed in a 3-coat plaster job is called the _____ coat.

   A. brown
   B. scratch
   C. hard
   D. white

45. The one of the following symbols that represents a steel section which is MOST similar in appearance to a W section is

   A. U
   B. L
   C. I
   D. Z

46. A plate used to connect two steel angles in a roof truss is known as a(n)

   A. angle iron
   B. gusset plate
   C. bearing plate
   D. tie bar

47. Steel beams are COMMONLY anchored to brick walls by

   A. government anchors
   B. tie rods
   C. eye bars
   D. anchor bolts

48. Rivet holes are lined up with a

   A. set screw
   B. ginnywink
   C. drift pin
   D. trivet

49. A sewer that carries BOTH storm water and sewage is called a _____ sewer.

   A. sanitary
   B. flush
   C. combined
   D. mixed

50. A fresh air inlet for a house drainage system would be connected to the system

   A. just ahead of the house trap
   B. at each horizontal branch line
   C. at the top of the stack through the roof
   D. at the trap of each water closet

KEY (CORRECT ANSWERS)

1.	D	11.	D	21.	A	31.	D	41.	D
2.	A	12.	C	22.	B	32.	D	42.	B
3.	B	13.	B	23.	C	33.	B	43.	A
4.	B	14.	C	24.	A	34.	D	44.	B
5.	C	15.	D	25.	D	35.	A	45.	C
6.	A	16.	D	26.	C	36.	C	46.	B
7.	C	17.	C	27.	B	37.	A	47.	A
8.	D	18.	A	28.	B	38.	B	48.	C
9.	C	19.	A	29.	C	39.	D	49.	C
10.	C	20.	B	30.	C	40.	B	50.	A

TEST 2

DIRECTIONS: Each question or incomplete statement is followed by several suggested answers or completions. Select the one that BEST answers the question or completes the statement. *PRINT THE LETTER OF THE CORRECT ANSWER IN THE SPACE AT THE RIGHT.*

Questions 1-5.

DIRECTIONS: Column I consists of a list of trades, and Column II lists tools used in those trades. In the space at the right, opposite the number of the trade in Column I, write the letter preceding the tool of the trade in Column II.

COLUMN I		COLUMN II	
1. Carpenter	A.	Mop	1.____
2. Plumber	B.	Hawk	2.____
3. Plasterer	C.	Miter box	3.____
4. Bricklayer	D.	Shave-hook	4.____
5. Roofer	E.	Jointing tool	5.____

Questions 6-7.

DIRECTIONS: Questions 6 and 7 refer to the mortar joints shown below.

6. The mortar joint MOST frequently used on common brickwork is   6.____
   A. 1   B. 2   C. 3   D. 4

7. The mortar joint which would NOT usually be made unless an outside scaffold was used is   7.____
   A. 1   B. 2   C. 3   D. 4

8. A rectangular yard is 50'0" long by 8'6" wide.   8.____
   The area of the yard is, in square feet,
   A. 420.0   B. 422.5   C. 425.0   D. 427.5

9. A rectangular court is 23'0" long by 9'6" wide. The length of the diagonal is MOST NEARLY

   A. 24'8" B. 24'10" C. 25'2" D. 25'6"

10. Concrete weighs 150 pounds per cubic foot.
    A slab of concrete 6'0" long by 3'6" wide by 1'4" thick weighs MOST NEARLY _____ pounds.

    A. 4150 B. 4200 C. 4250 D. 4300

11. A building 32'0" by 65'0" occupies a lot 60'0" by 110'0". The ratio of building area to lot area is MOST NEARLY

    A. 0.32 B. 0.33 C. 0.34 D. 0.35

12. When painting wood, puttying of nail holes and cracks is done

    A. before any painting is started
    B. after the priming coat is applied
    C. after the finish coat is applied
    D. at any stage in the painting

13. The process of pouring paint from one container to another in order to mix it is known as

    A. bleeding B. boxing C. cutting D. stirring

14. Paint is *thinned* with

    A. linseed oil   B. turpentine
    C. varnish   D. gasoline

15. A wood screw which can be tightened by a wrench is known as a _____ screw.

    A. lag B. Philips C. carriage D. monkey

16. To permit easy removal of forms from concrete, the inside surfaces of the forms are often coated with

    A. paint B. oil C. water D. asphalt

17. Sixteen pieces of 2 x 4 lumber, each 10'6" long, contain a total of _____ FBM.

    A. 110 B. 111 C. 112 D. 113

18. The consistency of concrete is measured with a

    A. Vicat needle   B. slump cone
    C. hook gage   D. bourdon gage

19. End-matched lumber would MOST likely be used for

    A. sheathing B. roofing C. flooring D. siding

20. A post or shore is to be placed midway between columns to support the formwork for a reinforced concrete girder. The post should be cut

    A. short, so that wedging is required
    B. to exact length

C. long, so that it will have to be driven into place
D. in two pieces, to permit jackknifing into place

21. Batter boards are set by a

    A. mason   B. plumber   C. roofer   D. surveyor

22. Of the following terms, all of which refer to tools, the one which is LEAST related to the others is

    A. back   B. box-end   C. cross-cut   D. rip

23. Of the following tools, the one which is LEAST like the others is

    A. brace and bit
    B. draw-knife
    C. plans
    D. spoke-shave

24. When wood splits easily, it is advisable to drill a hole for each nail. The hole for the nail should be _____ the nail.

    A. larger in diameter than
    B. smaller in diameter than
    C. exactly the same diameter as
    D. less than one-quarter the length of

25. The length of a 10-penny nail, in inches, is

    A. $2\frac{1}{2}$ B. 3   C. $3\frac{1}{2}$ D. 4

26. The decimal equivalent of 31/64 of an inch is MOST NEARLY

    A. 0.45   B. 0.46   C. 0.47   D. 0.48

27. Of the following, the one which is BEST classified as an abrasive is

    A. a saw   B. a chisel   C. graphite   D. sandpaper

28. Of the following construction materials, the one which would MOST likely be stored directly on the ground is

    A. brick   B. cement   C. steel   D. wood

29. The strength of brick walls is based upon the type of mortar used.
    The relative strength of the various types of mortar, in descending order, is

    A. cement, lime, cement-lime
    B. lime, cement-lime, cement
    C. cement-lime, cement, lime
    D. cement, cement-lime, lime

30. Coating reinforcing rods with oil before placing them in the forms is

    A. *good* practice, because it prevents rusting
    B. *poor* practice, because it makes the rods difficult to handle
    C. *good* practice if the forms are oiled
    D. *poor* practice, because it destroys the bond between the concrete and the rods

31. If the mixing plant should break down after one-half the concrete has been mixed for a floor, the BEST thing to do would be to

   A. take the concrete out of the forms and throw it away
   B. spread the available concrete evenly over the floor area
   C. block off one-half of the floor area and place the available concrete in the blocked-off area
   D. keep mixing the concrete in the forms with shovels until the plant is repaired

32. Splicing of reinforcing bars is accomplished by

   A. using wire ties
   B. underlapping the bars
   C. hooking the bars
   D. using metal clips

33. A sanitary sewer carries

   A. storm water only
   B. sewage only
   C. sewage and storm water
   D. the discharge from a sewage plant

34. A neat line

   A. is the result of good workmanship
   B. is used in concrete construction only
   C. defines an outer limit of a structure
   D. defines an outer limit of excavation for a structure

35. Continued trowelling of a cement-finish floor for a building is

   A. *good* practice, because it provides a smooth floor
   B. *poor* practice, because it produces a slippery floor
   C. *poor* practice, because it brings the fines to the surface
   D. *good* practice, because it insures proper mixing of the cement finish

36. In reinforced concrete form work, a beveled chamfer strip is used to

   A. reinforce the outside of the forms
   B. reinforce the inside of the forms
   C. seal leaks in the forms
   D. do none of the foregoing

37. Cracks in lumber due to contraction along annual rings are known as

   A. checks
   B. wanes
   C. pitch pockets
   D. dry rot

38. Honeycombing is MOST likely to occur in construction involving

   A. steel   B. concrete   C. wood   D. masonry

39. Floor beams are sometimes crowned to

   A. provide arch action
   B. eliminate deflection
   C. strengthen the floor
   D. provide a more nearly level floor than would be provided by straight beams

40. In brickwork, a rowlock course consists of

    A. headers
    B. stretchers
    C. bricks laid on edge
    D. bricks laid so that the longest dimension is vertical

41. The term *bond,* as used in bricklaying, refers to

    A. structure only
    B. pattern only
    C. structure and pattern
    D. color and finish of individual bricks

42. Concrete is a mixture of cement,

    A. fine aggregate, coarse aggregate, and water
    B. sand, and water
    C. stone, and water
    D. sand, and stone

43. Consistency, when used in connection with concrete, refers to the

    A. seven-day strength
    B. twenty-eight day strength
    C. initial set before forms are removed
    D. plasticity of freshly mixed concrete

44. Brick may be used for the facing material in both faced walls and veneered walls. The distinction between the two types of walls relates to

    A. bonding or lack of bonding between facing and backing
    B. type of material in facing and backing
    C. relative thickness of facing and backing
    D. the type of mortar used

45. A plaster *key* is NOT formed on _____ lath.

    A. wood   B. metal
    C. expanded metal   D. gypsum

46. Of the following, the BEST tool to use to make a hole in a coping stone is a

    A. star drill   B. coping saw
    C. pneumatic grinder   D. diamond wheel dresser

47. Roughing refers to work performed by a

    A. carpenter   B. bricklayer
    C. plumber   D. roofer

48. A post supporting a handrail is known as a

    A. tread   B. riser   C. newel   D. bevel

49. The live load on a floor is 40 pounds per square foot. The floor joists are on a 14'0" span and are spaced 2'6" on centers.
   The maximum live load carried by a joist, in pounds, is MOST NEARLY
   A. 700   B. 933   C. 1167   D. 1400

50. Of the following terms, the one LEAST related to the others is
   A. ground
   B. purlin
   C. rafter
   D. ridge board

KEY (CORRECT ANSWERS)

1. C	11. A	21. D	31. C	41. C
2. D	12. B	22. B	32. A	42. A
3. B	13. B	23. A	33. B	43. D
4. E	14. B	24. B	34. C	44. A
5. A	15. A	25. B	35. C	45. D
6. C	16. B	26. D	36. D	46. A
7. A	17. C	27. D	37. A	47. C
8. C	18. B	28. A	38. B	48. C
9. B	19. C	29. D	39. D	49. D
10. B	20. A	30. D	40. C	50. A

EXAMINATION SECTION
TEST 1

DIRECTIONS: Each question or incomplete statement is followed by several suggested answers or completions. Select the one that BEST answers the question or completes the statement. *PRINT THE LETTER OF THE CORRECT ANSWER IN THE SPACE AT THE RIGHT.*

1. The MOST commonly used method for site measurement is

    A. baseline B. direct
    C. triangulation D. pacing

    1._____

2. Which of the following is NOT a purpose of shrubs in landscaping?

    A. Reinforcing pathway alignments
    B. Providing supplementary low-level baffles and screens
    C. To furnish floral and foliage display
    D. Stabilizing slopes

    2._____

3. Of the following, _____ is TYPICALLY performed during the research stage of the planning design process.

    A. site analysis B. schematic studies
    C. photography D. adjustment

    3._____

4. The MAXIMUM allowable ratio (inches) of a vertical riser's height to the width of the tread in outdoor steps is

    A. 4 1/2 to 17 B. 5 to 16 C. 6 to 14 D. 8 to 10

    4._____

5. Which of the following steps in the implementation of site development would normally occur FIRST?

    A. Environmental impact assessment
    B. Site-structure plan
    C. Topographical survey
    D. Conceptual plan

    5._____

6. Drains should be placed farthest apart when installed in

    A. clay B. silt C. loam D. sand

    6._____

7. Approximately how many *secondary* tree species should be used to accentuate the theme tree of a site?

    A. 1-2 B. 3-5 C. 7-10 D. 10-12

    7._____

8. Technically, all land extending to within a 20-100 mile radius of a given site is said to be contained within the site's

    A. area B. domain C. region D. sector

    8._____

9. If a handful of moist soil feels silky or soapy and can be molded, but is not cohesive, it is MOST likely

   A. silty-loam B. marl
   C. clay D. clay-loam

10. In lawn areas, the MINIMUM allowable gradient is considered to be _____%.

    A. 1 B. 3 C. 5 D. 7

11. Which of the following plants is MOST suitable for raised bed planting?

    A. Foxglove B. Warley rose
    C. Bluebell D. Tulip

12. Each land-use region has an established north-west reference marker, known as the

    A. principal meridian B. line of demarcation
    C. range line D. base line

13. A private local road has been constructed at a width of 16 feet and consists of 2 lanes. Approximately how many dwellings is the road designed to serve?

    A. 1-5 B. 1-20 C. 5-21 D. Over 51

14. Of the following design concepts, _____ is BEST suited to large-scale urban planning.

    A. mass collection B. interconnection
    C. asymmetry D. repetition

15. What is the term for a publicly-owned strip of ground in which a street or road is placed?

    A. Place B. Right-of-way
    C. Artery D. Boulevard

16. _____ is NOT considered to be a basic element of the preliminary design process.

    A. Design principle B. Form composition
    C. Spatial composition D. Material composition

17. Where ground forms or structures impinge, plantings should be

    A. angular B. screened
    C. enframed D. compressed

18. Typically, slip lanes in arterial medians will measure _____ feet in width.

    A. 8 B. 10 C. 12 D. 16

19. Which of the following is normally performed during the synthesis stage of the planning-design process?

    A. Accommodation
    B. Performance observation
    C. Preparation of construction documents
    D. Review of governing regulations

20. In designing walkways, the general rule is to allow _____ feet of width for each pedestrian.

    A. 1   B. 2   C. 3   D. 4

21. If certain urban plantings might suffer from the effect of *frost pockets,* the BEST precaution is to

    A. use wind-hardy plants
    B. plant as close to structures as possible
    C. use shade-bearing plants
    D. leave gaps in enclosing walls

22. A landscaped pond or lake is first excavated along _____ lines, with a widened perimeter shelf.

    A. sloped   B. curved   C. parallel   D. straight

23. What is the term for the horizontal distance across a slope?

    A. Grain   B. Cross   C. Rip   D. Run

24. Direct building frontage and/or driveway connections are BEST suited to

    A. collectors   B. ways
    C. arteries   D. sub-collectors

25. Each of the following is a purpose for grading that falls within the *enhancement* category EXCEPT

    A. creating space
    B. accommodating circulation
    C. screening views
    D. providing visual interest

KEY (CORRECT ANSWERS)

1.	B	11.	B
2.	D	12.	A
3.	C	13.	B
4.	D	14.	C
5.	C	15.	B
6.	D	16.	D
7.	B	17.	D
8.	C	18.	C
9.	A	19.	A
10.	A	20.	B

21. D
22. D
23. D
24. B
25. B

TEST 2

DIRECTIONS: Each question or incomplete statement is followed by several suggested answers or completions. Select the one that BEST answers the question or completes the statement. *PRINT THE LETTER OF THE CORRECT ANSWER IN THE SPACE AT THE RIGHT.*

1. As a general rule, which of the following types of tree arrangements should be avoided in landscaping?   1.____

    A. Irregular   B. Mixed   C. Clustered   D. Geometric

2. The usual standard for the spacing of roadway lights is _____ feet.   2.____

    A. 25   B. 50   C. 100   D. 200

3. Of the following tree species, which grows MOST slowly?   3.____

    A. Beech
    C. Eucalyptus
    B. Magnolia
    D. Acacia

4. What is the term for the minimum distance that any portion of a structure must be located from a given property line?   4.____

    A. Cut   B. Setback   C. Tangent   D. Easement

5. If no handrail is provided, the MAXIMUM allowable gradient for a walkway is considered to be _____%.   5.____

    A. 3   B. 5   C. 8   D. 10

6. What is the term for a strip of land between a sidewalk and the curb of a street?   6.____

    A. Boulevard
    C. Avenue
    B. Easement
    D. Way

7. Which of the following types of retaining walls TYPICALLY makes use of struts?   7.____

    A. Crib
    C. Interceptor
    B. Diaphragm
    D. Piling

8. The total fee for designer services should be separated into all of the following categories EXCEPT _____ fee.   8.____

    A. final completion
    C. partial completion
    B. commencement
    D. retainer

9. Which of the following soil types is MOST likely to become waterlogged in winter?   9.____

    A. Gravelly
    C. Silt
    B. Clay loam
    D. Sand

10. Earth that is removed or excavated from a site is termed   10.____

    A. cut   B. slag   C. ballast   D. fill

11. Which of the following ground covers would require dry soil?   11.____

    A. Lily of the valley
    C. English ivy
    B. Woodruff
    D. Blue fescue

12. To _____ would NOT be in accordance with sound water management.

    A. minimize grading
    B. detain surface runoff in swales or ponds
    C. confine development to lowlands
    D. provide for sheet flow

13. Where two arterial roadways intersect, the strength of provided lighting should be APPROXIMATELY _____ footcandles.

    A. .2   B. .4   C. .6   D. .8

14. What type of soil consists of a mixture of clay, sand, and silt in balanced proportions?

    A. Peat   B. Marl   C. Topsoil   D. Loam

15. Of the following types of road surfaces, _____ will require the highest crown or cross-gradient.

    A. concrete   B. gravel
    C. bituminous   D. compacted earth

16. Where lines or elements of a given site are NOT parallel to each other, _____ site measurement is most often recommended.

    A. baseline   B. direct
    C. triangulation   D. pacing

17. Which of the following is performed during the analysis stage of the planning-design process?

    A. Schematic studies   B. Program development
    C. Data collection   D. Impact assessment

18. Sections of land that extend east and west of the established north-south reference line are numbered as

    A. townships   B. metes   C. ranges   D. parcels

19. Which of the following types of soils has the GREATEST capacity for water retention?

    A. Light loam   B. Sandy peat
    C. Stiff clay   D. Coarse sand

20. The normal width of one lane on a public road is _____ feet.

    A. 6-8   B. 8-10   C. 10-12   D. 12-16

21. Vines are used in landscaping for each of the following purposes EXCEPT to

    A. stabilize slopes and dunes
    B. cool exposed walls
    C. soften architectural lines
    D. provide foliage displays

22. A _____ is NOT a type of construction drawing. 22._____

    A. layout plan
    B. master plan
    C. planting plan
    D. details sketch

23. Which of the following volumetric components is MOST concerned with use? 23._____

    A. Base plane
    B. Vertical space dividers
    C. Sight-line meridian
    D. Overhead plane

24. Approximately _____% of soil shrinkage is considered normal in compacted earth fills. 24._____

    A. 1-2   B. 3-5   C. 7-10   D. 12-15

25. The study of a design's THIRD dimension is termed 25._____

    A. form composition
    B. mass collection
    C. spatial composition
    D. verge initialization

KEY (CORRECT ANSWERS)

1.	D	11.	D
2.	C	12.	C
3.	B	13.	D
4.	B	14.	D
5.	C	15.	B
6.	A	16.	C
7.	B	17.	B
8.	B	18.	C
9.	B	19.	B
10.	A	20.	C

21. C
22. B
23. A
24. B
25. C

TEST 3

DIRECTIONS: Each question or incomplete statement is followed by several suggested answers or completions. Select the one that BEST answers the question or completes the statement. *PRINT THE LETTER OF THE CORRECT ANSWER IN THE SPACE AT THE RIGHT.*

1. Which of the following plants, growing at an undeveloped site, would indicate wet, acid soil?

   A. Spaghnum mosses B. Thistle
   C. Silverweed D. Heather

2. Of the following types of outdoor walls, _____ is typically MOST expensive to construct.

   A. random ashlar B. squared rubble
   C. brick D. coursed ashlar

3. Which of the following steps in a project's design phase would occur FIRST?

   A. Construction documents B. Functional diagrams
   C. Preliminary design D. Master plan

4. Approximately _____ persons per hour can be accommodated by a 2-foot width of community walkway.

   A. 800 B. 1700 C. 3300 D. 5500

5. _____ is a means of creating unity in a landscape design.

   A. Alternation B. Mass collection
   C. Inversion D. Repetition

6. Typically, the standard width for a handicapped parking stall measures _____ feet.

   A. 8 B. 10 C. 12 D. 14

7. The MAXIMUM allowable gradient of landscaped swales is _____ %.

   A. 1 B. 2 C. 4 D. 6

8. All land extending to within a 0-5 mile radius of a given site is said to be contained within the site's

   A. sector B. vicinity C. area D. zone

9. A *township* is usually comprised of _____ sections, each of which is approximately 1 mile square.

   A. 12 B. 36 C. 64 D. 144

10. To avoid atmospheric pollution among urban plantings, it is BEST to avoid the use of

    A. conifers B. vines
    C. fruit bearers D. angiosperms

11. _____ soil is MOST likely alkaline and experiences excessive drainage.

   A. Chalky
   B. Clay-loam
   C. Sandy
   D. Infertile compact

12. Of the following vine species, which grows MOST quickly?

   A. Star jasmine
   B. Bougainvillea
   C. Honeysuckle
   D. Memorial rose

13. The dominant character and identity of a neighborhood is provided by its

   A. ground cover
   B. canopy trees
   C. shrubs
   D. intermediate trees

14. Which of the following types of outdoor lighting materials will have the LONGEST normal life?

   A. Fluorescent
   B. Tungsten
   C. Halogen
   D. Sodium

15. A flight of outdoor steps with a 5-inch riser has a tread-riser gradient of 10-12%. As a mean, the normal step stride of a user would be APPROXIMATELY _____ inches.

   A. 16   B. 20   C. 24   D. 32

16. Each of the following is a commonly invoked reason to adapt landscaping to a given landform EXCEPT to

   A. make use of existing drainageways
   B. increase carrying capacity
   C. reduce the cost of earthwork
   D. prevent topsoil erosion

17. Which of the following plants is MOST suitable for rock garden planting?

   A. Daffodil
   B. Silver fleece
   C. Chrysanthemum
   D. Thrift

18. On a mulched or planted embankment, 1 on _____ is typically considered to be the MAXIMUM angle of repose.

   A. 1   B. 1 1/2   C. 2   D. 3

19. Which of the following is performed during the operation stace of the planning-design process?

   A. Consolidation
   B. Performance observation
   C. Comparative analysis
   D. Review of governing regulations

20. For outdoor steps, _____ to _____ is considered to be the preferred ratio (inches) of a vertical riser's height to the width of the tread.

   A. 4 1/2; 17   B. 5; 16   C. 6; 14   D. 8; 10

21. The dominant plants in a site's mass planting should be used 21.____

   A. at protruding points
   B. to provide shade
   C. in recessive bays
   D. as screens

22. Which of the following plants, growing at an undeveloped site, would indicate potentially fertile soil? 22.____

   A. Rushes
   B. Stinging nettle
   C. Reeds
   D. Furze

23. If equipped with a handrail, a short walkway may be pitched to a MAXIMUM allowable gradient of _____%. 23.____

   A. 5   B. 12   C. 15   D. 22

24. A private local road has been constructed at a width of 12 feet, and consists of 1 lane. Approximately how many dwellings is the road designed to serve? 24.____

   A. 1-5   B. 1-15   C. 5-30   D. 10-21

25. The document which identifies the existing and proposed elevations of a site's ground plane(s) is the 25.____

   A. section
   B. elevation
   C. preliminary design
   D. grading plane

KEY (CORRECT ANSWERS)

1.	A	11.	A
2.	D	12.	C
3.	B	13.	B
4.	C	14.	A
5.	D	15.	A
6.	D	16.	B
7.	C	17.	D
8.	C	18.	C
9.	B	19.	B
10.	A	20.	B

21. A
22. B
23. C
24. A
25. D

EXAMINATION SECTION
TEST 1

DIRECTIONS: Each question or incomplete statement is followed by several suggested answers or completions. Select the one that BEST answers the question or completes the statement. *PRINT THE LETTER OF THE CORRECT ANSWER IN THE SPACE AT THE RIGHT.*

1. The population or level of activity that can be sustained for a given length of time without depletion of the resources or breakdown of the biological systems of a land-water area is a quality known as

    A. specified yield
    B. carrying capacity
    C. biodiversity
    D. climax community

2. Typically, the MAXIMUM angle of repose of any landscaped surface is 1 on

    A. 1
    B. 1 1/2
    C. 2
    D. 3

3. Each land-use region has an established east-west reference marker, known as the

    A. principle meridian
    B. line of demarcation
    C. range line
    D. base line

4. A site's intermediate trees should be installed

    A. along pathway boundaries
    B. to provide a spatial ceiling
    C. near structural boundaries
    D. in the open

5. If bicycle use is anticipated, a typical low-volume community walkway should be APPROXIMATELY _____ feet in width.

    A. 4
    B. 5
    C. 6
    D. 7

6. Ground covers are used in landscaping for

    A. definition of use areas
    B. accentuating points and features
    C. unification of site
    D. reinforcement pathway alignments

7. The exercise of eminent domain over a property can be made more palatable by all of the following provisions EXCEPT

    A. granting the owner tenancy when long-range acquisition is in the public interest
    B. using only after open negotiation has been attempted
    C. using only for the final 50% of land required when a holdout has blocked acquisition
    D. purchasing with leaseback for conditional uses

8. Which of the following is NOT a typical characteristic of the dominant species in a mass planting?

    A. Taller
    B. Softer in color
    C. Coarser
    D. More bulky

9. The recommended paving width of a private local street that serves 21-50 dwellings is _____ feet and _____ lanes.

   A. 12; 2   B. 16; 1   C. 18; 2   D. 24; 2

10. Which of the following types of road surfaces will require the LOWEST cross-gradient?

    A. Concrete
    B. Gravel
    C. Bituminous
    D. Earth

11. Which of the following soil types is considered BEST for horticultural purposes?

    A. Sandy loam
    B. Peat
    C. Calcareous
    D. Medium loam

12. When possible, all road and drive intersections should be constructed at an angle of APPROXIMATELY _____ degrees.

    A. 30   B. 45   C. 60   D. 90

13. What is the term for the study of the EXACT location of all the edges and lines of a design?

    A. Form composition
    B. Mass collection
    C. Spatial composition
    D. Verge initialization

14. The *theme* tree of a site should be all of the following EXCEPT

    A. requiring little care
    B. indigenous
    C. deciduous
    D. moderately fast-growing

15. Typically, the standard width for a normal (not compact) parking stall measures _____ feet.

    A. 8   B. 10   C. 12   D. 14

16. Technically, all land extending to within a 5-20 mile radius of a given site is said to be contained within the site's

    A. vicinity   B. district   C. area   D. zone

17. Under normal conditions, the compacted topsoil layer used for new lawn construction should be APPROXIMATELY _____ inches thick.

    A. 2   B. 4   C. 6   D. 8

18. Which of the following steps in a project's design phase would occur LAST?

    A. Construction documents
    B. Functional diagrams
    C. Preliminary design
    D. Master plan

19. Usually, which of the following steps in the implementation of site development would occur LAST?

    A. Environmental impact assessment
    B. Site-structure plan
    C. Topographical survey
    D. Conceptual plan

20. As a rule of thumb for outdoor steps constructed in regular flights, the sum of the height of 2 risers plus the depth of a single tread will equal _____ inches.

    A. 18   B. 26   C. 38   D. 42

21. Each of the following is typically considered a means of creating order in a design composition EXCEPT

    A. mass collection   B. symmetry
    C. inversion   D. asymmetry

22. Which of the following soil types is MOST likely to suffer from a mineral deficiency?

    A. Loam   B. Clay   C. Sandy   D. Peat

23. The level of an enclosed body of water can be controlled by a sliding gate known as a

    A. weir   B. bilge   C. outfall   D. dam

24. Which of the following plants, growing at an undeveloped site, would indicate potentially fertile soil?

    A. Silverweed   B. Wild strawberry
    C. Thistle   D. Chickweed

25. Of the following types of streets, a(n) _____ is designed to be a safe, pleasant low-speed connection between motor courts and residential streets.

    A. artery   B. sub-collector
    C. place   D. lane

KEY (CORRECT ANSWERS)

1.	B	11.	D
2.	B	12.	D
3.	D	13.	A
4.	D	14.	C
5.	C	15.	B
6.	A	16.	A
7.	C	17.	B
8.	B	18.	A
9.	C	19.	B
10.	A	20.	B

21. C
22. C
23. A
24. D
25. B

TEST 2

DIRECTIONS: Each question or incomplete statement is followed by several suggested answers or completions. Select the one that BEST answers the question or completes the statement. *PRINT THE LETTER OF THE CORRECT ANSWER IN THE SPACE AT THE RIGHT.*

1. A landscaped beach should slope to a depth of AT LEAST _____ feet before reaching the deep-cut line. 1._____

    A. 3 B. 6 C. 9 D. 12

2. All exterior volumes are formed by each of the following volumetric components EXCEPT 2._____

    A. base plane
    B. vertical space dividers
    C. sight-line meridian
    D. overhead plane

3. Earth fill used on landscaped sites should be placed in uniform layers of loose material, each measuring APPROXIMATELY _____ inches in depth. 3._____

    A. 2-4 B. 6-8 C. 12-16 D. 18-24

4. In the planning-design process, a comprehensive program is USUALLY developed during the stage known as 4._____

    A. analysis B. commission C. synthesis D. research

5. Where an arterial roadway meets a collector, the strength of provided lighting should be APPROXIMATELY _____ foot-candles. 5._____

    A. .2 B. .4 C. .6 D. .8

6. Which of the following is NOT considered to be one of the three most basic design principles used by site designers? 6._____

    A. Order B. Dominance C. Rhythm D. Unity

7. Perrons or stepped ramps should be used on rough-terrain slopes whose grade is APPROXIMATELY _____ %. 7._____

    A. 5-10 B. 10-15 C. 15-25 D. 25-35

8. The principal units of land within most counties are 8._____

    A. townships
    B. ranges
    C. municipalities
    D. sections

9. If a handful of moist soil is sticky, easily molded, and can be *polished* by sliding it between your finger and thumb, it is MOST likely 9._____

    A. silt
    B. medium-loam
    C. clay-loam
    D. silty loam

10. For topographical surveys, the map MOST often used by site planners covers an area of approximately 68 square miles, with a scale of about 1 inch per 10._____

    A. 500 feet
    B. 2000 feet
    C. 1 mile
    D. 1.5 miles

11. Typically, supplementary tree species at a site are used to demarcate or differentiate areas of unique landscaping quality according to each of the following criteria EXCEPT

    A. special need
    B. use
    C. hydrology
    D. topography

12. If intermediate turn-arounds are not provided, the length of a cul-de-sac should NOT exceed (approximately) _____ feet.

    A. 250   B. 500   C. 1000   D. 2000

13. Which of the following is performed during the construction stage of the planning-design process?

    A. Contract award
    B. Review of possibilities
    C. Development of implementation methods
    D. Review of governing regulations

14. The paved surface of a walkway should have a longitudinal or cross-gradient of AT LEAST _____ %.

    A. 1   B. 2   C. 3   D. 4

15. What is the term for balance that is achieved without bilateral symmetry?

    A. Inversion
    B. Distribution balance
    C. Occult balance
    D. Skewed balance

16. The use of shrubs and low-branching trees should be avoided within a MINIMUM distance of _____ feet from all traffic intersections.

    A. 10   B. 50   C. 100   D. 250

17. All of the following are advantages to using ramps, rather than steps, to connect the planes of a developed site EXCEPT

    A. easier to ascend/descend
    B. more suitable for all climates
    C. cheaper to construct
    D. more of a unifier than a divider

18. Which of the following soil types has the GREATEST natural angle of repose?

    A. Damp clay
    B. Dry alluvial soil
    C. Compact earth
    D. Fine, dry sand

19. At a developed site, the functional size requirement, in square feet, for a single person standing alone is

    A. 3   B. 5   C. 8   D. 10

20. Which of the following is a means of creating rhythm in a landscape design?

    A. Symmetry
    B. Gradation
    C. Dominance
    D. Interconnection

21. The recommended paving width of a private local street that serves over 50 dwellings is _____ feet and _____ lanes.

    A. 16; 1   B. 18; 2   C. 20; 2   D. 24; 2

22. Sloped sites generally BEST lend themselves to _____ plan patterns.

    A. geometric   B. contoured
    C. cell-bud   D. crystalline

23. Which of the following is NOT a fundamental principle of water-edge detailing?

    A. Allowance for wave action
    B. Diversion of strong currents
    C. Armoring banks against swift flows
    D. Preclusion of flooding

24. Generally, daytime temperature variations due strictly to elevation average about _____ °F for every 1000 feet.

    A. 3   B. 5   C. 12   D. 15

25. Which of the following is NOT usually a purpose of preliminary design?

    A. Studying coordination of all elements of the design
    B. Providing designer and clients with a comprehensive view of the entire design
    C. Studying appearance and aesthetics of design
    D. Delimitation of relative material cost estimates

KEY (CORRECT ANSWERS)

1.	B		11.	C
2.	C		12.	C
3.	B		13.	A
4.	C		14.	A
5.	B		15.	C
6.	B		16.	C
7.	C		17.	B
8.	A		18.	C
9.	C		19.	B
10.	B		20.	B

21. C
22. B
23. B
24. A
25. D

TEST 3

DIRECTIONS: Each question or incomplete statement is followed by several suggested answers or completions. Select the one that BEST answers the question or completes the statement. *PRINT THE LETTER OF THE CORRECT ANSWER IN THE SPACE AT THE RIGHT.*

1. Of the following tree species, which grows MOST quickly? 1.____
   A. Walnut B. Silver maple
   C. Lombardy poplar D. Gingko

2. Which of the following types of retaining walls TYPICALLY makes use of tie beams? 2.____
   A. Crib B. Cantilever
   C. Diaphragm D. Piling

3. Which of the following is the MOST common site development principle in cold regions? 3.____
   A. Breeze funneling
   B. Plant screening
   C. Water catchment and storage
   D. Creation of enclosed courts

4. A handrail is recommended for a flight of outdoor steps consisting of _____ or more risers. 4.____
   A. 4 B. 6 C. 8 D. 12

5. In the planning-design process, a definition of services is USUALLY transacted during the _____ stage. 5.____
   A. construction B. research
   C. operation D. commission

6. The recommended divider height for the provision of privacy while seated is _____ feet. 6.____
   A. 3 B. 4 1/2 C. 5 D. 6 1/2

7. *Intermediate* trees are NOT used for 7.____
   A. enframing B. understory screening
   C. unification D. windbreak

8. If a handful of moist soil is gritty but soils the fingers and can be pressed roughly into a ball, it is MOST likely 8.____
   A. sandy loam B. silty clay
   C. clay-loam D. sand

9. When site soils are impervious or overly porous, the compacted topsoil layer used for new lawn construction should be APPROXIMATELY _____ inches thick. 9.____
   A. 2-4 B. 4-6 C. 6-8 D. 8-12

10. Which of the following types of outdoor lighting materials has the HIGHEST potential lamp wattage?

    A. Fluorescent
    B. Mercury/fluorescent
    C. Tungsten/halogen
    D. Sodium

11. The MOST powerful space definers and enclosers are

    A. plantings
    B. walls
    C. earth forms
    D. structures

12. For a parking compound that includes two or more courts, an approximate area-capacity calculation that considers added features such as approach ramps, distributor loops, etc. will allow _____ square feet of paved area per standard car.

    A. 40   B. 80   C. 120   D. 300

13. *Dominance* in a landscaped design is typically established through contrasts in each of the following EXCEPT

    A. position   B. size   C. texture   D. color

14. _____ site measurement is recommended when there are many different points along an axis which need to be located and drawn.

    A. Baseline
    B. Direct
    C. Triangulation
    D. Pacing

15. On a sketch, the outline of a landscaped water body should be shown as

    A. curvilinear
    B. unconfined
    C. perpendicular
    D. angular

16. A _____ is NOT generally used as a vertical divider at a site.

    A. baffle   B. enframer   C. backdrop   D. screen

17. Typically, what is the recommended width, in feet, of a public 2-lane road?

    A. 12   B. 16   C. 18   D. 22

18. Of the following plants, _____ growing at an undeveloped site would indicate dry, sandy, or gravelly soil.

    A. silverweed
    B. foxglove
    C. rushes
    D. furze

19. Emphasis is commonly given to traffic circulation routes through the use of each of the following EXCEPT

    A. supplementary planting
    B. modulated ground forms
    C. canopy trees
    D. increased levels of lighting

20. What is the term for a strip of land within a privately-owned lot to which others have the right of access?

   A. Boulevard
   B. Easement
   C. Run
   D. Right-of-way

21. The document which gives the horizontal dimensions of all the elements and areas of a site design is called the _____ plan.

   A. grading
   B. master
   C. commission
   D. layout

22. The floor level of habitable structures surrounding a water body should be held above the _____ -year flood stage.

   A. 10   B. 50   C. 100   D. 500

23. Which of the following would have the HOTTEST surface temperature under direct summer sunlight?

   A. Concrete walkway
   B. Mulched easement
   C. Gravel roadway
   D. Bituminous roadway

24. The statement of a design's material composition is specifically an element of the

   A. impact assessment
   B. construction drawings
   C. site survey
   D. master plan

25. The MAXIMUM angle of repose on a lawn area is 1 on

   A. 1   B. 1 1/2   C. 2   D. 3

KEY (CORRECT ANSWERS)

1. C
2. A
3. D
4. B
5. D

6. B
7. C
8. A
9. C
10. B

11. B
12. D
13. A
14. A
15. A

16. B
17. C
18. B
19. C
20. B

21. D
22. C
23. D
24. D
25. D

READING COMPREHENSION
UNDERSTANDING AND INTERPRETING WRITTEN MATERIAL
EXAMINATION SECTION
TEST 1

DIRECTIONS: Each question or incomplete statement is followed by several suggested answers or completions. Select the one that BEST answers the question or completes the statement. *PRINT THE LETTER OF THE CORRECT ANSWER IN THE SPACE AT THE RIGHT.*

Questions 1-3.

DIRECTIONS: Questions 1 through 3 are to be answered SOLELY on the basis of the following paragraph.

The aging housing inventory presents a broad spectrum of conditions, from good upkeep to unbelievable deterioration. Buildings, even relatively good buildings, are likely to have numerous minor violations rather than the gross and evident sanitary violations of an earlier age. Except for the serious violations in a relatively small number of slum buildings, the task is to deal with masses of minor violations that, though insignificant in themselves, amount in the aggregate to major deprivations of health and comfort to tenants. Caused by wear and tear, by the abrasions of time, and aggravated by neglect, these conditions do not readily yield to the dramatic *vacate and restore* measures of earlier times. Moreover, the lines between *good* and *bad* housing have become blurred in many parts of our cities; we find a range of *shades of gray* blending into each other. Different kinds of code enforcement efforts may be required to deal with different degrees of deterioration.

1. The above passage suggests that code enforcement efforts may have to be

    A. developed to cope with varying levels of housing dilapidation
    B. aimed primarily at the serious violations in slum buildings
    C. modeled on the *vacate and restore* measures of earlier times
    D. modified to reduce unrealistic penalties for petty violations

1.____

2. According to the above passage, during former times some buildings had sanitary violations which were

    A. irreparable and minor
    B. blurred and gray
    C. flagrant and obvious
    D. insignificant and numerous

2.____

3. According to the above passage, the aging housing stock presents a

    A. great number of rent-controlled buildings
    B. serious problem of tenant-caused deterioration
    C. significant increase in buildings without intentional violations
    D. wide range of physical conditions

3.____

Questions 4-5.

DIRECTIONS: Questions 4 and 5 are to be answered SOLELY on the basis of the following passage.

In general, housing code provisions relating to the safe and sanitary maintenance of dwelling units prescribe the maintenance required for foundations, walls, ceilings, floors, windows, doors, stairways, and also the facilities and equipment required in other sections. The more recent codes have, in addition, extensive provisions designed to ensure that the unit be maintained in a rat-free and rat-proof condition. Also, as an example of new approaches in code provisions, one proposed Federal model housing code prohibits the landlord from terminating vital services and utilities except during temporary emergencies or when actual repairs or maintenance are in process. This provision may be used to prevent a landlord from turning off utility services as a technique of self-help eviction or as a weapon against rent strikes.

4. According to the above passage, the more recent housing codes have extensive provisions designed to

   A. maintain a reasonably fire-proof living unit
   B. prohibit tenants from participating in rent strikes
   C. maintain the unit free from rats
   D. prohibit tenants from using lead-based paints

5. According to the above passage, one housing code would permit landlords to terminate vital services during

   A. a rent strike
   B. an actual eviction
   C. a temporary emergency
   D. the planning of repairs and maintenance

Questions 6-8.

DIRECTIONS: Questions 6 through 8 are to be answered SOLELY on the basis of the following passage.

City governments have long had building codes which set minimum standards for building and for human occupancy. The code (or series of codes) makes provisions for standards of lighting and ventilation, sanitation, fire prevention, and protection. As a result of demands from manufacturers, builders, real estate people, tenement owners, and building-trades unions, these codes often have established minimum standards well below those that the contemporary society would accept as a rock-bottom minimum. Codes often become outdated so that meager standards in one era become seriously inadequate a few decades later as society"s concept of a minimum standard of living changes. Out-of-date codes, when still in use, have sometimes prevented the introduction of new devices and modern building techniques. Thus, it is extremely important that building codes keep pace with changes in the accepted concept of a minimum standard of living.

6. According to the above passage, all of the following considerations in building planning would probably be covered in a building code EXCEPT

   A. closet space as a percentage of total floor area
   B. size and number of windows required for rooms of differing sizes
   C. placement of fire escapes in each line of apartments
   D. type of garbage disposal units to be installed

7. According to the above passage, if an ideal building code were to be created, how would the established minimum standards in it compare to the ones that are presently set by city governments?
   They would

   A. be lower than they are at present
   B. be higher than they are at present
   C. be comparable to the present minimum standards
   D. vary according to the economic group that sets them

8. On the basis of the above passage, what is the reason for difficulties in introducing new building techniques?

   A. Builders prefer techniques which represent the rock-bottom minimum desired by society.
   B. Certain manufacturers have obtained patents on various building methods to the exclusion of new techniques.
   C. The government does not want to invest money in techniques that will soon be out-dated.
   D. New techniques are not provided for in building codes which are not up-to-date.

Questions 9-11.

DIRECTIONS: Questions 9 through 11 are to be answered SOLELY on the basis of the following paragraph.

When constructed within a multiple dwelling, such storage space shall be equipped with a sprinkler system and also with a system of mechanical ventilation in no way connected with any other ventilating system. Such storage space shall have no opening into any other part of the dwelling except through a fireproof vestibule. Any such vestibule shall have a minimum superficial floor area of fifty square feet, and its maximum area shall not exceed seventy-five square feet. It shall be enclosed with incombustible partitions having a fire-resistive rating of three hours. The floor and ceiling of such vestibule shall also be of incombustible material having a fire-resistive rating of at least three hours. There shall be two doors to provide access from the dwelling,to the car storage space. Each such door shall have a fire-resistive rating of one and one-half hours and shall be provided with a device to prevent the opening of one door until the other door is entirely closed.

9. According to the above paragraph, the one of the following that is REQUIRED in order for cars to be permitted to be stored in a multiple dwelling is a(n)

   A. fireproof vestibule   B. elevator from the garage
   C. approved heating system   D. sprinkler system

10. According to the above paragraph, the one of the following materials that would NOT be acceptable for the walls of a vestibule connecting a garage to the dwelling portion of a building is

   A. 3" solid gypsum blocks
   B. 4" brick
   C. 4" hollow gypsum blocks, plastered both sides
   D. 6" solid cinder concrete blocks

10.____

11. According to the above paragraph, the one of the following that would be ACCEPTABLE for the width and length of a vestibule connecting a garage that is within a multiple dwelling to the dwelling portion of the building is

   A. 3'8" x 13'0"   B. 4'6" x 18'6"
   C. 4'9" x 14'6"   D. 4'3" x 19'3"

11.____

Questions 12-13.

DIRECTIONS: Questions 12 and 13 are to be answered SOLELY on the basis of the following paragraph.

It shall be unlawful to place, use, or maintain in a condition intended, arranged, or designed for use, any gas-fired cooking appliance, laundry stove, heating stove, range or water heater or combination of such appliances in any room or space used for living or sleeping in any new or existing multiple dwelling unless such room or space has a window opening to the outer air or such gas appliance is vented to the outer air. All automatically operated gas appliances shall be equipped with a device which shall shut off automatically the gas supply to the main burners when the pilot light in such appliance is extinguished. A gas range or the cooking portion of a gas appliance incorporating a room heater shall not be deemed an automatically operated gas appliance. However, burners in gas ovens and broilers which can be turned on and off or ignited by non-manual means shall be equipped with a device which shall shut off automatically the gas supply to those burners when the operation of such non-manual means fails.

12. According to the above paragraph, an automatic shut-off device is NOT required on a gas

   A. hot water heater   B. laundry dryer
   C. space heater   D. range

12.____

13. According to the above paragraph, a gas-fired water heater is permitted

   A. only in kitchens   B. only in bathrooms
   C. only in living rooms   D. in any type of room

13.____

Questions 14-18.

DIRECTIONS: Questions 14 through 18 are to be answered SOLELY on the basis of the information contained in the statement below.

No multiple dwelling shall be erected to a height in excess of one and one-half times the width of the widest street on which it faces, except that above the level of such height, for each one foot that the front wall of such dwelling sets back from the street line, three feet shall be added to the height limit of such dwelling, but such dwelling shall not exceed in maximum height three feet plus one and three-quarter times the width of the widest street on which it faces.

Any such dwelling facing a street more than one hundred feet in width shall be subject to the same height limitations as though such dwelling faced a street one hundred feet in width.

14. The MAXIMUM height of a multiple dwelling set back five feet from the street line and facing a 60 foot wide street is feet.

    A. 60   B. 90   C. 105   D. 165

15. The MAXIMUM height of a multiple dwelling set back six feet from the street line and facing a 120 foot wide street is _____ feet.

    A. 198   B. 168   C. 120   D. 105

16. The MAXIMUM height of a multiple dwelling is

    A. 100 ft.   B. 150 ft.   C. 178 ft.   D. unlimited

17. The MAXIMUM height of a multiple dwelling set back 10 feet from the street line and facing a 110 foot wide street is feet.

    A. 178   B. 180   C. 195   D. 205

18. The MAXIMUM height of a multiple dwelling set back eight feet from the street line and facing a 90 foot wide street is feet.

    A. 135   B. 147   C. 178   D. 159

Questions 19-23.

DIRECTIONS: Questions 19 through 23 are to be answered SOLELY on the basis of the following statement.

The number of persons accommodated on any story in a lodging house shall not be greater than the sum of the following components,

   a. 22 persons for each full multiple of 22 inches in the smallest clear width for each means of egress approved by the department, other than fire escapes
   b. 20 persons for each lawful fire escape accessible from such story.

19. The MAXIMUM number of persons that may be accommodated on a story in a lodging house depends on the

    A. number of lawful fire escapes *only*
    B. number of approved means of egress *only*
    C. smallest clear width in each approved means of egress *only*
    D. number of lawful fire escapes and sum total of smallest clear widths in each approved means of egress

20. The MAXIMUM number of persons that may be accommodated on a story of a lodging house having one lawful fire escape and a sum total of 44 inches in the smallest clear widths of the two approved means of egress is

    A. 20   B. 22   C. 42   D. 64

21. The MAXIMUM number of persons that may be accommodated on a story of a lodging house having two lawful fire escapes and a sum total of 60 inches in the smallest clear width of the approved means of egress is

   A. 64   B. 84   C. 100   D. 106

22. The MAXIMUM number of persons that may be accommodated on a story of a lodging house having one lawful fire escape and a sum total of 33 inches in the smallest clear width of the approved means of egress is

   A. 42   B. 53   C. 64   D. 73

23. The MAXIMUM number of persons that may be accommodated on a story of a lodging house having two lawful fire escapes and two approved means of egress, with 40 inches and 44 inches in the smallest clear widths, respectively, is

   A. 84   B. 104   C. 106   D. 108

Questions 24-25.

DIRECTIONS: Questions 24 and 25 are to be answered SOLELY on the basis of the following paragraph.

Though the recent trend toward apartment construction may appear to be the Region's response to large-lot zoning and centralized industry, it really is not. It is mainly a function of the age of the population. Most of the apartments are occupied by one- and two-person families young people out of school but without a family of their own and older people whose children have grown. Both groups have been increasing in number; and, in this Region, they characteristically live in apartments. It is this increased demand for apartments and the simultaneous decrease in demand for one-family houses that dramatically raised the percentage of building permits issued for multi-family housing units from 36 percent in 1977 to 67 percent in 1981. The fact that three-fourths of the apartments were built in the Core between 1977 and 1981 at the same time as the Core was losing population underscores the failure of the apartment boom to slow the outward spread of the population.

24. According to the above paragraph, one of the reasons for the increase in the number of building permits issued for multi-family construction in the City Metropolitan Region is

   A. that workers in industry want to live close to their jobs
   B. an increase in the number of elderly people living in the Region
   C. the inability of many families to afford the large lots necessary to build private homes
   D. the new zoning ordinance made it easier to build apartments

25. According to the above paragraph, the apartment construction boom

   A. increased the population density in the Core
   B. spurred a population shift to the suburbs
   C. did not halt the outward flow of the population from the Core
   D. was most significant in the outer areas of the Region

KEY (CORRECT ANSWERS)

1. A
2. C
3. D
4. C
5. C

6. A
7. B
8. D
9. D
10. B

11. C
12. D
13. D
14. C
15. B

16. C
17. A
18. D
19. D
20. D

21. B
22. A
23. C
24. B
25. C

TEST 2

DIRECTIONS: Each question or incomplete statement is followed by several suggested answers or completions. Select the one that BEST answers the question or completes the statement. *PRINT THE LETTER OF THE CORRECT ANSWER IN THE SPACE AT THE RIGHT.*

Questions 1-4.

DIRECTIONS: Questions 1 through 4 are to be answered SOLELY on the basis of the following paragraph.

Although the suburbs have provided housing and employment for millions of additional families since 1950, many suburban communities have maintained controls over the kinds of families who can live in them. Suburban attitudes have been formed by reaction against a perception of crowded, harassed city life and threatening alien city people. As population, taxable income, and jobs have left the cities for the suburbs, the *urban crisis* of substandard housing, declining levels of education and public services, and decreasing employment opportunities has been created. The crisis, however, is not urban at all, but national, and in part a result of the suburban policy that discourages outward movement by the urban poor.

1. According to the above paragraph, the quality of urban life 1.____

   A. is determined by public opinion in the cities
   B. has worsened in recent years
   C. is similar to rural life
   D. can be changed by political means

2. According to the above paragraph, suburban communities have 2.____

   A. tried to show that the urban crisis is really a national crisis
   B. avoided taking a position on the urban crisis
   C. been involved in causing the urban crisis
   D. been the innocent victims of the urban crisis

3. According to the above paragraph, the poor have 3.____

   A. become increasingly sophisticated in their attempts to move to the suburbs
   B. generally been excluded from the suburbs
   C. lost incentive for betterment of their living conditions
   D. sought improvement of the central cities

4. As used in the above paragraph, the word perception means MOST NEARLY 4.____

   A. development   B. impression
   C. opposition   D. uncertainty

Questions 5-8.

DIRECTIONS: Questions 5 through 8 are to be answered SOLELY on the basis of the following paragraph.

The concentration of publicly assisted housing in central cities -- because the suburbs do not want them and effectively bar them -- is usually rationalized by a solicitous regard for keeping intact the city neighborhoods cherished by low-income groups. If one accepted this as valid, the devotion of minorities to blighted city neighborhoods in preference to suburban employment and housing would be an historic first. Certainly no such devotion was visible among the millions who have deserted their city neighborhoods in the last 25 years even if it meant an arduous daily trip from the suburbs to their jobs in the cities.

5. The writer implies that MOST poor people

   A. prefer isolation
   B. fear change
   C. are angry
   D. seek betterment

6. The general tone of the paragraph is BEST characterized as

   A. uncertain   B. skeptical   C. evasive   D. indifferent

7. As used in the above paragraph, the word <u>rationalize</u> means MOST NEARLY

   A. dispute   B. justify   C. deny   D. locate

8. According to the above paragraph, publicly assisted housing is concentrated in the central cities PRIMARILY because

   A. city dwellers are unable to find satisfactory housing
   B. deterioration of older housing has increased in recent years
   C. suburbanites have opposed the movement of the poor to the suburbs
   D. employment opportunities have decreased in the suburbs

Questions 9-11.

DIRECTIONS: Questions 9 through 11 are to be answered SOLELY on the basis of the following paragraph.

In recent years, new and important emphasis has been placed upon the maximum use of conservation and rehabilitation techniques in carrying out programs of urban renewal and revitalization. In urban renewal projects where existing structures are hopelessly deteriorated or land uses are incompatible with the community's overall plans, the entire area may be acquired, cleared, and sold for redevelopment. However, where existing structures are basically sound but have deteriorated to the point where they are a <u>blighting</u> influence on the neighborhood, they may be salvaged through a program of rehabilitation and reconditioning.

9. According to the above paragraph, the one of the following which is MOST likely to cause area-wide razing of the buildings in urban renewal programs is

   A. a program of rehabilitation and reconditioning
   B. concerted insistence by landlords and tenants that certain buildings be bulldozed
   C. an inability of community groups to agree on priorities for staged clearance
   D. land use contrary to the community's general plan

10. According to the above paragraph, rehabilitation of structures may take place if

    A. new conservation and rehabilitation techniques are used
    B. salvaging all the buildings in the entire area is hopeless
    C. the community wishes to preserve historic structures
    D. the existing buildings are structurally sound

11. As used in the above paragraph, the word <u>blighting</u> means MOST NEARLY 11.____

   A. ruining   B. infrequent   C. recurrent   D. traditional

Questions 12-13.

DIRECTIONS: Questions 12 and 13 are to be answered SOLELY on the basis of the following paragraphs.

We must also find better ways to handle the relocation of people uprooted by projects. In the past, many renewal plans have foundered on this problem, and it is still the most difficult part of the community development. Large-scale replacement of low-income residents -- many ineligible for public housing -- has contributed to deterioration of surrounding communities. However, thanks to changes in housing authority procedures, relocation has been accomplished in a far more satisfactory fashion. The step-by-step community development projects we advocate in this plan should bring further improvement.

But additional measures will be necessary. There are going to be more people to be moved; and, with the current shortage of apartments, large ones especially, it is going to be tougher to find places to move them to. The city should have more freedom to buy or lease housing that comes on the market because of normal turnover and make it available to relocatees.

12. According to the above paragraphs, one of the reasons a neighborhood may deteriorate is that 12.____

   A. there is a scarcity of large apartments
   B. step-by-step community development projects have failed
   C. people in the given neighborhood are uprooted from their homes
   D. a nearby renewal project has an inadequate relocation plan

13. From the above paragraphs, one might conclude that the relocation phase of community renewal has been improved. 13.____

   A. by changes in housing authority procedures
   B. by development of step-by-step community development projects
   C. through expanded city powers to buy housing for relocation
   D. by the addition of huge sums of money

Questions 14-15.

DIRECTIONS: Questions 14 and 15 are to be answered SOLELY on the basis of the following paragraphs.

Provision of decent housing for the lower half of the population (by income) was thus taken on as a public responsibility. Public housing was to assist the poorest quarter of urban families while the 221(d)(3) Housing Program would assist the next quarter. But limited funds meant that the supply of subsidized housing could not stretch nearly far enough to help this half of the population. Who were to be left out in the rationing process which was accomplished by the sifting of applicants for housing on the part of public and private authorities?

Discrimination on the grounds of race or color is not allowed under Federal law. In all sections of the country, encouragingly, housing programs are found which follow this law to the letter. Yet, housing programs in some cities still suffer from the residue of racial segregation policies and attitudes that for years were condoned or even encouraged.

Some sifting in the 221(d)(3) Housing Program follows the practice of many public housing authorities, the imposition of requirements with respect to character. This is a delicate matter. To fill a project overwhelmingly with broken families, alcoholics, criminals, delinquents, and other problem tenants would hardly make it a wholesome environment. Yet the total exclusion of such families is hardly an acceptable alternative. To the extent this exclusion is practiced, the very people whose lives are described in order to persuade lawmakers and the public to instigate new programs find the door shut in their faces when such programs come into being. The proper balance is difficult to achieve, but society's neediest families surely should not be totally denied the opportunities for rejuvenation in subsidized housing.

14. From the above paragraphs, it can be assumed that the 221(d)(3) Housing Program

    A. served a population earning more than the median income
    B. served a less affluent population than is served by public housing
    C. excludes all problem families from its projects
    D. is a subsidized housing program

15. According to this text, the provision of housing for the poor

    A. has not been completely accomplished with public monies
    B. is never influenced by segregationist policies
    C. is limited to providing housing for only the neediest families
    D. is primarily the responsibility of the Federal government

16. Five hundred persons attended a public hearing at which a proposed public housing project was being considered. Less than half favored the project while the majority opposed the project.
    According to the above statement, it is REASONABLE to conclude that

    A. the proposal stimulated considerable community interest
    B. the public housing project was disapproved by the city because a majority opposed it
    C. those who opposed the project lacked sympathy for needy persons
    D. the supporters of the project were led by militants

17. A vacant lot close to a polluted creek is for sale. Two buyers compete. One owns an adjacent factory which provides 300 high paying unskilled jobs. He needs to expand or move from the city. If he expands, he will provide 300 additional jobs. The other is a community group in a changing residential area close by. They hope to stabilize the neighborhood by bringing in new housing. They would build an apartment building with 100 dwelling units on the lot.
    According to the above paragraph, it is REASONABLE to conclude that

    A. jobs are more important than housing
    B. there is conflict between the factory owners and the neighborhood group
    C. the neighborhood group will not succeed in stabilizing the area by constructing new housing
    D. the polluted creek should be cleaned up

18. The housing authority faces every problem of the private developer, and it must also assume responsibilities of which private building is free. The authority must account to the community; it must conform to federal regulations; it must provide durable buildings of good standard at low cost; it must overcome the prejudices against public operations, of contractors, bankers, and prospective tenants. These authorities are being watched by anti-housing enthusiasts for the first error of judgment or the first evidence of high costs, to be torn to bits before a Congressional committee.
On the basis of this statement, it would be MOST correct to state that

   A. private builders do not have the opposition of contractors, bankers, and prospective tenants
   B. Congressional committees impede the progress of public housing by petty investigations
   C. a housing authority must deal with all the difficulties encountered by the private builder
   D. housing authorities are no more immune from errors in judgment than private developers

19. Another factor that has considerably added to the city's housing crisis has been the great influx of low-income workers and their families seeking better employment opportunities during wartime and defense boom periods. The circumstances of these families have forced them to crowd into the worst kind of housing and have produced on a renewed scale the conditions from which slums flourish and grow.
On the basis of this statement, one would be justified in stating that

   A. the influx of low-income workers has aggravated the slum problem
   B. the city has better employment opportunities than other sections of the country
   C. the high wages paid by our defense industries have made many families ineligible for tenancy in public housing projects
   D. the families who settled in the city during wartime and the defense build-up brought with them language and social customs conducive to the growth of slums

20. Much of the city felt the effects of the general postwar increase of vandalism and street crime, and the greatly expanded public housing program was no exception. Projects built in congested slum areas with a high incidence of delinquency and crime were particularly subjected to the depredations of neighborhood gangs. The civil service watchmen who patrolled the projects, unarmed and neither trained nor expected to perform police duties, were unable to cope with the situation.
On the basis of this statement, the MOST accurate of the following statements is:

   A. Neighborhood gangs were particularly responsible for the high incidence of delinquency and crime in congested slum areas having public housing programs
   B. Civil service watchmen who patrolled housing projects failed to carry out their assigned police duties
   C. Housing projects were not spared the effects of the general postwar increase of vandalism and street crime
   D. Delinquency and crime affected housing projects in slum areas to a greater extent than other dwellings in the same area

21. Another peculiar characteristic of real estate is the absence of liquidity. Each parcel is a discrete unit as to size, location, rental, physical condition, and financing arrangements. Each property requires investigation, comparison of rents with other properties, and individualized haggling on price and terms.
On the basis of this statement, the LEAST accurate of the following statements is:

    21.____

   A. Although the size, location, and rent of parcels vary, comparison with rents of other properties affords an indication of the value of a particular parcel
   B. Bargaining skill is the essential factor in determining the value of a parcel of real estate
   C. Each parcel of real estate has individual peculiarities distinguishing it from any other parcel
   D. Real estate is not easily converted to other types of assets

22. In part, at least, the charges of sameness, monotony, and institutionalism directed at public housing projects result from the degree in which they differ from the city's normal housing pattern. They seem alike because their very difference from the usual makes them stand apart.
In many respects, there is considerably more variety between public housing projects than there is between different streets of apartment houses or tenements throughout the city.
On the basis of this statement, it would be LEAST accurate to state that:

    22.____

   A. There is considerably more variety between public housing projects than there is between different streets of tenements throughout the city
   B. Public housing projects differ from the city's normal housing pattern to the degree that sameness, monotony, and institutionalism are characteristic of public buildings
   C. Public housing projects seem alike because their deviation from the usual dwellings draws attention to them
   D. The variety in structure between public housing projects and other public buildings is related to the period in which they were built

23. The amount of debt that can be charged against the city for public housing is limited by law. Part of the city's restricted housing means goes for cash subsidies it may be required to contribute to state-aided projects. Under the provisions of the state law, the city must match the state's contributions in subsidies; and while the value of the partial tax exemption granted by the city is counted for this purpose, it is not always sufficient.
On the basis of this statement, it would be MOST accurate to state that:

    23.____

   A. The amount of money the city may spend for public housing is limited by annual tax revenues
   B. The value of tax exemptions granted by the city to educational, religious, and charitable institutions may be added to its subsidy contributions to public housing projects
   C. The subsidy contributions for state-aided public housing projects are shared equally by the state and the city under the provisions of the state law
   D. The tax revenues of the city, unless supplemented by state aid, are insufficient to finance public housing projects

24. Maintenance costs can be minimized and the useful life of houses can be extended by building with the best and most permanent materials available. The best and most permanent materials in many cases are, however, much more expensive than materials which require more maintenance. The most economical procedure in home building has been to compromise between the capital costs of high quality and enduring materials and the maintenance costs of less desirable materials.
On the basis of this statement, one would be justified in stating that:

    A. Savings in maintenance costs make the use of less durable and less expensive building materials preferable to high quality materials that would prolong the useful life of houses constructed from them
    B. Financial advantage can be secured by the home builder if he judiciously combines costly but enduring building materials with less desirable materials which, however, require more maintenance
    C. A compromise between the capital costs of high quality materials and the maintenance costs of less desirable materials makes it easier for a home builder to estimate construction expenditures
    D. The most economical procedure in home building is to balance the capital costs of the most permanent materials against the costs of less expensive materials that are cheaper to maintain

24.___

25. Personnel selection has been a critical problem for local housing authorities. The pool of qualified workers trained in housing procedures is small, and the colleges and universities have failed to grasp the opportunity for enlarging it. While real estate experience makes a good background for management of a housing project, many real estate men are deplorably lacking in understanding of social and governmental problems. Social workers, on the other hand, are likely to be deficient in business judgment.
On the basis of this statement, it would be MOST accurate to state that:

    A. Colleges and universities have failed to train qualified workers for proficiency in housing procedures
    B. Social workers are deficient in business judgment as related to the management of a housing project
    C. Real estate experience makes a person a good manager of a housing project
    D. Local housing authorities have been critical of present methods of personnel selection

25.___

KEY (CORRECT ANSWERS)

1. B
2. C
3. B
4. B
5. D

6. B
7. B
8. D
9. D
10. D

11. A
12. D
13. A
14. D
15. A

16. A
17. B
18. C
19. A
20. C

21. B
22. B
23. C
24. B
25. A

READING COMPREHENSION
UNDERSTANDING AND INTERPRETING WRITTEN MATERIAL
EXAMINATION SECTION
TEST 1

DIRECTIONS: Each question or incomplete statement is followed by several suggested answers or completions. Select the one that BEST answers the question or completes the statement. *PRINT THE LETTER OF THE CORRECT ANSWER IN THE SPACE AT THE RIGHT.*

Questions 1-3.

DIRECTIONS: Questions 1 through 3, inclusive, are to be answered in accordance with the following paragraph.

All cement work contracts, more or less, in setting. The contraction in concrete walls and other structures causes fine cracks to develop at regular intervals. The tendency to contract increases in direct proportion to the quantity of cement in the concrete. A rich mixture will contract more than a lean mixture. A concrete wall which has been made of a very lean mixture and which has been built by filling only about one foot in depth of concrete in the form each day will frequently require close inspection to reveal the cracks.

1. According to the above paragraph,

    A. shrinkage seldom occurs in concrete
    B. shrinkage occurs only in certain types of concrete
    C. by placing concrete at regular intervals, shrinkage may be avoided
    D. it is impossible to prevent shrinkage

1.____

2. According to the above paragraph, the one of the factors which reduces shrinkage in concrete is the

    A. volume of concrete in wall
    B. height of each day's pour
    C. length of wall
    D. length and height of wall

2.____

3. According to the above paragraph, a rich mixture

    A. pours the easiest
    B. shows the largest amount of cracks
    C. is low in cement content
    D. need not be inspected since cracks are few

3.____

Questions 4-6.

DIRECTIONS: Questions 4 through 6, inclusive, are to be answered SOLELY on the basis of the following paragraph.

It is best to avoid surface water on freshly poured concrete in the first place. However, when there is a very small amount present, the recommended procedure is to allow it to evaporate before finishing. If there is considerable water, it is removed with a broom, belt, float, or by other convenient means. It is never good practice to sprinkle dry cement, or a mixture of cement and fine aggregate, on concrete to take up surface water. Such fine materials form a layer on the surface that is likely to dust or hair check when the concrete hardens.

4. The MAIN subject of the above passage is

    A. surface cracking of concrete
    B. evaporation of water from freshly poured concrete
    C. removing surface water from concrete
    D. final adjustments of ingredients in the concrete mix

4.___

5. According to the above passage, the sprinkling of dry cement on the surface of a concrete mix would MOST LIKELY

    A. prevent the mix from setting
    B. cause discoloration on the surface of the concrete
    C. cause the coarse aggregate to settle out too quickly
    D. cause powdering and small cracks on the surface of the concrete

5.___

6. According to the above passage, the thing to do when considerable surface water is present on the freshly poured concrete is to

    A. dump the concrete back into the mixer and drain the water
    B. allow the water to evaporate before finishing
    C. remove the water with a broom, belt, or float
    D. add more fine aggregate but not cement

6.___

Questions 7-9.

DIRECTIONS: Questions 7 through 9, inclusive, are to be answered ONLY in accordance with the information given in the paragraph below.

Before placing the concrete, check that the forms are rigid and well braced and place the concrete within 45 minutes after mixing it. Fill the forms to the top with the wearing-course concrete. Level off the surfaces with a strieboard. When the concrete becomes stiff but still workable (in a few hours), finish the surface with a wood float. This fills the hollows and compacts the concrete and produces a smooth but gritty finish. For a non-gritty and smoother surface (but one that is more slippery when wet), follow up with a steel trowel after the water sheen from the wood-troweling starts to disappear. If you wish, slant the tread forward a fraction of an inch so that it will shed rain water.

7. Slanting the tread a fraction of an inch gives a surface that will

    A. have added strength
    B. not be slippery when wet
    C. shed rain water
    D. not have hollows

7.___

8. In addition to giving a smooth but gritty finish, the use of a wood float will tend to   8._____

   A. give a finish that is slippery when wet
   B. compact the concrete
   C. give a better wearing course
   D. provide hollows to retain rain water

9. Which one of the following statements is most nearly correct?   9._____

   A. Having checked the forms, one may place the concrete immediately after mixing same.
   B. One must wait at least 15 minutes after mixing the concrete before it may be placed in the forms.
   C. A gritty compact finish and one which is more slippery when wet will result with the use of a wood float.
   D. A steel trowel used promptly after a wood float will tend to give a non-gritty smooth finish.

Questions 10-11.

DIRECTIONS: Questions 10 and 11 are to be answered SOLELY on the basis of information contained in the following paragraph.

Tools and plastering methods have changed very little over the years. Most of the changes are mere improvements of the basic tools. The tools formerly made by hand are now machine-made and are *rigidly* constructed of light, but strong, materials in contrast to the clumsy constructions of the early types. The power-driven mixers and hoisting equipment used on large plastering jobs today produce better mortars and lighten the tasks involved.

10. According to the above paragraph, present day tools used for plastering   10._____

    A. have made plastering much more complicated than it used to be
    B. are heavier than the old-fashioned tools they replaced
    C. produce poorer results but speed up the job
    D. are lighter and stronger than the hand-made tools of the past

11. As used in the above paragraph, the word *rigidly* means MOST NEARLY   11._____

    A. feeble   B. weakly   C. firmly   D. flexibly

Questions 12-18.

DIRECTIONS: Questions 12 through 18 are to be answered in accordance with the following paragraphs.

SURFACE RENEWING OVERLAYS

A surface renewing overlay should consist of material which can be constructed in very thin layers. The material must fill surface voids and provide an impervious skid-resistant surface. It must also be sufficiently resistant to traffic abrasion to provide an economical service life.

Materials meeting these requirements are:
- a. Asphalt concrete having small particle size
- b. Hot sand asphalts
- c. Surface seal coats

Fine-graded asphalt concrete or hot sand asphalt can be constructed in layers as thin as one-half inch and fulfill all requirements for surface renewing overlays. They are recommended for thin resurfacing of pavements having high traffic volumes, as their service lives are relatively long when constructed properly. They can be used for minor leveling, they are quiet riding, and their appearance is exceptionally pleasing. Seal coats or slurry seals may fulfill surface requirements for low traffic pavements.

12. A surface renewing overlay must fill surface voids, provide an impervious skid-resistant surface, and

    A. be resistant to traffic abrasion
    B. have small particle size
    C. be exceptionally pleasing in appearance
    D. be constructed in half-inch layers

13. An *impervious skid-resistant surface* means a surface that is

    A. rough to the touch and fixed firmly in place
    B. waterproof and provides good gripping for tires
    C. not damaged by skidding vehicles
    D. smooth to the touch and quiet riding

14. The number of types of materials that can be constructed in very thin layers and are also suitable for surface renewing overlays is

    A. 1 B. 2 C. 3 D. 4

15. The SMALLEST thickness of asphalt concrete or hot sand asphalt that can fulfill all requirements for surface renewing overlays is _____ inch(es).

    A. ¼ B. ½ C. 1 D. 2

16. The materials that are recommended for thin resurfacing of pavements having high traffic volumes are

    A. those that have relatively long service lives
    B. asphalt concretes with maximum particle size
    C. surface seal coats
    D. slurry seals with voids

17. Fine-graded asphalt concrete and hot sand asphalt are quiet riding and are also

    A. recommended for low traffic pavements
    B. used as slurry seal coats
    C. suitable for major leveling
    D. exceptionally pleasing in appearance

18. The materials that may fulfill surface requirements for low traffic pavements are 18.____

    A. fine-graded asphalt concretes
    B. hot sand asphalts
    C. seal coats or slurry seals
    D. those that can be used for minor leveling

Questions 19-25.

DIRECTIONS: Questions 19 through 25 are to be answered SOLELY on the basis of the paragraphs below.

OPEN-END WRENCHES

Solid, non-adjustable wrenches with openings in one or both ends are called open-end wrenches. Wrenches with small openings are usually shorter than wrenches with large openings. This proportions the lever advantage of the wrench to the bolt or stud and helps prevent wrench breakage or damage to the bolt or stud.

Open-end wrenches may have their jaws parallel to the handle or at angles anywhere up to 90 degrees. The average angle is 15 degrees. This angular displacement variation permits selection of a wrench suited for places where there is room to make only a part of a complete turn of a nut or bolt. Handles are usually straight, but may be curved. Those with curved handles are called S-wrenches. Other open-end wrenches may have offset handles. This allows the head to reach nut or bolt heads that are sunk below the surface.

There are a few basic rules that you should keep in mind when using wrenches. They are:
   I.   ALWAYS use a wrench that fits the nut properly. Otherwise, the wrench may slip, or the nut may be damaged.
   II. Keep wrenches clean and free from oil. Otherwise, they may slip, resulting in possible serious injury to you or damage to the work.
   III. Do NOT increase the leverage of a wrench by placing a pipe over the handle. Increased leverage may damage the wrench or the work.

19. Open-end wrenches 19.____

    A. are adjustable
    B. are solid
    C. always have openings at both ends
    D. are always S-shaped

20. Wrench proportions are such that wrenches with _____ openings have _____ handles. 20.____

    A. larger; shorter   B. smaller; longer
    C. larger; longer   D. smaller; thicker

21. The average angle between the jaws and the handle of a wrench is _____ degrees. 21.____

    A. 0   B. 15   C. 22   D. 90

22. Offset handles are intended for use MAINLY with   22.___

    A. offset nuts
    B. bolts having fine threads
    C. nuts sunk below the surface
    D. bolts that permit limited swing

23. The wrench which is selected should fit the nut properly because this   23.___

    A. prevents distorting the wrench
    B. insures use of all wrench sizes
    C. avoids damaging the nut
    D. overstresses the bolt

24. Oil on wrenches is   24.___

    A. *good* because it prevents rust
    B. *good* because it permits easier turning
    C. *bad* because the wrench may slip off the nut
    D. *bad* because the oil may spoil the work

25. Extending the handle of a wrench by slipping a piece of pipe over it is considered   25.___

    A. *good* because it insures a tight nut
    B. *good* because less effort is needed to loosen a nut
    C. *bad* because the wrench may be damaged
    D. *bad* because the amount of tightening can not be controlled

KEY (CORRECT ANSWERS)

1.	D	11.	C
2.	B	12.	A
3.	B	13.	B
4.	C	14.	C
5.	D	15.	B
6.	C	16.	A
7.	C	17.	D
8.	B	18.	C
9.	A	19.	B
10.	D	20.	C

21.	B
22.	C
23.	C
24.	C
25.	C

TEST 2

DIRECTIONS: Each question or incomplete statement is followed by several suggested answers or completions. Select the one that BEST answers the question or completes the statement. *PRINT THE LETTER OF THE CORRECT ANSWER IN THE SPACE AT THE RIGHT.*

Questions 1-3.

DIRECTIONS: Questions 1 through 3 are to be answered SOLELY on the basis of the following passage.

A utility plan is a floor plan which shows the layout of a heating, electrical, plumbing, or other utility system. Utility plans are used primarily by the persons reponsible for the utilities, but they are important to the craftsman as well. Most utility installations require the leaving of openings in walls, floors, and roofs for the admission or installation of utility features. The craftsman who is, for example, pouring a concrete foundation wall must study the utility plans to determine the number, sizes, and locations of the openings he must leave for piping, electric lines, and the like.

1. The one of the following items of information which is LEAST likely to be provided by a utility plan is the

   A. location of the joists and frame members around stairwells
   B. location of the hot water supply and return piping
   C. location of light fixtures
   D. number of openings in the floor for radiators

2. According to the passage, the persons who will *most likely* have the GREATEST need for the information included in a utility plan of a building are those who

   A. maintain and repair the heating system
   B. clean the premises
   C. paint housing exteriors
   D. advertise property for sale

3. According to the passage, a repair crew member should find it MOST helpful to consult a utility plan when information is needed about the

   A. thickness of all doors in the structure
   B. number of electrical outlets located throughout the structure
   C. dimensions of each window in the structure
   D. length of a roof rafter

1.____

2.____

3.____

Questions 4-9.

DIRECTIONS: Questions 4 through 9 are to be answered SOLELY on the basis of the following passage.

The basic hand-operated hoisting device is the tackle or purchase, consisting of a line called a fall, reeved through one or more blocks. To hoist a load of given size, you must set up a rig with a safe working load equal to or in excess of the load to be hoisted. In order to do this, you must be able to calculate the safe working load of a single part of line of given size, the safe working load of a given purchase which contains a line of given size, and the minimum size of hooks or shackles which you must use in a given type of purchase to hoist a given load. You must also be able to calculate the thrust which a given load will exert on a gin pole or a set of shears inclined at a given angle, the safe working load which a spar of a given size used as a gin pole or as one of a set of shears will sustain, and the stress which a given load will set up in the back guy of a gin pole or in the back guy of a set of shears inclined at a given angle.

4. The above passage refers to the lifting of loads by means of

    A. erected scaffolds
    B. manual rigging devices
    C. power-driven equipment
    D. conveyor belts

5. It can be concluded from the above passage that a set of shears serves to

    A. absorb the force and stress of the working load
    B. operate the tackle
    C. contain the working load
    D. compute the safe working load

6. According to the above passage, a spar can be used for a

    A. back guy   B. block   C. fall   D. gin pole

7. According to the above passage, the rule that a user of hand-operated tackle MUST follow is to make sure that the safe working load is AT LEAST

    A. equal to the weight of the given load
    B. twice the combined weight of the block and falls
    C. one-half the weight of the given load
    D. twice the weight of the given load

8. According to the above passage, the two parts that make up a tackle are

    A. back guys and gin poles
    B. blocks and falls
    C. rigs and shears
    D. spars and shackles

9. According to the above passage, in order to determine whether it is safe to hoist a particular load, you MUST

    A. use the maximum size hooks
    B. time the speed to bring a given load to a desired place
    C. calculate the forces exerted on various types of rigs
    D. repeatedly lift and lower various loads

Questions 10-15.

DIRECTIONS: Questions 10 through 15 are to be answered SOLELY on the basis of the following set of instructions.

PATCHING SIMPLE CRACKS IN A BUILT-UP ROOF

If there is a visible crack in built-up roofing, the repair is simple and straightforward:

1. With a brush, clean all loose gravel and dust out of the crack, and clean three or four inches around all sides of it.
2. With a trowel or putty knife, fill the crack with asphalt cement and then spread a layer of asphalt cement about 1/8 inch thick over the cleaned area.
3. Place a strip of roofing felt big enough to cover the crack into the wet cement and press it down firmly.
4. Spread a second layer of cement over the strip of felt and well past its edges.
5. Brush gravel back over the patch.

10. According to the above passage, in order to patch simple cracks in a built-up roof, it is necessary to use a

    A. putty knife and a drill
    B. knife and pliers
    C. tack hammer and a punch
    D. brush and a trowel

11. According to the above passage, the size of the area that should be clear of loose gravel and dust before the asphalt cement is first applied should

    A. be the exact size of the crack itself
    B. extend three or four inches on all sides of the crack
    C. be 1/8 inch greater than the size of the crack itself
    D. extend the length of the roofing strip

12. According to the above passage, loose gravel and dust in the crack should be removed with a

    A. brush   B. felt pad   C. trowel   D. dust mop

13. Assume that both layers of asphalt cement needed to patch the crack are of the same thickness.
    The total thickness of asphalt cement used in the patch should be MOST NEARLY _____ inch.

    A. 1/2   B. 1/3   C. 1/4   D. 1/8

14. According to the instructions in the above passage, how large should the strip of roofing felt be cut?

    A. Three of four inches square
    B. Smaller than the crack and small enough to be surrounded by cement on all sides of the strip
    C. Exactly the same size and shape of the area covered by the wet cement
    D. Large enough to completely cover the crack

15. The final or finishing action to be taken in patching a simple crack in a built-up roof is to

    A. clean out the inside of the crack
    B. spread a layer of asphalt a second time
    C. cover the crack with roofing felt
    D. cover the patch of roofing felt and cement with gravel

Questions 16-17.

DIRECTIONS: Questions 16 and 17 are to be answered SOLELY on the basis of the information given in the following paragraph.

Supplies are to be ordered from the stockroom once a week. The standard requisition form, Form SP21, is to be used for ordering all supplies. The form is prepared in triplicate, one white original and two green copies. The white and one green copy are sent to the stockroom, and the remaining green copy is to be kept by the orderer until the supplies are received.

16. According to the above paragraph, there is a limit on the

    A. amount of supplies that may be ordered
    B. day on which supplies may be ordered
    C. different kinds of supplies that may be ordered
    D. number of times supplies may be ordered in one year

17. According to the above paragraph, when the standard requisition form for supplies is prepared,

    A. a total of four requisition blanks is used
    B. a white form is the original
    C. each copy is printed in two colors
    D. one copy is kept by the stock clerk

Questions 18-21.

DIRECTION: Questions 18 through 21 are to be answered SOLELY on the basis of the following passage.

The Oil Pollution Act for U. S. waters defines an *oily mixture* as 100 parts or more of oil in one million parts of mixture. This mixture is not allowed to be discharged into the prohibited zone. The prohibited zone may, in special cases, be extended 100 miles out to sea but, in general, remains at 50 miles offshore. The United States Coast Guard must be contacted to report all *oily mixture* spills. The Federal Water Pollution Control Act provides for a fine of $10,000 for failure to notify the United States Coast Guard. An employer may take action against an employee if the employee causes an *oily mixture* spill. The law holds your employer responsible for either cleaning up or paying for the removal of the oil spillage.

18. According to the Oil Pollution Act, an *oily mixture* is defined as one in which there are _____ parts or more of oil in _____ parts of mixture.

    A. 50; 10,000   B. 100; 10,000
    C. 100; 1,000,000   D. 10,000; 1,000,000

19. Failure to notify the proper authorities of an *oily mixture* spill is punishable by a fine. Such fine is provided for by the

    A. United States Coast Guard
    B. Federal Water Pollution Control Act
    C. Oil Pollution Act
    D. United States Department of Environmental Protection

20. According to the law, the one responsible for the removal of an *oily mixture* spilled into U.S. waters is the 20.____

    A. employer
    B. employee
    C. U.S. Coast Guard
    D. U.S. Pollution Control Board

21. The *prohibited zone,* in general, is the body of water 21.____

    A. within 50 miles offshore
    B. beyond 100 miles offshore
    C. within 10,000 yards of the coastline
    D. beyond 10,000 yards from the coastline

Questions 22-25.

DIRECTIONS: Questions 22 through 25 are to be answered SOLELY on the basis of the following paragraph.

    Synthetic detergents are materials produced from petroleum products or from animal or vegetable oils and fats. One of their advantages is the fact that they can be made to meet a particular cleaning problem by altering the foaming, wetting, and emulsifying properties of a cleaner. They are added to commonly used cleaning materials such as solvents, water, and alkalies to improve their cleaning performance. The adequate wetting of the surface to be cleaned is paramount in good cleaning performance. Because of the relatively high surface tension of water, it has poor wetting ability, unless its surface tension is decreased by addition of a detergent or soap. This allows water to flow into crevices and around small particles of soil, thus loosening them.

22. According to the above paragraph, synthetic detergents are made from all of the following EXCEPT 22.____

    A. petroleum products   B. vegetable oils
    C. surface tension oils   D. animal fats

23. According to the above paragraph, water's poor wetting ability is related to 23.____

    A. its low surface tension
    B. its high surface tension
    C. its vegetable oil content
    D. the amount of dirt on the surface to be cleaned

24. According to the above paragraph, synthetic detergents are added to all of the following EXCEPT 24.____

    A. alkalines   B. water   C. acids   D. solvents

25. According to the above paragraph, altering a property of a cleaner can give an advantage in meeting a certain cleaning problem.
    The one of the following that is NOT a property altered by synthetic detergents is the cleaner's

    A. flow ability
    B. foaming property
    C. emulsifying property
    D. wetting ability

25.___

KEY (CORRECT ANSWERS)

1.	A		11.	B
2.	A		12.	A
3.	B		13.	C
4.	B		14.	D
5.	A		15.	D
6.	D		16.	D
7.	A		17.	B
8.	B		18.	C
9.	C		19.	B
10.	D		20.	A

21. A
22. C
23. B
24. C
25. A

GRAPHS, MAPS, SKETCHES

EXAMINATION SECTION
TEST 1

DIRECTIONS: Each question or incomplete statement is followed by several suggested answers or completions. Select the one that BEST answers the question or completes the statement. *PRINT THE LETTER OF THE CORRECT ANSWER IN THE SPACE AT THE RIGHT.*

Questions 1-7.

DIRECTIONS: Questions 1 to 7, inclusive, are based on information contained on Chart A.

1. Puerto Ricans were the LARGEST number of people in 1.____

   A. 1975   B. 1973   C. 1979   D. 1971

2. At some time between 1974 and 1975, two groups had the same number of persons. These two groups were 2.____

   A. Puerto Rican and Black
   B. Caucasian and Black
   C. Oriental and Black
   D. Puerto Rican and Caucasian

3. In the same year that the Black population reached its GREATEST peak, the LOWEST number of people residing in Revere were of the following group or groups: 3.____

   A. Puerto Rican and Caucasian
   B. Oriental
   C. Puerto Rican
   D. Puerto Rican and Oriental

4. The group which showed the GREATEST increase in population from 1970 to 1979 is 4.____

   A. Puerto Rican
   B. Caucasian
   C. Oriental
   D. not determinable from the graph

5. In 1977, the Black population was higher by APPROXIMATELY 20% over 5.____

   A. 1972   B. 1976   C. 1974   D. 1978

6. The SMALLEST number of people in 1973 were 6.____

   A. Puerto Rican and Black
   B. Oriental and Black
   C. Puerto Rican and Caucasian
   D. Puerto Rican and Oriental

7. The percent increase in population of Puerto Ricans from 1971 to 1978 is *most nearly* 7._____

   A. 34% B. 18% C. 62% D. 80%

CHART A

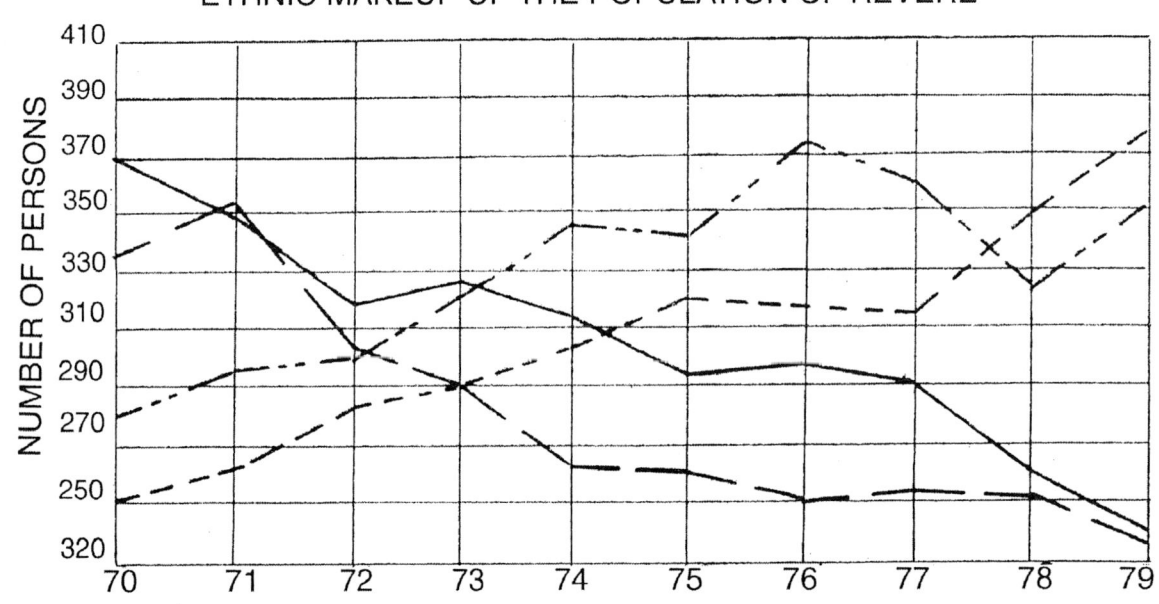

ETHNIC MAKEUP OF THE POPULATION OF REVERE

PUERTO RICAN – – – –
CAUCASIAN ————
ORIENTAL — —
BLACK —··—

KEY (CORRECT ANSWERS)

1. C
2. D
3. B
4. A
5. A
6. D
7. A

TEST 2

DIRECTIONS: Each question or incomplete statement is followed by several suggested answers or completions. Select the one that BEST answers the question or completes the statement. *PRINT THE LETTER OF THE CORRECT ANSWER IN THE SPACE AT THE RIGHT.*

Questions 1-2.

DIRECTIONS: Questions 1 and 2 are based on information contained on Chart B.

1. The percent of Black middle students attending overcrowded schools in the period 1967 to 1968 is *most nearly*

    A. 34.6   B. 37.6   C. 44.0   D. 47.5

    1._____

2. The percent growth in total school enrollment between 1960-61 and 1967-68 is *most nearly*

    A. 37.6
    B. 45.7
    C. 35.8
    D. cannot be determined from data given

    2._____

CHART B

Summary: School Utilization and Enrollment

PRIMARY SCHOOLS

	1960-61	1967-68
NUMBER OF / PERCENT SCHOOLS / UTILIZATION	20/105	20/102
ENROLLMENT/CAPACITY	16685/15842	18204/17813
UTILIZATION: OVER/UNDER	NET +1942/-1099	NET +2045/-1654
	NO. +843	NO. +391
	%	%
WHITE ENROLLMENT	3645 21.8	3146 17.2
NEGRO ENROLLMENT	12691 76.1	14304 78.5
PUERTO RICAN ENROLLMENT	349 2.1	754 4.1

MIDDLE SCHOOLS

	1960-61	1967-68
NUMBER OF / PERCENT SCHOOLS / UTILIZATION	3/101	5/96
ENROLLMENT/CAPACITY	4869/4808	7502/7811
UTILIZATION: OVER/UNDER	NET +235/-174	NET +276/-585
	NO. +61	NO. -309
	%	%
WHITE ENROLLMENT	1478 30.4	1717 22.8
NEGRO ENROLLMENT	3279 67.3	5228 69.6
PUERTO RICAN ENROLLMENT	112 2.3	557 7.4

HIGH SCHOOLS

	1960-61	1967-68
NUMBER OF / PERCENT SCHOOLS / UTILIZATION	2/78	3/107
ENROLLMENT/CAPACITY	1791/2300	6003/5847
UTILIZATION: OVER/UNDER	NET +157-524	NET +985/-829
	NO. -509	NO. +156
	%	%
WHITE ENROLLMENT	1106 61.8	3266 54.4
NEGRO ENROLLMENT	650 36.3	2561 42.6
PUERTO RICAN ENROLLMENT	35 2.0	176 2.9

Detail: School Utilization and Enrollment 1967-1968

PRIMARY SCHOOLS

PRIMARY SCHOOLS	CONSTRUCTION — DATES AND TYPE[a]	GRADES	AVERAGE YRS OVER OR UNDER GRADE	SPECIAL PROGRMS	ENROLLMENT TOTAL	WHITE NO	WHITE %	NEGRO NO	NEGRO %	PUERTO RICAN NO	PUERTO RICAN %	CAPACITY TOTAL	AVAIL– SHORT+	% OF UTIL	OTHER ROOMS
PS 15	1939	K-6	-.1	T,AS	565	2	.3	523	92.5	40	7.0	669	- 104	84.4	18 (NOTE M)
PS 30	1965	K-6	+1.2	T,AS	1605	854	53.2	748	46.6	3	.2	1099	+ 506	146.0	6 PORTABLES
PS 35	1931	K-6	+.6	AS	640	345	53.9	259	40.4	36	5.6	702	- 62	91.1	
PS 36	1924,63	K-6	-.3	SS	703	9	1.2	684	97.2	10	1.6	509	+ 194	138.1	6 PORTABLES
PS 37	1912,42,64	K-6	+.7	MES,AS	615	61	9.9	544	88.4	10	1.6	419	+ 196	146.7	
PS 40	1914,28,63	K-6	-.8	SS,MES	1058	-	-	994	93.9	55	5.1	869	+ 189	121.7	6 (NOTE N)
PS 45	1936	K-6	-.6	SS	986	7	.7	949	96.2	30	3.0	856	+ 130	115.1	6 PORTABLES
PS 46	1922	K-6	+.2	SP	495	-	-	482	97.3	3	.6	633	- 137	78.3	1 (NOTE O)
PS 50	1904	K-6	+1.5	T,AS	772	10	2.0	593	76.8	63	8.1	833	- 61	92.8	
PS 80	1964	K-6	-1.1		1052	116	15.0	574	54.5	57	5.5	1197	- 62	87.8	
PS 82	1906	K-6	+1.3		440	375	85.2	21	4.7	44	10.0	378	+ 62	116.4	2 (NOTE P)
PS 95	1915,25	K-6	-1.0	SS	1274	489	38.2	647	50.7	138	10.8	1320	- 46	96.5	
PS 116	1925,64	K-6	-.0	SS	914	-	-	902	98.6	10	1.0	1067	- 153	85.6	
PS 118	1923,32	K-6	-1.2	T	887	28	3.1	832	93.7	27	3.0	1089	- 202	81.4	
PS 123	1928,32,64	K-6	-1.2	SS	1565	41	2.6	1448	92.5	76	4.8	1103	+ 462	141.8	12 PORTABLES
PS 134	1928,38	K-6	-.9	T	1067	42	3.9	959	89.8	66	6.1	761	+ 306	140.2	
PS 136	1928,37	K-6	-.7	T	987	10	1.0	950	96.2	27	2.7	1301	- 314	75.8	1 (NOTE Q)
PS 140	1929,38,63	K-6	-.8	SS	1160	46	3.9	1098	94.6	16	1.3	1241	- 81	93.4	
PS 160	1939	K-6	-.6	SS	1019	11	1.0	1006	98.6	2	.6	1030	- 11	98.9	
PS 178	1951	K-6	+1.8	SS	400	268	67.0	91	22.7	41	10.2	738	- 338	54.2	
TOTAL PRIMARY SCHOOLS—	20				18204	3146	17.2	14304	78.5	754	4.1	17813	+ 2045	102.1	
													- 1654		

MIDDLE SCHOOLS

MIDDLE SCHOOLS	CONSTRUCTION	GRADES	AVG	SPECIAL	TOTAL	WHITE NO	WHITE %	NEGRO NO	NEGRO %	PR NO	PR %	CAP	AVAIL	% UTIL	
IS 8	1963	6-8	-.5	SS,PI	1562	325	20.8	1124	71.9	113	7.2	1523	+ 39	102.5	
IS 59	1956	6-7	-.1	PI,T,AS	1633	621	38.0	846	51.8	166	10.1	1396	+ 237	116.9	
IS 72	1967	6-7	-	T,AS	1396	210	15.0	1111	83.8	75	5.3	1647	- 251	84.7	
IS 142	1930,38	6-8	-1.5	SS	1096	21	1.9	1064	97.1	11	1.0	1333	- 231	82.2	
JS 192	1963	7-9	-.8		1815	540	29.7	1083	59.6	192	10.5	1912	- 97	94.9	
TOTAL MIDDLE SCHOOLS—	5				7502	1717	22.8	5228	69.6	557	7.4	7811	+ 276	96.0	
													- 585		

HIGH SCHOOLS

HIGH SCHOOLS	CONSTRUCTION	GRADES	AVG	SPECIAL	TOTAL	WHITE NO	WHITE %	NEGRO NO	NEGRO %	PR NO	PR %	CAP	AVAIL	% UTIL	
SPRINGFLD GDNS	1965	9-12	-.3		4277	2758	64.4	1462	34.1	57	1.3	3292	+ 985	129.9	
JAMAICA VOC	1896-C	9-12	-2.9		644	382	59.3	235	36.4	27	4.1	895	- 251	71.9	
M WILSON VOC	1942	9-12	-3.7		1082	126	11.6	864	79.8	92	8.5	1660	- 578	65.1	
TOTAL HIGH SCHOOLS—	3				6003	3266	54.4	2561	42.6	176	2.9	5847	+ 985	102.6	
													- 829		

NOTES

1. INCLUDES ENROLLMENT AND CAPACITY AT ANNEX (PS 170) IN QUEENS PLANNING DISTRICT 8
a. EXCEPT AS NOTED ALL SCHOOLS ARE OF FIREPROOF CONSTRUCTION
c. NOT FIREPROOF
x. NOT AVAILABLE

CODE

T: TRANSITIONAL SCHOOL
AS: AFTER SCHOOL STUDY CENTER
SS: SPECIAL SERVICE SCHOOL
MES: MORE EFFECTIVE SCHOOL
SP: SPECIAL PRIMARY SCHOOL
PI: PILOT INTERMEDIATE SCHOOL

NOTES

M IN ROCHDALE VILLAGE
N 4 PORTABLES, 2 IN UNION METHODIST CHURCH
O IN BROOKS MEMORIAL METHODIST CHURCH
P AT 139-35 88TH STREET
Q IN GRACE METHODIST EPISCOPAL CHURCH

KEY (CORRECT ANSWERS)

1. B
2. C

TEST 3

DIRECTIONS: Each question or incomplete statement is followed by several suggested answers or completions. Select the one that BEST answers the question or completes the statement. *PRINT THE LETTER OF THE CORRECT ANSWER IN THE SPACE AT THE RIGHT.*

Questions 1-4.

DIRECTIONS: Questions 1 to 4, inclusive, are based on the information contained on Chart C.

1. What percent of all households in 1960 are Puerto Rican households with incomes of $6,000 or more per year?

   A. 38%   B. 57%   C. 6%   D. 0.6%

   1.____

2. The median income in all households in 1960 is in the range of

   A. $3,000 - $5,999
   B. $6,000 - $9,999
   C. $10,000 - $14,999
   D. cannot be determined from data given

   2.____

3. The total number of white persons living in one or two person households in 1960 is

   A. 13,126   B. 28,884   C. 24,704   D. 46.5

   3.____

4. Which of the following statements is MOST likely to be true?

   A. In 1970, the majority of the population in the above data is white.
   B. The majority of households in 1960 have incomes under $6,000.
   C. There are 8668 people in 1960 in households with incomes under $3,000.
   D. The majority of households in 1960 with incomes under $2,000 are white.

   4.____

CHART C

Population and Housing Data

Housing Units

	TOTAL	1 ROOM	2 ROOMS	3 ROOMS	4 ROOMS	5 ROOMS	6+ ROOMS
TOTAL HOUSING UNITS - 1960	57611	1484	2492	10491	9074	8409	25661
TOTAL OCCUPIED HOUSING UNITS	56187						
RENTER OCCUPIED - TOTAL	23040						
PUBLICLY AIDED	1048	-	44	240	553	199	12
OWNER OCCUPIED - TOTAL	33147	-	-	-	-	-	-
PUBLICLY AIDED	-	-	-	-	-	-	-
PUBLIC HOUSING - 1970							
PUBLIC RENTER	1434	-	44	321	736	300	33
PUBLICLY AIDED RENTER	65	-	-	22	26	17	-
PUBLICLY AIDED OWNER	6075	-	3	2770	2214	568	520

Income 1960

	PERSONS IN HOUSEHOLD						TOTAL NUMBER OF HOUSEHOLDS
	1	2	3	4	5	6+	
WHITE HOUSEHOLDS							
UNDER $2000	1652	1153	276	143	122	58	3346
$2000 - $2999	459	717	176	67	58		1477
$3000 - $5999	1472	3018	1688	1290	944		8412
$6000 - $9999	501	3520	2649	1936	1900		10506
$10000 - $14999	75	1378	1255	1069	1144		4925
$15000 AND OVER	17	476	535	637	680		2345
NEGRO AND OTHER NON-WHITE HOUSEHOLDS							
UNDER $2000	494	664	386	303	444		2291
$2000 - $2999	237	453	315	192	280		1477
$3000 - $5999	587	2368	1721	1304	2313		8293
$6000 - $9999	98	1735	1984	1650	2465		7932
$10000 - $14999	13	370	567	679	1370		3025
$15000 AND OVER	1	23	82	116	435		656
PUERTO RICAN HOUSEHOLDS							
UNDER $2000	9	7	2	11	11		45
$2000 - $2999	4	17	14	12			32
$3000 - $5999	10	42	45	26	71		169
$6000 - $9999	-	8	35	30	112		219
$10000 - $14999	-	-	5	21	53		87
$15000 AND OVER	-	-	4	3	19		26
ALL HOUSEHOLDS							
UNDER $2000	2155	1824	664	457	577		5682
$2000 - $2999	700	1170	493	273	340		2986
$3000 - $5999	2069	5403	3454	2620	3328		16874
$6000 - $9999	599	5297	4668	3616	4477		18457
$10000 - $14999	92	1754	1857	1769	2567		8041
$15000 AND OVER	17	499	621	756	1134		3027

Population Growth

(line graph showing population from 1950 to 1970, axis 0 to 250,000)

Ethnic Make-up (in percent)

(bar charts for White, Black, Puerto Rican)

Households 1960 (in percent)

	% OF ALL HOUSEHOLDS	PERSONS IN HOUSEHOLDS					
		1	2	3	4	5	6+
White	56	14	33	21	17	9	7
Black	43	7	23	20	19	13	18
Puerto Rican	1	4	13	17	18	21	27
All Households	100%	12	23	20	17	12	12

KEY (CORRECT ANSWERS)

1. D
2. B
3. C
4. D

TEST 4

DIRECTIONS: Each question or incomplete statement is followed by several suggested answers or completions. Select the one that BEST answers the question or completes the statement. *PRINT THE LETTER OF THE CORRECT ANSWER IN THE SPACE AT THE RIGHT.*

Questions 1-4.

DIRECTIONS: Questions 1 through 4, inclusive, are based on information contained on Chart D.

1. The percentage of households by ethnic make-up in 1960 was *most nearly* 1._____

   A. 16% white, 12% Black and other non-white, 16% Puerto Rican, and 56% not reported
   B. 39% white, 26% Black and other non-white, and 35% Puerto Rican
   C. 95% white, 3% Black and 2% Puerto Rican
   D. 99% white, 1% Black and other non-white, and 0% Puerto Rican

2. In 1960, the predominant age group was in the age range of 2._____

   A. 5-15   B. 25-44   C. 45-64   D. 0-15

3. In 1960, the LARGEST singular and discrete income group consisted of households with the following characteristics: 3._____

   A. Black and other non-white households of 3 persons with total earnings of between $6,000 and $9,999
   B. White households with 3 persons with total earnings from under $2,000 to $5,999
   C. White households of 2 persons with total earnings between $6,000 and $9,999
   D. White households with total earnings under $2,000

4. The percent population increase between 1950 and 1970 was most nearly 4._____

   A. 56%   B. 30%   C. 25%   D. 33%

CHART D

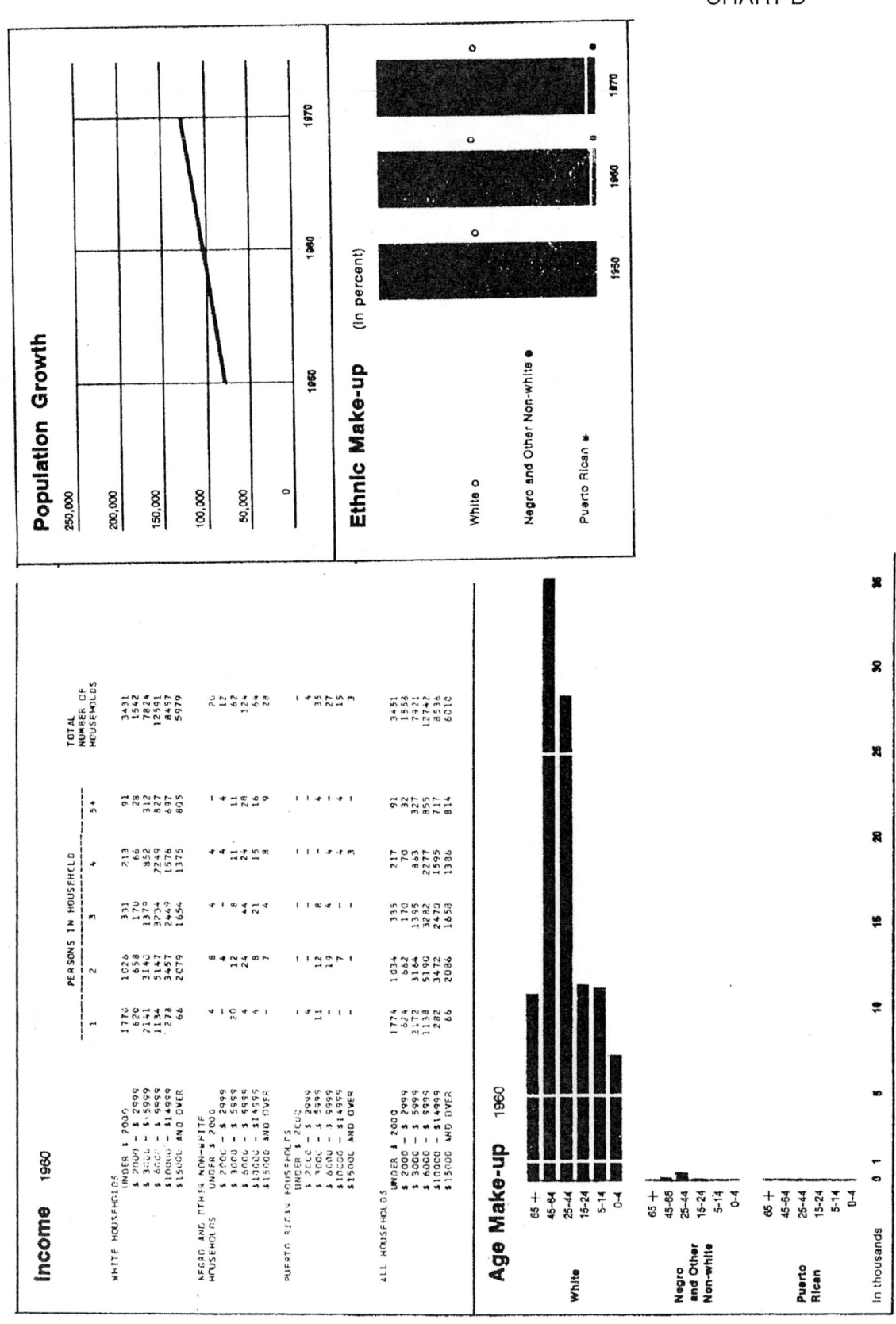

Population Growth

(line graph showing growth from 1950 to 1970, y-axis 0 to 250,000)

Ethnic Make-up (in percent)

Bar charts for 1950, 1960, 1970

White ○
Negro and Other Non-white ●
Puerto Rican ∗

Income 1960

	1	2	3	4	5+	TOTAL NUMBER OF HOUSEHOLDS
WHITE HOUSEHOLDS						
UNDER $2000	1770	1026	331	213	91	3431
$2000 - $2999	620	658	170	66	28	1542
$3000 - $5999	2141	3140	1370	852	312	7824
$6000 - $9999	1134	5147	3734	7249	827	12591
$10000 - $14999	1278	3457	2449	1576	697	8457
$15000 AND OVER	66	2079	1654	1375	805	5979
NEGRO AND OTHER NON-WHITE HOUSEHOLDS						
UNDER $2000	4	8	4	4	4	24
$2000 - $2999	—	4	4	4	—	12
$3000 - $5999	30	12	8	11	11	62
$6000 - $9999	4	24	44	24	28	124
$10000 - $14999	4	8	21	15	16	64
$15000 AND OVER	4	7	4	8	9	28
PUERTO RICAN HOUSEHOLDS						
UNDER $2000	—	—	—	—	—	4
$2000 - $2999	14	12	8	—	4	35
$3000 - $5999	11	19	4	4	4	27
$6000 - $9999	—	7	1	4	1	15
$10000 - $14999	—	—	—	3	—	3
$15000 AND OVER	—	—	—	—	—	—
ALL HOUSEHOLDS						
UNDER $2000	1774	1034	335	217	91	3451
$2000 - $2999	624	662	170	70	32	1558
$3000 - $5999	2172	3164	1395	863	327	7721
$6000 - $9999	1138	5190	3282	2277	855	12742
$10000 - $14999	282	3472	2470	1595	717	8536
$15000 AND OVER	66	2086	1658	1386	814	6010

Age Make-up 1960

Bar chart in thousands (0 to 36)

White: 65+, 45-64, 25-44, 15-24, 5-14, 0-4
Negro and Other Non-white: 65+, 45-64, 25-44, 15-24, 5-14, 0-4
Puerto Rican: 65+, 45-64, 25-44, 15-24, 5-14, 0-4

KEY (CORRECT ANSWERS)

1. D
2. C
3. C
4. A

TEST 5

DIRECTIONS: Each question or incomplete statement is followed by several suggested answers or completions. Select the one that BEST answers the question or completes the statement. *PRINT THE LETTER OF THE CORRECT ANSWER IN THE SPACE AT THE RIGHT.*

Questions 1-3.

DIRECTIONS: Questions 1 through 3, inclusive, are based on information contained on Zoning Map E. Zoning Map E is drawn to scale. Candidates are to scale off measurements.

1. One-third of Block A (shaded area) has already been developed as a public housing project. It is proposed that a second development be built on the remainder of the site. The approximate size of the proposed site, in acres, is *most nearly* (43,650 sq.ft. = 1 acre)

    A. 5.9 B. 55 C. 1.8 D. 10.3

    1.____

2. If Site B were developed for housing and 40% of the site was covered by buildings, the amount of open space would be *most nearly* _____ acres.

    A. 2.5 B. 6.3 C. 3.8 D. 2.7

    2.____

3. A new elementary school will have to be built to accommodate the children from the two proposed projects at A and B.
If the new school must be within 1/2 mile walk of any point in either project, which would be the *most likely* site?

    A. 1 B. 2 C. 3 D. 4

    3.____

2 (#5)

ZONING MAP E

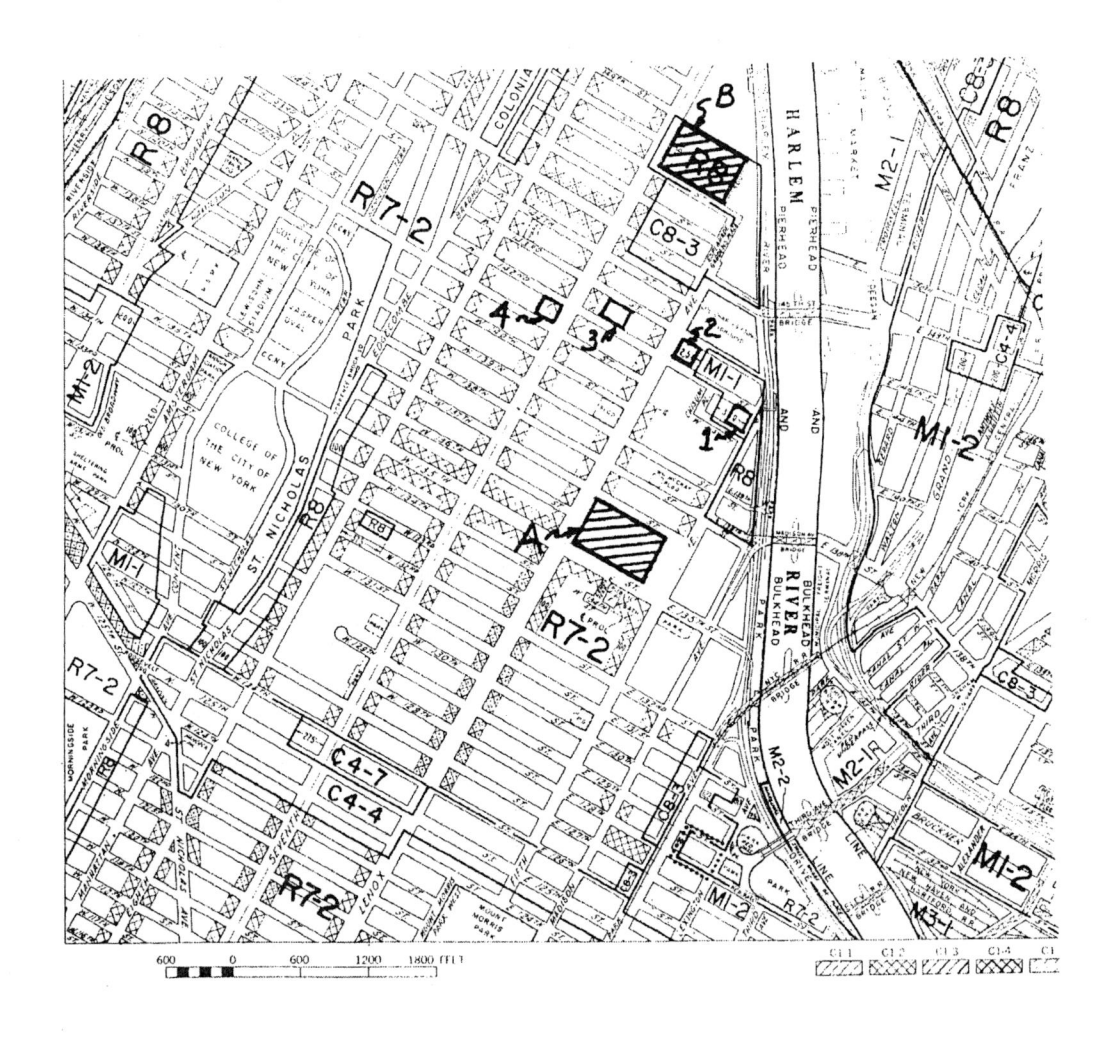

KEY (CORRECT ANSWERS)

1. A
2. C
3. B

TEST 6

DIRECTIONS: Each question or incomplete statement is followed by several suggested answers or completions. Select the one that BEST answers the question or completes the statement. *PRINT THE LETTER OF THE CORRECT ANSWER IN THE SPACE AT THE RIGHT.*

Questions 1-2.

DIRECTIONS: Questions 1 and 2 are to be answered in accordance with the Coast and Geodetic Map F.

1. The difference in elevation between the lowest and highest point of Ewen Park is *most nearly* _____ feet.   1.____

   A. 100   B. 25   C. 200   D. 50

2. Given: The scale of the map is as shown.   2.____
   The distance between the College of Mt. St. Vincent and Ewen Park is *most nearly* _____ feet.

   A. 2,000   B. 6,000   C. 24,000   D. 12,000

COAST & GEODETIC MAP F

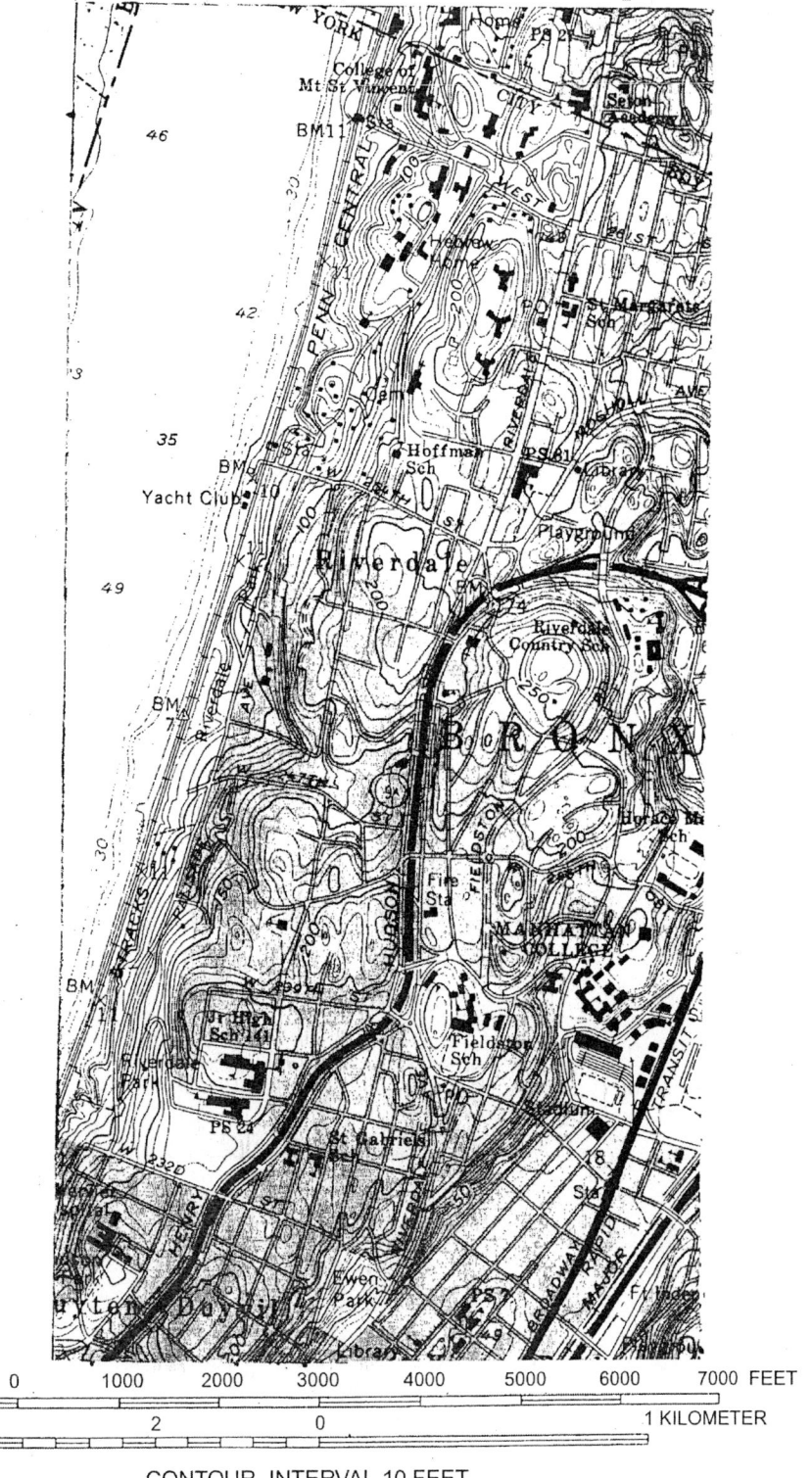

CONTOUR INTERVAL 10 FEET

KEY (CORRECT ANSWERS)

1. A
2. D

TEST 7

DIRECTIONS: Each question or incomplete statement is followed by several suggested answers or completions. Select the one that BEST answers the question or completes the statement. *PRINT THE LETTER OF THE CORRECT ANSWER IN THE SPACE AT THE RIGHT.*

Questions 1-3.

DIRECTIONS: Questions 1 to 3, inclusive, are based on information contained on Sketch G, a birds-eye view of a proposed development.

NOTE: The attached single family homes in the periphery are one-story high and contain 1,000 square feet. They are square buildings.

1. The dimension A of this single family attached home is *most nearly* _____ feet.   1._____
   A. 20   B. 32   C. 50   D. 100

2. The dimension B of the road is *most nearly* _____ feet.   2._____
   A. 25   B. 48   C. 75   D. 100

3. The dimension C of the courtyard is *most nearly* _____ feet.   3._____
   A. 40   B. 85   C. 57   D. 150

SKETCH G

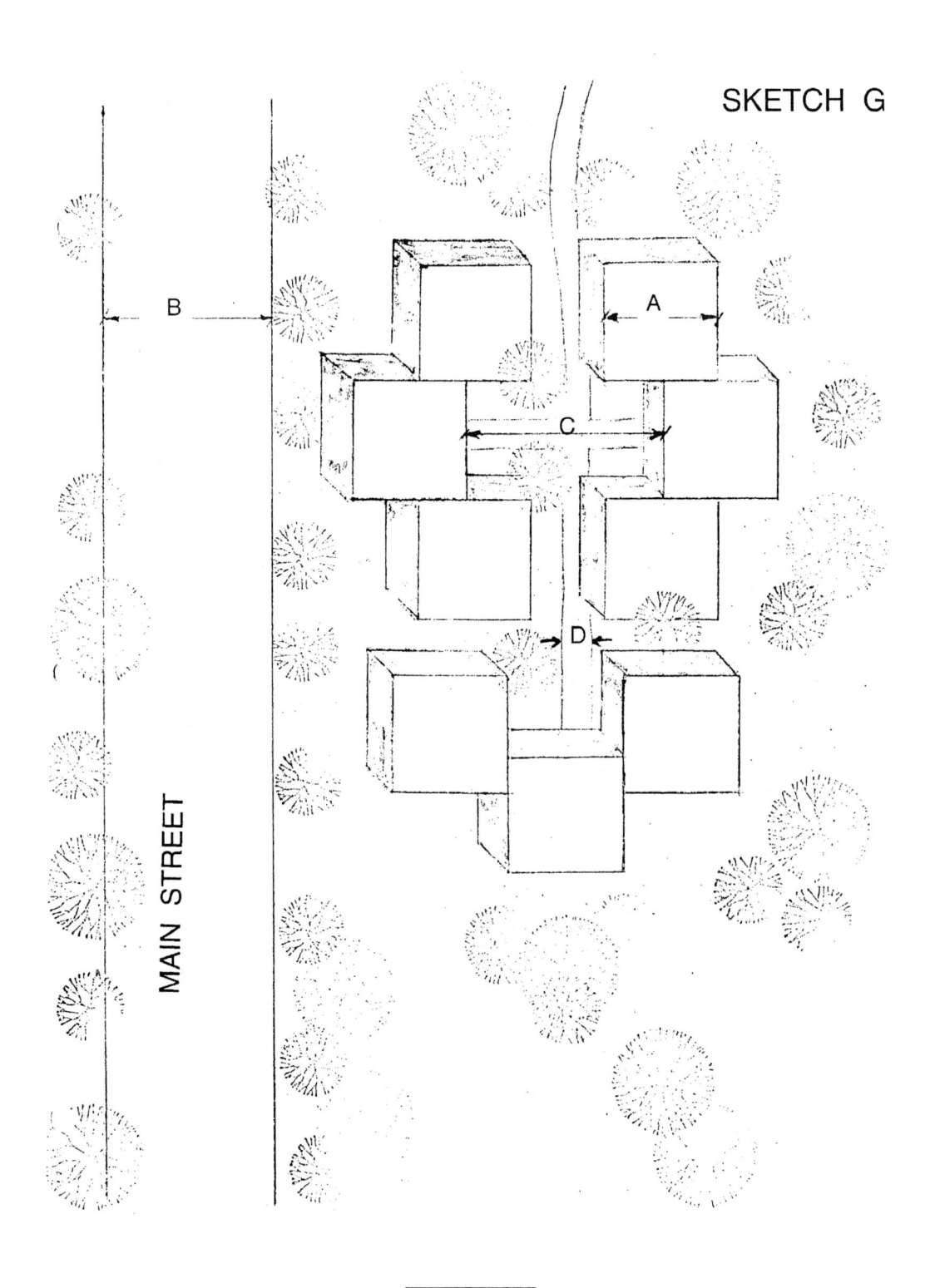

MAIN STREET

KEY (CORRECT ANSWERS)

1. B
2. B
3. C

INTERPRETING STATISTICAL DATA GRAPHS, CHARTS AND TABLES
EXAMINATION SECTION
TEST 1

DIRECTIONS: Each question or incomplete statement is followed by several suggested answers or completions. Select the one that BEST answers the question or completes the statement. *PRINT THE LETTER OF THE CORRECT ANSWER IN THE SPACE AT THE RIGHT.*

Questions 1-10.

DIRECTIONS: Questions 1 through 10 are to be answered SOLELY on the basis of the following tables, which contain data concerning the Green Valley Region, a fictional area.

HOUSING PATTERNS, GREEN VALLEY REGION 1990-2000

TABLE I

TYPE OF HOUSING	SUBURBS 1990	SUBURBS 2000	TOWNS 1990	TOWNS 2000	REGION TOTAL* 1990	REGION TOTAL* 2000
Multi-unit Dwellings	2,600	5,200	9,300	10,900	13,700	18,800
Single-unit Dwellings	15,100	17,700	11,000	11,400	43,700	46,900
Mobile Dwellings	300	?	900	1,800	14,700	31,400
TOTAL	18,000	23,600	21,200	24,100	72,100	97,100

*NOTE: Region totals include other categories in addition to suburbs and towns.

TABLE II
SUBSTANDARD HOUSING, GREEN VALLEY REGION
(INCLUDED IN FIGURES IN TABLE I, ABOVE)

	1990-800 UNITS	2000-1,200 UNITS
Multi-unit	64%	54%
Single-unit	33%	28%
Mobile	3%	18%

1. If the single-unit dwellings in towns in 1990 each contained an average of 5.1 rooms, the total number of rooms in this category was MOST NEARLY

   A. 56,000   B. 61,000   C. 561,000   D. 651,000

2. The number of mobile dwellings in the suburbs in 2000 was

   A. 500   B. 600   C. 700   D. 800

3. From 1990 to 2000, the total number of all Green Valley Region housing units increased by MOST NEARLY

   A. 31%   B. 34%   C. 37%   D. 40%

4. For 2000, what was the TOTAL number of substandard multi-unit dwellings?

   A. 548　　　B. 573　　　C. 623　　　D. 648

5. In the towns from 1990 to 2000, the type of housing having the LARGEST proportionate increase was

   A. mobile
   B. multi-unit
   C. single-unit
   D. substandard

6. In 2000, the TOTAL number of dwellings which were NOT substandard was

   A. 95,300　　　B. 95,900　　　C. 96,200　　　D. 96,500

7. Assume that in 1990, 3.5 persons was the average occupancy in the towns in each kind of dwelling.
   Thus, the population of the towns in the Green Valley Region in 1990 was

   A. 73,600　　　B. 73,800　　　C. 74,000　　　D. 74,200

8. Which of the following statements concerning mobile dwellings is CORRECT?
   In

   A. 2000, mobile dwellings were the largest category of substandard dwellings
   B. 1990, the number of mobile dwellings in suburbs was greater by 30% than the number in towns
   C. the Green Valley Region during the period 1990-00, the number of mobile dwellings increased by 50%
   D. 1990, the total number of mobile dwellings in the Green Valley Region was less than 25% of the total number of all dwellings

9. Assume that of the single-unit dwellings not in suburbs and towns in 1990, 20% were in villages.
   Therefore, the number of single-unit dwellings in villages in 1990 was

   A. 2,480　　　B. 3,070　　　C. 3,520　　　D. 4,110

10. Assume that in the Green Valley Region the following changes were expected in 2004 as compared to 2000: the number of suburban dwellings was increased by 30%; the number of town dwellings was decreased by 15%.
    Therefore, the ratio of suburban dwellings to town dwellings expected for 2004 was MOST NEARLY

    A. 3:2　　　B. 4:3　　　C. 5:4　　　D. 6:5

KEY (CORRECT ANSWERS)

1. A   6. B
2. C   7. D
3. B   8. D
4. D   9. C
5. A   10. A

TEST 2

Questions 1-6.

DIRECTIONS: Questions 1 through 6 are to be answered SOLELY on the basis of the graph below which presents data on two demographic characteristics and the rate of new home construction in Empire State during the period 1995 through 2006.

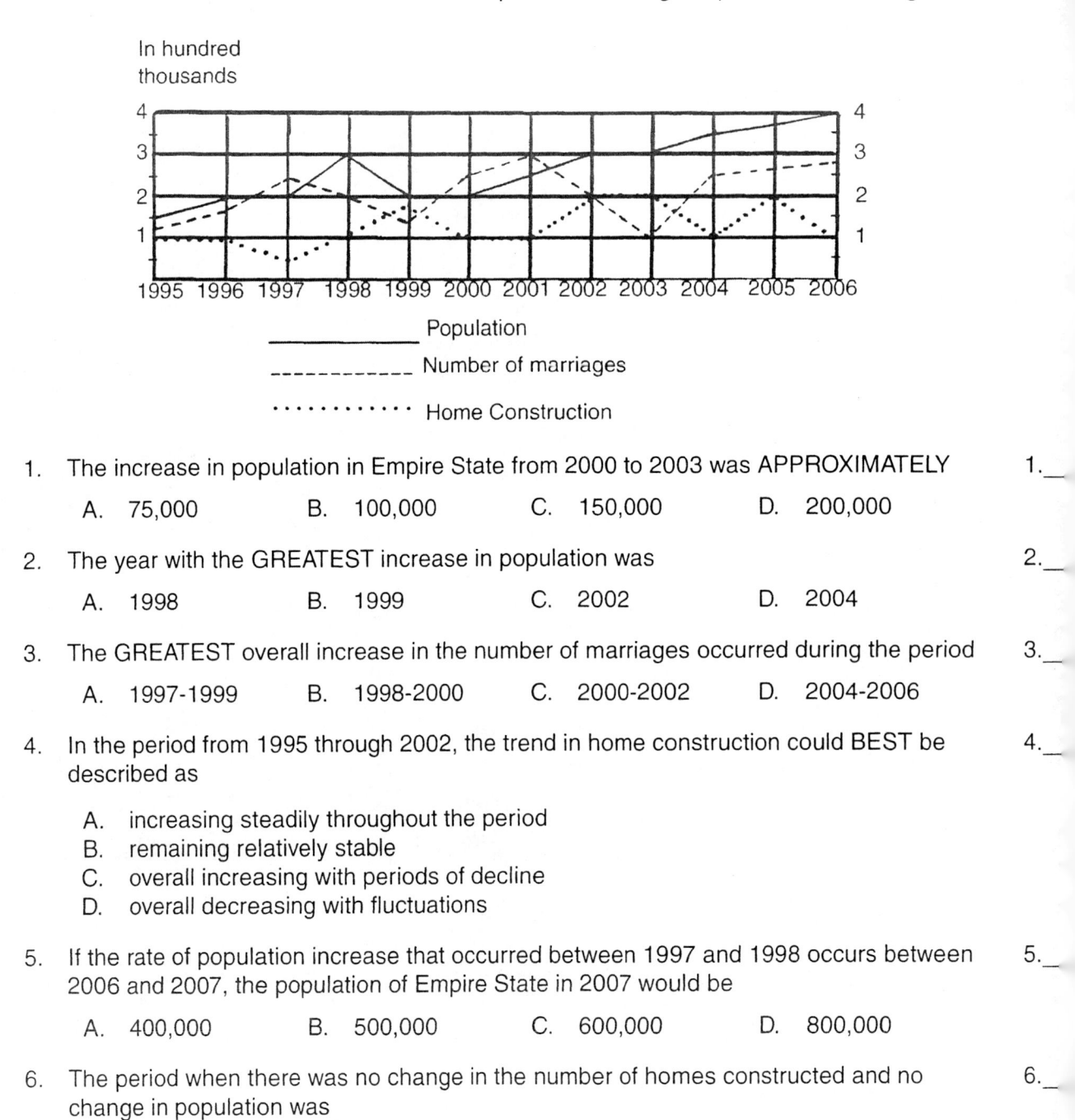

In hundred thousands

_____ Population

_ _ _ _ _ _ _ Number of marriages

· · · · · · · · · Home Construction

1. The increase in population in Empire State from 2000 to 2003 was APPROXIMATELY

    A. 75,000   B. 100,000   C. 150,000   D. 200,000

2. The year with the GREATEST increase in population was

    A. 1998   B. 1999   C. 2002   D. 2004

3. The GREATEST overall increase in the number of marriages occurred during the period

    A. 1997-1999   B. 1998-2000   C. 2000-2002   D. 2004-2006

4. In the period from 1995 through 2002, the trend in home construction could BEST be described as

    A. increasing steadily throughout the period
    B. remaining relatively stable
    C. overall increasing with periods of decline
    D. overall decreasing with fluctuations

5. If the rate of population increase that occurred between 1997 and 1998 occurs between 2006 and 2007, the population of Empire State in 2007 would be

    A. 400,000   B. 500,000   C. 600,000   D. 800,000

6. The period when there was no change in the number of homes constructed and no change in population was

    A. 1996-1997   B. 1999-2000   C. 2000-2001   D. 2002-2003

KEY (CORRECT ANSWERS)

1. B
2. A
3. B
4. C
5. C
6. D

TEST 3

Questions 1-6.

DIRECTIONS: Questions 1 through 6 are to be answered SOLELY on the basis of the information given in the graph below, which presents data on the rate of new office construction in the uptown, midtown, and downtown areas of Gotham City for the period from 1968 through 2001.

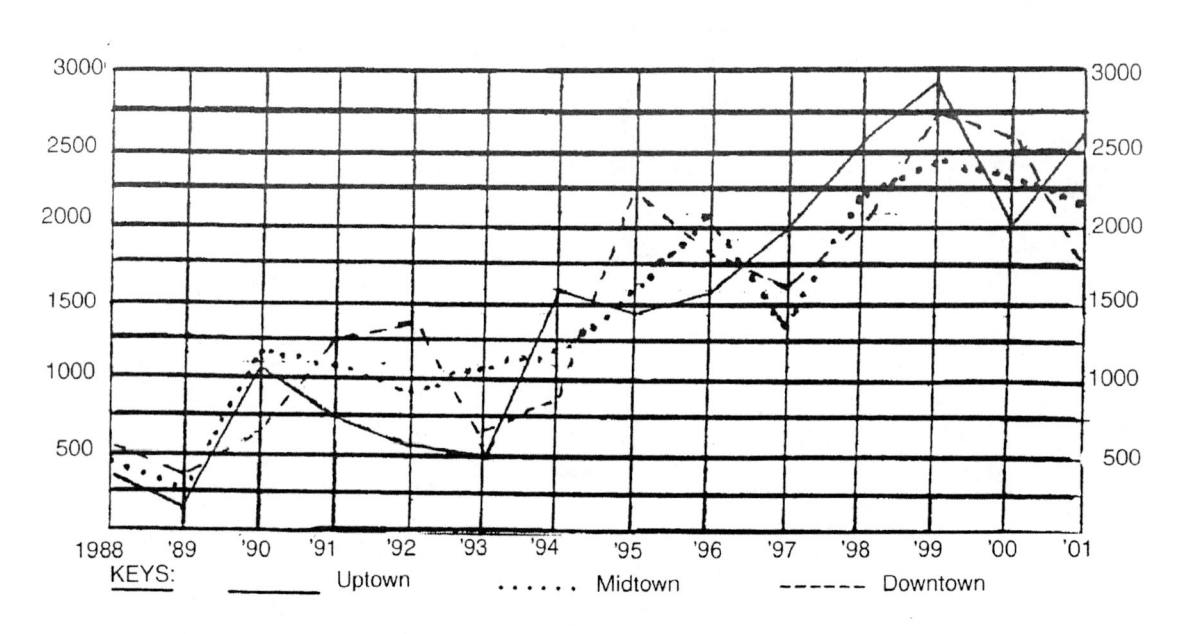

1. The amount of office space which was constructed in Gotham City in the year 1997 is MOST NEARLY _____ square feet.

   A. 2,100,000
   B. 3,500,000
   C. 4,900,000
   D. 5,700,000

2. In which of the following years was the LEAST amount of office space constructed in the downtown area?

   A. 1988   B. 1991   C. 1993   D. 1995

3. The year with the GREATEST amount of new office construction was

   A. 1990   B. 1994   C. 1999   D. 2001

4. In the years 1995 through 1999, the overall trend in new uptown office space construction could BEST be described as

   A. generally stable
   B. steadily increasing with small annual fluctuations
   C. generally increasing with large annual fluctuations
   D. steadily decreasing with major annual fluctuations

5. The GREATEST increase in percentage of new office space construction occurred in the year

   A. 1998   B. 1995   C. 1992   D. 1990

6. Consider the relationship between the amount of midtown office construction in 1990 and 1994.
If the same relationship exists in 2001 and 2005, the amount of midtown office construction in 2005 would be _____ square feet.

    A. 1,300,000
    B. 1,600,000
    C. 2,100,000
    D. 2,500,000

6.____

KEY (CORRECT ANSWERS)

1. C
2. A
3. C
4. B
5. D
6. C

TEST 4

Questions 1-7.

DIRECTIONS: Questions 1 through 7 are to be answered SOLELY on the basis of the information and the table below which lists the minimum and average monthly rents paid for various kinds of apartments in 3 groups of housing projects in City Z.

MINIMUM AND AVERAGE MONTHLY RENTS FOR VARIOUS KINDS OF APARTMENTS IN HOUSING PROJECTS IN CITY Z

Size of Apartment	Group I Projects Minimum	Group I Projects Average	Group II Projects Minimum	Group II Projects Average	Group III Projects Minimum	Group III Projects Average
2 rooms	$167.00	$178.00	$196.00	$216.60	$212.60	$229.00
3 rooms	$208.00	$223.20	$232.60	$253.00	$245.00	$260.60
4 rooms	$237.00	$248.00	$285.00	$315.00	$299.00	$329.80
5 rooms	$278.00	$296.60	$338.00	$355.00	$358.00	$387.00
6 rooms or more	$321.00	$344.40	$380.00	$418.00	$421.00	$462.00

Names of Group I Projects: Allen, Belton, Carlton, Grand, Ramsey, Redwood, Sandford, Trent

Names of Group II Projects: Alden, Berton, Carry, Gerrard, Long, Randall, Tallwood, Tenth St., Thomas Ave.

Names of Group III Projects: Astor Lane, Edgewood, Kennelly, Lange, Roosevelt, Summerset, Turner, Westgate

Each of Questions 1 through 7 gives the name of a housing project, the monthly rent paid by a tenant in that project, and the size of the tenant's apartment. You are to compare the information in each question with the table and lists of projects, and then mark A, B, C, or D in the answer space at the right in accordance with the following instructions:

- A. If the rent in the question is the minimum for this size apartment in this project, mark your answer A.
- B. If the rent in the question is higher than the minimum rent for this size apartment in this project but lower than the average rent, mark your answer B.
- C. If the rent in the question is exactly the same as the average rent for this size apartment in this project, mark your answer C.
- D. If the rent in the question is higher than the average rent for this size apartment in this project, mark your answer D.

SAMPLE QUESTION: Astor Lane Project, 2 rooms, $217.00

According to the lists of projects, the Astor Lane Project is in Group III. In the table above, under Group III Projects and across the line reading *2 rooms,* the minimum rent is $212.60 and the average rent is $229.00. Thus, the rent paid by this tenant is higher than the minimum rent but lower than the average rent. Therefore, the answer is B.

1. Randall Project, 4 rooms, $285.00   1.____
2. Trent Project, 6 rooms, $328.20   2.____
3. Lange Project, 3 rooms, $264.60   3.____
4. Alden Project, 5 rooms, $355.00   4.____
5. Summerset Project, 4 rooms, $337.00   5.____
6. Grand Project, 2 rooms, $181.60   6.____
7. Carry Project, 6 rooms, $407.00   7.____

KEY (CORRECT ANSWERS)

1. A
2. B
3. D
4. C
5. D
6. D
7. B

TEST 5

Questions 1-8.

DIRECTIONS: Questions 1 through 8 are to be answered SOLELY on the basis of the information given below. Assume that apartments of the sizes indicated in the questions exist in the projects named. In each question, the title of the Resident Employee, the size of the apartment he occupies, and the project he lives in are given. Choose from the options at the right in each question the monthly rental the Resident Employee pays.

MONTHLY RENTALS FOR RESIDENT EMPLOYEES IN STATE PROJECTS				
	Group I Projects		Group II Projects	
	Supt. & Asst. Supt	All Other Employees	Supt. & Asst. Supt	All Other Employees
2 rooms	$186	$170	$188	$172
3 rooms	$194	$182	$200	$188
4 rooms	$206	$194	$224	$212
5 rooms	$228	$212	$254	$238
6 rooms	$240	$228	$262	$250
7 rooms or more	$252	$236	$272	$256

<u>Names of Group I Projects</u>: Amsterdam, Astoria, Bland, Bronx River, Brownsville, Carver, Cypress Hills, Farragut, Forest, Gowanus, Ingersoll, Johnson, King, Lincoln, Marcy, Melrose, Patterson, Redfern, Smith, Soundview, Wald, Whitman.

<u>Names of Group II Projects</u>: Albany, Audubon, Baychester, Bronx River Add., Bushwick, Butler, Castle Hill, Chelsea, Douglass, Douglass Add., Drew-Hamilton, Edgemere, Haber, Howard, Independence, Manhattanville, Marlboro, Mill Brook, Murphy, Rutgers, Stapleton, Sumner, White, Williams, Plaza, Wilson, Wise Towers

1. Maintenance Man
   2-room apartment
   Manhattanville Project

   A. $170   B. $172   C. $186   D. $188

2. Housing Caretaker
   3-room apartment
   Baychester Project

   A. $172   B. $182   C. $188   D. $200

3. Maintenance Man
   6-room apartment
   Redfern Project

   A. $228   B. $238   C. $240   D. $250

4. Assistant Superintendent
   3-room apartment
   Lincoln Project

   A. $182   B. $188   C. $194   D. $200

5. Housing Caretaker
   4-room apartment
   Stapleton Project

   A. $182   B. $194   C. $206   D. $212

6. Assistant Superintendent
   5-room apartment
   Drew-Hamilton Project

   A. $212   B. $228   C. $238   D. $254

7. Housing Fireman
   8-room apartment
   Gowanus Project

   A. $238   B. $252   C. $256   D. $292

8. Superintendent
   6-room apartment
   Whitman Project

   A. $238   B. $240   C. $252   D. $262

KEY (CORRECT ANSWERS)

1. B
2. C
3. A
4. C
5. D
6. D
7. A
8. B

ZONING ORDINANCES IN RELATION TO THE HOUSING INSPECTION

	Page
I. Background of Zoning	1
II. Definitions	2
III. Zoning Objectives	3
IV. What Zoning Cannot Do	4
V. Content of the Ordinance	4
VI. Bulk and Height requirements	5
VII. Yard Requirements	5
VIII. Off street Parking	6
IX. Nonconforming Uses	6
X. Variances	6
XI. Exceptions	7
XII. Administration	7
XIII. How Zoning Can Benefit the Housing Inspector	7
XIV. Example of Zoning and Housing Relationships	8

ZONING ORDINANCES IN RELATION TO THE HOUSING INSPECTION

Zoning is essentially a means of ensuring that a community's hind uses are compatibly located for the health, safety, and general welfare of the community. Experience has shown that some types of controls are needed in order to provide orderly growth in relation to the community plan for development. Just as a capital improvement program governs public improvements such as streets, parks, and other recreational facilities, schools, and public buildings, so zoning governs the planning program with respect to the use of public and private property.

When a person buys or builds a house or other structure in a municipality that has a zoning ordinance in effect, he is presumed to know and obliged by law to comply with the zoning regulations governing the use of buildings and land in the section of the community in which his property is located. If he either erects a structure or converts a house or building that is within that particular district by the local zoning ordinance into another type of use he still has acquired no property right to continue the forbidden use. An example would be the conversion of a single family residence into multifamily units. Even if the owner has obtained a building permit for this work already completed, the building permit would be voided, because the work was started in violation of the zoning code and because a building permit can be valid' only when issued for a lawful purpose. The building inspector is therefore obliged to refuse issuance of a building permit if the proposed work is in violation of the zoning ordinance.

It is very important that the housing inspector know the general nature of zoning regulations, since properties in violation of both the housing code and the zoning ordinance must be brought into full compliance with the zoning ordinance before the housing code can be enforced. In many cases the housing inspector may be able to eliminate some of the properties in violation of the housing code through enforcement of the zoning ordinance.

I. Background of Zoning

Zoning regulations have been used for several centuries. In the early settlement of our country, gunpowder mills and storehouses were prohibited from being located within the heavily populated portions of town, owing to the frequent fires and explosions. Later, zoning took the form of fire districts, and under implied legislative powers, wooden buildings were prohibited from certain sections of the municipality.

Massachusetts passed one of the first zoning laws in 1692. This law authorized Boston, Salem, Charlestown, and certain other market towns in the province to assign certain locations in each town for the establishment of slaughterhouses and still houses for currying of leather.

Act and Resolves of the Province of Massachusetts Bay 1692-93 C. 23

"Be it ordained and enacted by the Governor, Council and Representatives convened in General Court or Assembly, and by the authority of the same,

Sect. 1 That the selectmen of the towns of Boston, Salem, and Charlestown respectively, or other market towns in the province, with two or more justices of the peace dwelling in the town, or two of the next justices of the country, shall at or before the last day of March, one thousand six hundred ninety-three, assign some certain places of the said towns (where it may be least offensive) for the erecting or setting up of slaughterhouses for the killing of all meat, still houses, and houses for trying of tallow and currying of leather (which houses may be erected of timber, the law referring to building with brick or stone not withstanding) and shall cause an entry to be made in the town book of what places shall be by them so assigned, and make known the same by posting it up in some public places of the town; by which houses and places respectively, and no other, all butchers, slaughter men, distillers, chandlers, and curriers shall exercise and practice their respective trades and mysteries; on pain that any butcher or slaughter man transgressing of this act by killing of meat in any other place, for every conviction thereof before one or more justices of the peace, shall forfeit and pay the sum of twenty shillings (shilling worth about l2-l6¢); and any distiller, chandler or currier offending against this act, for every conviction thereof before their majesties justices at the general sessions of the peace for the county, shall forfeit and pay the sum of five pounds (a pound equals 20 shillings and was worth somewhere between $2.40 and $3.20); one-third part of said forfeitures to be the use of the majesties for the support of the government of the province and incident charges thereof, one-third to the poor of the town when such offense shall be committed, and the other third to him or them that shall inform and sue for the same ....

II. Definitions

A. Accessory Structure - A detached building or structure in a secondary or subordinate capacity from the main or principal building or structure on the same premises. Example: garage behind a single-family dwelling.

B. Accessory Use - A use incidental and subordinate to the principal use of a structure. Example: a home-located physician's office.

C. Alteration - A change or rearrangement of the structural parts of a building, or an expansion or enlargement of the building.

D. Building Area - That portion of the lot remaining available for construction after all required open space and yard requirements are met.

E. Dwelling - Any enclosed space that is wholly or partially used or intended to be used for living or sleeping by human occupants provided that temporary housing shall not be regarded as a dwelling. Temporary housing is defined as any tent, trailer, mobile home, or any other shelter designed to be transportable and not attached to the ground, to another structure, or to any utility system on the same premises for more than 30 consecutive days.

F. Dwelling, Two Family - A structure containing two dwelling units and designed for occupancy by no more than two families.

G. Dwelling, Multifamily - A residential structure equipped with more than two dwelling units.

H. Dwelling Unit - Any room or group of rooms located within a dwelling and forming a single habitable unit with facilities that are used or intended to be used by a single family for living, sleeping, cooking, and eating.

I. Exception - Sometimes called "special use." An exception is a land use that can be made compatible with a district upon the imposition by the board of adjustment of special provisions covering its development, even though it would not otherwise be permitted in the district. Example: Fire substation being permitted to locate in a residential area.

J. Family - One or more individuals living together and sharing common living, sleeping, cooking, and eating facilities.

K. Home Occupation - An occupation conducted in a dwelling unit subject to the restrictions of the zoning ordinance. Limitations of interest to housing inspectors are the following: (a) Only the occupant or members of his family residing on the premises shall be engaged in the occupation, (b) the home occupation use shall be subordinate to its use for residential purposes and shall not occupy more than 25 per cent of the floor area of the dwelling unit, (c) the home occupation shall not be conducted in an accessory structure, (d) no offensive noise, glare, vibration, heat, smoke, dust, or odor shall be produced.

L. Lot- Parcel of land considered as a unit devoted to either a particular use or to occupancy by a building and its accessory structures.

M. Lot Depth - The average horizontal distance between the front and rear lot line measured at right angles to the structure.

N. Lot Width - The average horizontal distance between the sides of a lot measured at right angles to the lot depth.

O. Nonconforming Use - (a) Use of a building or use of land that does not conform to the regulations of the district in which located. (b) Nonconforming use also means a building or land use that does not conform to the regulations of the district in which the building or land is but that is nevertheless legal since it existed before enactment of the ordinance.

P. Open Space - Unoccupied space that is open to the sky and on the same lot with the building.

Q. Variance - Easing or lessening of the terms of the zoning ordinance by a public body so that relief for hardships will be provided but with the public interest still protected.

Inspectors should refer to the definitions in the zoning ordinance of their municipality for additions and changes.

III. Zoning Objectives

As stated earlier, the purpose of a zoning ordinance is to ensure that the land uses within the community are regulated not only for the health, safety, and welfare of the community but also in keeping with the comprehensive plan for community development. The objectives contained in the zoning ordinance that help to achieve a development providing for the health, safety, and welfare are the following:

A. Regulate Height, Bulk, and Area of Structure. In order to provide established standards of healthful housing within the community, regulations dealing with building heights, lot coverage, and floor areas must be established. These regulations then ensure that adequate natural lighting, ventilation, privacy, and recreational area for children will be realized. These are all fundamental physiological needs that have been determined to be necessary for a healthful environment.

Safety from fires is enhanced because of building separations needed to meet yard and open-space requirements.

Through prescribing minimum lot area per dwelling unit, population density controls are established.

B. Avoid Undue Levels of Noise, Vibration, Glare, Air Pollution, and Odor. By providing land use category districts, these environmental stresses upon the individual can be reduced. As in the first item, the absence of these stresses has been determined to be a fundamental physiological individual need.

C. Lessen Street Congestion Through Off-Street Parking and Off-Street Loading Requirement.

D. Facilitate Adequate Provisions of Water, Sewerage, Schools, Parks, and Playgrounds.

E. Secure Safety From Flooding.

F. Conserve Property Values. Through careful enforcement of the provisions property values will be stabilized and conserved.

IV. What Zoning Cannot Do

In order to understand more fully the difference between zoning and the other devices such as subdivision regulations, building codes, and housing ordinances, the housing inspector must know the things that cannot be accomplished by a zoning ordinance.

Items that cannot be accomplished in a zoning ordinance include:

A. Correcting Existence of Overcrowding or Substandard Housing. Zoning is not retroactive and cannot correct conditions such as those cited. These are corrected through enforcement of a minimum standards housing code.

B. Materials and Methods of Construction. Materials and methods of construction are enforced through the building codes rather than through zoning.

C. Cost of Construction. Quality of construction and hence construction costs are often regulated through deed restrictions or covenants. Zoning does, however, stabilize property values in an area by prohibiting incompatible development such as the location of a heavy industry in the midst of a well-established subdivision.

D. Subdivision Design and Layout. Design and layout of subdivisions as well as provisions for parks and streets are controlled through subdivision regulations.

V. Content of the Ordinance

Zoning ordinances establish districts of whatever size, shape, and number the municipality deems best for carrying out the purposes of the zoning ordinance. Most cities use three major districts: residential, commercial, and industrial. These three may then be subdivided into many sub districts, depending on local conditions. These districts specify the principal and accessory uses, exceptions, and prohibitions.

In general these permitted land uses are based on intensity of land use, a less intense land use being permitted in a more intense district but not vice versa. For example, a single-family residence is a less intense land use than a multifamily dwelling. A multifamily dwelling would not, however, be permitted in a single-family district.

In recent years, some ordinances are being partially based on performance standards rather than solely on land use intensity. For example, some types of industrial developments may be permitted in a less intense use district provided that the proposed land use creates no noise, glare, smoke, dust, vibration, or other environmental stress exceeding acceptable standards and provided further that adequate off street parking, screening, landscaping, and other similar measures are taken.

VI. Bulk and Height Requirements

To further achieve the earlier stated objectives of the zoning ordinance, other regulations within a particular zoning district are imposed to gain control of population densities and to provide adequate light, air, privacy, and other elements needed for a safe and healthy environment.

Most early zoning ordinances stated that within a particular district the height and bulk of any structure could not exceed certain dimensions and specified that dimensions for front, side, and rear yards must be provided. Today some zoning ordinances use floor area ratios for regulation. Floor area ratio is the relationship between the floor space of the structure and the size of the lot on which it is located. For example, a floor area ratio of 1 would permit either a two-story building covering 50 per cent of the lot, or a one-story building covering 100 per cent of the lot. This is illustrated in Figure 1. Other zoning ordinances specify the maximum amount of the lot that can be covered or else merely require that a certain amount of open space must be provided for each structure and leave the flexibility of the location to the builder. Still other ordinances, rather than specify a particular height for the structure, specify an angle of light obstruction within a particular district that will assure air and light to the surrounding structures. An example of this is shown in Figure 2.

VII. Yard Requirements

Zoning ordinances also contain yard requirements that are divided into front, rear, and side yard requirements. These requirements, in addition to stating the lot dimensions, usually designate the amount of setback

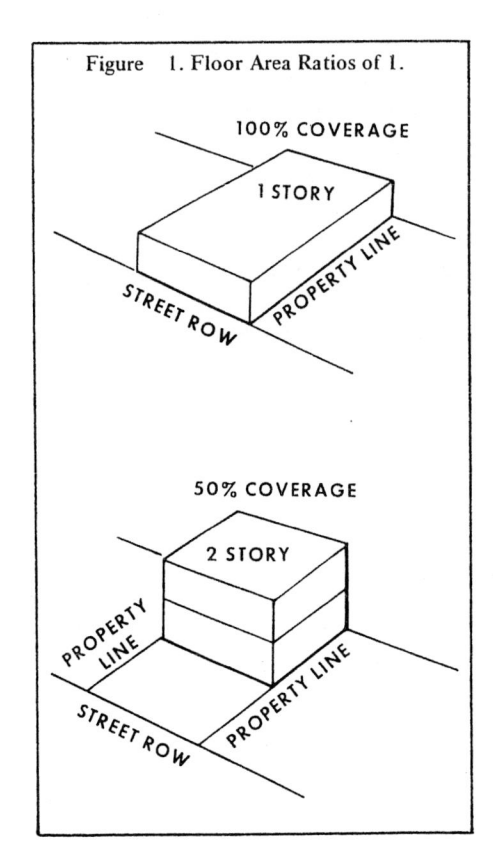

Figure 1. Floor Area Ratios of 1.

required. Most ordinances permit the erection of auxiliary buildings in rear yards provided they are located at stated distances from all lot lines and provided sufficient stated open space is maintained. If the property is a corner lot, additional requirements are set to allow visibility for motorists.

VIII. Off street Parking

Space for off street parking and off street loading is also contained in the ordinance. These requirements are based on standards relating floor space or seating capacity to land use. For example, a furniture store would require fewer off street parking spaces in relation to the floor area than a movie theater would.

IX. Nonconforming Uses

Since zoning is not retroactive, all zoning ordinances must contain a provision for nonconforming uses. If a use has already been established within a particular district before adoption of the ordinance, it must be permitted to continue. Provisions are, however, put into

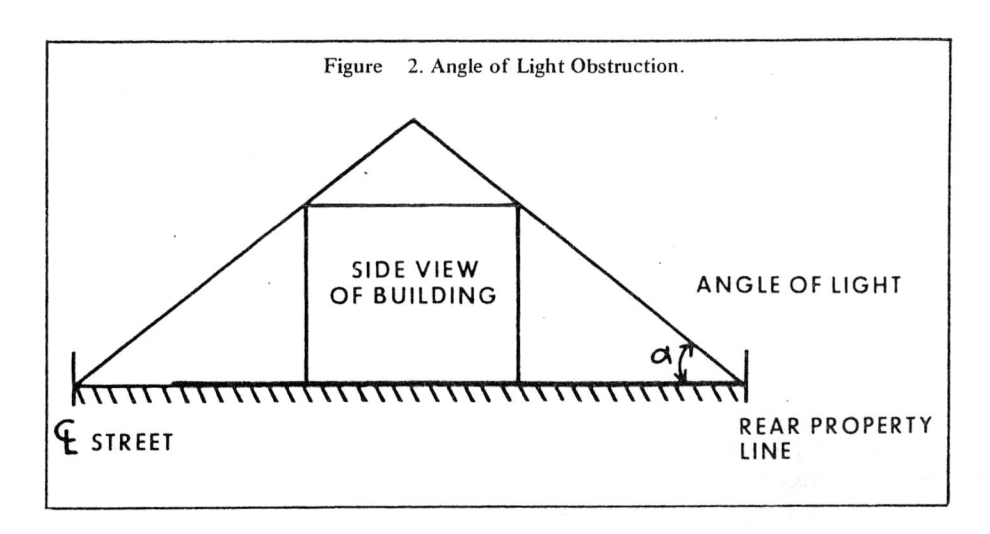

Figure 2. Angle of Light Obstruction.

The ordinance to aid in eliminating nonconforming use. These provisions generally prohibit the following: (1) An enlargement or expansion of the nonconforming uses, (2) reconstruction of the nonconforming use if more than a certain portion is destroyed, (3) resumption of the use after it has been abandoned for a period of specified time, and (4) changing the use to a higher classification or to another nonconforming use. Some zoning ordinances further provide a period of amortization during which the nonconforming land use must be phased out.

X. Variances

Zoning ordinances contain provisions for permitting variances and providing a method of granting these variances subject to certain specified conditions. A variance may be granted when, owing to a particular lot shape, topography, or other lot characteristics, an undue hardship would be imposed on the owner if the exact content of the ordinance is adhered to. For example, assume we have a piece of irregularly shaped property located in a district having the side yard requirements of 20 feet on a side and total lot size requirement of 10,000 square feet. Suppose that our property contains 10,200 feet and thus meets the area requirements; however, let us further assume that, owing to the irregular shape of the property, we can provide side yards of only 15 feet on a side. Since a hardship would be imposed if the exact letter of the law is held to, the zoning board of adjustment could be asked for a variance. Since there is sufficient total open area and since a lessening of the ordinance is not detrimental to the surrounding property, a variance would probably be granted.

Before a variance can be granted, it must be shown that (1) there is a practical hardship, (2) that the variance is needed for the owner to realize a reasonable return on the property, (3) that the original intent of the ordinance will be adhered to, (4) that the character of the neighborhood will not be changed, and (5) that the public's safety and welfare will be preserved.

XI. Exceptions

An exception is often confused with a variance. In every city there are some necessary uses that do not correspond to the permitted land uses within the district. The zoning code recognizes, however, that if proper safeguards were to be provided, these uses would not have a detrimental effect on the district. An example would be a fire substation, which could be permitted in a residential area provided the station house is designed to resemble a residential dwelling and further provided the property is properly landscaped.

XII. Administration

The key man in the zoning process is the zoning inspector, since he must come in contact with each case. In many cases the zoning inspector may also be the building inspector or the housing inspector. Since the building inspector or housing inspector is already in the field making inspections, it is relatively easy for him to check compliance with a zoning ordinance. This compliance can be checked by comparing the actual land use against that allowed for the area and shown on the zoning map.

Each zoning ordinance has a map as a part of the ordinance giving the permitted usage for each block. By taking a copy of this map with him, the inspector can make a preliminary check of the land use in the field. If the use does not conform, the inspector must then check with the Zoning Board to see if the property in question was a "nonconforming use" at the time of passage of the ordinance and if an exception has been granted. In cities where up-to-date records of existing nonconforming uses and exceptions granted are maintained, the inspector can check the use in the field against the records.

When violation is observed and the property owner is duly notified of the violation, he then has the right of hearing before a Zoning Board of Adjustment (sometimes also called the Zoning Board of Appeals). The Board may uphold the zoning enforcement officer or may rule in favor of the property owner. If the action of the zoning enforcement officer is upheld, the property owner may, if he so desires, seek relief through the courts; otherwise the violation will be corrected to conform to the zoning code.

XIII. How Zoning Can Benefit the Housing Inspector

It is of critical importance for the housing inspector, the building inspector, and the zoning inspector to work closely together in cities where these positions and responsibilities are separate. Experience has shown that when illegal conversions or uses of properties occur, these illegally converted properties are often among the most substandard encountered in the city and often contain especially dangerous housing code violations.

In communities where the zoning code is enforced effectively, the resulting zoning compliance in new and existing housing helps advance, as well as sustain, many of the minimum standards of the housing code such as occupancy, ventilation, light, and unimpeded egress. By the same token, building or housing inspectors can often aid the zoning inspector by helping eliminate some nonconforming uses through code enforcement.

XIV. Example of Zoning and Housing Relationships

The following cases will illustrate these relationships:

A Case 1

Two and one-half-story, 13-room house. Originally it had these features:

a Five-room dwelling unit on first floor including a three-piece bathroom.

b Eight-room dwelling unit occupying the second and third floors including one bathroom of three pieces on the second floor. The second and third floors are served by only one staircase.

c Two oil burners, one heating first floor, the other the second and third floors.

It is located in a residential zoning district where two-family housing is the maximum use permitted.

Five years later, while making a regular inspection, the zoning officer found this house in the process of being converted into a three-family use in violation of the zoning ordinance. The owner has already done these things.

a Made second floor into a separate five-room dwelling unit.

b Started converting the three rooms on the third floor into another apartment by:

1. Installing a three-piece bathroom, 35 square feet in area, against the windowless west wall of the center bedroom, the habitable area being thus reduced to 40 square feet, and setting up the remainder of the area as the living room by providing a coffee table, lamp, and two overstuffed chairs;

2. Putting in a wall kitchenette consisting of a sink with cold water and a stove, plus a table, lamp, and cupboards in the rear bedroom that is 60 square feet in area;

3. Equipping the front bedroom that is 90 square feet in size with two beds, chest of drawers, and other bedroom furnishings for two.

He admitted, however, that he had not checked on state tenement house law requirements since he did not realize multiple dwellings of three families or more are covered by this law.

Question: How many violations (either housing or zoning) can you find?

Answer: As a result of these actions by the owner, the house now has one more dwelling unit than is permitted by the zoning ordinance in this residential district and also contains these obvious housing code violations:

(a) Threatened over occupancy of the third-floor dwelling unit (only 190 square feet available, but 250 square feet habitable floor space is the minimum required for two occupants).

(b) Size of the front bedroom inadequate by 30 square feet if it is used by two occupants. The back bedroom lacks the requirements needed for occupancy by one person (70 square feet). If a third person lived in the dwelling unit the minimum required habitable floor area would then become 350 square feet.

(c) The bathroom does not meet the light and ventilation requirements.

(d) The kitchen sink does not have hot water.

(e) No refrigerator is provided.

(f) From the description it sounds as if one might have to go through a sleeping room to reach the bathroom. This would be a violation.

(g) Both the second and third floor units are in violation since they lack two means of egress.

B Case 2

Assume that a three-family dwelling unit is the largest size permitted in the zoning district where the building in question is located. The housing inspector's investigation of the three-story dwelling from cellar to roof showed that it contained:

1. Four dwelling units, two with six rooms each and two with three rooms each.

2. Five families, three in separate dwelling units and the two on the third floor in one unit.

3. A bathroom and a kitchen on the second floor shared by two families.

4. The bathroom and kitchen on the third floor also being shared by two families.

5. Inadequate means of egress from the dwelling unit in the third floor.

Question: If you were the housing inspector, what actions would you take?

Answer: In this situation there are definite housing code violations. The housing inspector also knows there is a zoning violation. Because he knows that the property must meet zoning requirements before complying with the housing code, the inspector would refer this case to the zoning department for action.

The housing inspector should never speak for the zoning department and tell the owner that he is in violation of a zoning ordinance unless he and the zoning inspector are the same individual. The housing inspector should complete his housing inspection and leave. Responsibility for informing the owner of any zoning violation lies with the zoning department.

In this particular case, some housing code violations will be corrected through enforcement of zoning. However, there are still violations of requirements for egress, a third kitchen, and a third bathroom.

After compliance with the zoning ordinance has been obtained, the zoning department should notify the housing inspector so that he can then enforce any housing violations that may still exist.

C   Case 3

Mr. Jones, a zoning inspector, gets a report that at 1212 Oak Street the owner, Mr. Smith, is converting his single-family house into two apartments and has already started alterations. Investigations of the zoning map shows that in this district, apartments, up to four, are permitted if 1,500 square feet of open land area is provided for each apartment. Mr. Jones checks and finds that no building permit has been issued. A site investigation reveals that Mr. Smith has only 2,000 square feet of open area available. He then informs Mr. Smith that he is in violation of the zoning ordinance.

Mr. Smith then appeals to the Zoning Board of Adjustment for a variance to allow him to have two apartments even though he does not have the required 3,000 square feet 0 f open area. His appeal is denied by the board since no real hardship exists. As a result, Mr. Smith must rent the property as a single-family dwelling and is unable to recover the money he has already spent in starting alterations.

Discuss:

1.   The actions of Mr. Jones.

Answer: Mr. Jones was justified in citing Mr. Smith for a zoning violation since the proposed open area would have been inadequate.

2   The action of the Board of Adjustment.

Answer: The Board of Adjustment was also justified in upholding the zoning regulations. If the board had not acted in this manner, the crowding on this property could well have started deterioration in surrounding properties.

3   The action of Mr. Smith.

Answer: Mr. Smith had no legitimate complaint when the Board ruled against him. If he had first sought to obtain a building permit, as required by law, he would have been told that his proposed alterations would not meet zoning regulations and hence would not have suffered a monetary loss.

D   Case 4

Mr. Edwards requests a building permit to change a three-story single-family house into a two-family unit. Since two-family units are permitted in this district and he has sufficient open area, the permit is granted.

Six months later, the housing inspector, while making a systematic code enforcement inspection, finds that the converted house now has an apartment on each of the three floors. The bath on the second floor is shared by families on the second and third floors. This is a violation of the housing code.

Knowing that all the other houses on this street are only one- or two-family units, he also suspects a zoning violation. After returning to the office, he contacts the zoning department and learns that Mr. Edwards is in violation of the zoning ordinance as well as of the housing code.

Question: Which ordinance must be enforced first and why?

Answer: The zoning ordinance must be enforced first, since a zoning ordinance is a "primary" ordinance and determines the land use of a particular property. A housing code ordinance is a "secondary" ordinance and sets standards of residential usage on the property.

E Case 5

During a routine inspection, the housing inspector finds a house with three families, one of which is living in a cellar apartment.

Question: What actions should he take?

Answer: The inspector should immediately cite the owner for a violation of the ordinance and then follow through to see that the situation is corrected. If the family living in the cellar requires housing assistance as a result of corrective measures taken, the housing inspector should inform them of public agencies available for assistance.

F Case 6

During a routine inspection of a district zoned for up to three-family use, the housing inspector encounters a house that the owner says contains two dwelling units in addition to his own, and also one rooming unit. The inspector finds a cook stove in the "rooming unit."

Question: What actions should he take?

Answer: Although a rooming unit would be permitted in this district, the addition of a cook stove changes the rooming unit into a dwelling unit.

The inspector should refer this case to the zoning department for immediate action and then follow up for housing violations at a later date.

G Case 7

The housing inspector is investigating a complaint of alleged housing violations. The owner refuses to admit the inspector inside the building and becomes belligerent.

Question: What should the inspector do next?

Answer: The inspector should remain courteous and not lose his temper. If the inspector is not able to obtain permission to inspect without further arousing the owner, he should leave.

Since recent decisions of the U.S. Supreme Court have dictated the inclusion of requirements to obtain a search warrant in cases where entry to the inspector is denied, the inspector should obtain a warrant. He will then return at a later time with someone to serve the warrant.

H Case 8

During an inspection in July, the housing inspector finds a house that has been converted into two apartments. While checking the basement, he sees that the furnace appears in an unsafe condition. Further checking reveals that there is no provision for heat in the second apartment.

Question: What action should the inspector take since it is July and heat is not now needed. Besides, how does he know that the owner will not install heat before winter?

Answer: The inspector should cite the owner for a violation of the housing code anyway. In his notice of violations, because it is July, he can give the owner sufficient time to comply. He would also send a copy of the letter to the heating inspector for follow up.

I Case 9

During an inspection, the housing inspector is greeted at the door by a 10-year-old boy who is alone. The boy says it is all right to make the inspection.

Question: Should he? Why?

Answer: No. Permission to enter must be obtained from a responsible adult. Suppose that instead of the 10-year-old boy, he had found a 16-year-old girl.

Question: How would these change things? Why?

Answer: It would not change things, since the 16-year-old girl is not considered a responsible adult. For the protection of the inspector, some housing departments would not permit him to enter alone when the house is occupied by only a female, especially one under age.

J Case 10

During his inspections the housing inspector finds a house that has no bathroom but does have an outside pit privy.

Question: What action should be taken?

Answer: The inspector should issue a violation for lack of indoor toilet facilities and follow through the regular steps established by his housing department. A copy of the violation should also be sent to the health department for any actions that they may wish to take for elimination of the privy.

K Case 11

A number of violations are found in a residence, but the family is occupying the unit under a land purchase contract agreement with the landlord. The owner holds title until enough rent is paid to equal the sale price. The repairs needed are more than the family can afford and are such that the building should be declared unfit for occupancy. The family now has $2,000 worth of equity in the property.

Questions: What actions should the inspector take? Who is responsible for repairs? Who will lose money?

Answer: The inspector would cite the owner of record for a housing violation, since the owner of record is responsible for repairs. If the owner will not bring the building into compliance with the code, the building should be posted as unfit for habitation and the family removed.

The family buying will probably lose in this situation. Before contracting to buy, they should have obtained a certificate of inspection from the housing department showing any violations existing at the time of purchase.

L Case 12

The property at 112 East Street is owned by an out-of-state individual. The housing inspector found the property unfit for habitation and has had the family renting the property removed. The house is now vacant and the out-of-town owners will not make the repairs since the cost of the necessary

repairs would be too great in relation to the value of the property. The property is in an area that will probably be included in a future urban renewal project within the next few years.

Complaints have been made to the housing department by the neighbors that the house has its windows broken out and its doors broken open. Children play inside during the day and have almost set the building on fire several times. Moreover, vagrants occasionally sleep inside at night.

Question: What action would you take if you were the housing inspector?

Answer: After following standard department procedures, the housing inspector should recommend, that the house be demolished and this cost assessed as a lien against the property. If allowed to remain, the house will be a detriment to surrounding properties and also to the neighborhood.

M Case 13

During a routine inspection, you find a house with very poor premises sanitation and evidence of roaches, flies, and rats. The property meets minimum housing standards otherwise.

Question: What action can you take?

Answer: The action depends on local regulations and procedures. In many communities the housing program is organizationally located within the health department. In that case, the housing inspector would probably follow through in requiring elimination of the infestation. If the housing inspection program were located within a department other than the health department, the housing inspector may refer the case to the health department for action.

N Case 14

While making a systematic code inspection, the housing inspector encounters a lady who questions the inspector regarding his findings on the house next door, which she is sure is much worse than hers.

Question: How should the inspector deal with the lady?

Answer: The inspector must be very courteous and tactful in his conversation and inform her that he is not permitted to discuss his survey findings for other properties.

BUILDING ASPECTS OF A HOUSING INSPECTION

CONTENTS

		Page
I.	Background Factors	1
II.	Housing Construction Terminology	1
III.	Structure	4
IV.	Discussion of Inspection Techniques	15
V.	Noise as an Environmental Stress	17

BUILDING ASPECTS OF A HOUSING INSPECTION

The principle function of a house is to furnish protection from the elements. In its current stage, however, our civilization requires that a home provide not only shelter but also privacy, safety, and reasonable protection of our physical and mental health. A living facility that fails to offer these essentials through adequately designed and properly maintained interiors and exteriors cannot be termed "healthful housing."

I. Background Factors

In this chapter, a building will be considered in terms of its major components: heating, plumbing, and electrical systems. Each of these items will be examined in detail in future chapters. Attention will be given in this chapter to the portions of a building not visible upon completion of the ceiling, roof, and interior and exterior walls in order to give the reader an understanding of generally accepted construction practices. Emphasis, however, will be placed upon the visible interior and exterior parts of a completed dwelling that have a bearing on the soundness, state of repair, and safety of the dwelling both during intended use and in the event of a fire. These are some of the elements that the housing inspector must examine when making a thorough housing inspection.

II. Housing Construction Terminology

(Key to Component Parts Numbered in Figure 1)

A Fireplace

1 **Chimney** - A vertical masonry shaft of reinforced concrete or other approved non-combustible, heat resisting material enclosing one or more flues. It removes the products of combustion from solid, liquid, or gaseous fuel.

2 **Flue Liner** - The flue is the hole in the chimney. The liner, usually of terra cotta, protects the brick from harmful smoke gases.

3 **Chimney Cap** - This top is generally of concrete. It protects the brick from weather.

4 **Chimney Flashing** - Sheet-metal flashing provides a tight joint between chimney and roof.

5 **Firebrick** - An ordinary brick cannot withstand the heat of direct fire, and so special firebrick is used to line the fireplace.

6 **Ash Dump** - A trap door to let the ashes drop to a pit below, from where they may be easily removed.

7 **Cleanout Door** - The door to the ash pit or the bottom of a chimney through which the chimney can be cleaned.

8 **Chimney Breast** - The inside face or front of a fireplace chimney.

9 **Hearth** - The floor of a fireplace that extends into the room for safety purposes.

B Roof

10 **Ridge** - The top intersection of two opposite adjoining roof surfaces.

11 **Ridge Board** - The board that follows along under the ridge.

12 **Roof Rafters** - The structural members that support the roof.

13 **Collar Beam** - Really not a beam at all. A tie that keeps the roof from spreading. Connects similar rafters on opposite side of roof.

14 **Roof Insulation** - An insulating material (usually rock wool or fiberglas) in a blanket form placed between the roof rafters for the purpose of keeping a house warm in the winter, cool in the summer.

15 **Roof Sheathing** - The boards that provide the base for the finished roof.

Figure 1. Housing Construction Terminology

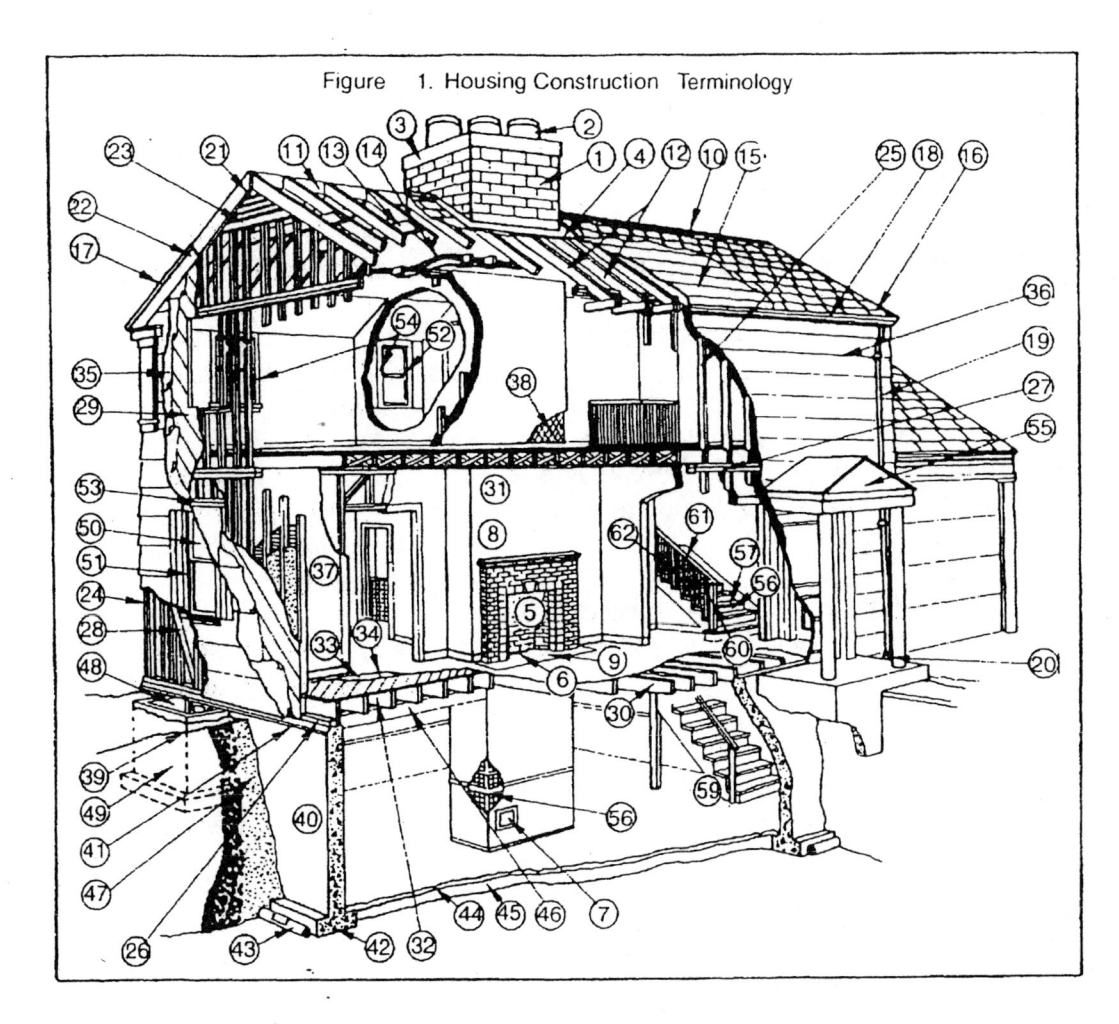

16 **Roofing** - The wood, asphalt, or asbestos shingles - or tile, slate or metal - that form the outer protection against the weather.

17 **Cornice** - A decorative element made up of molded members usually placed at or near the top of an exterior or interior wall.

18 **Gutter** - The trough that gathers rainwater from a roof.

19 **Downspouts** - The pipe that leads the water down from the gutter.

20 **Storm Sewer Tile** - The underground pipe that receives the water from the downspouts and carries it to the sewer.

21 **Gable** - The triangular end of a building with a sloping roof.

22 **Barage Board** - The fascia or board at the gable just under the edge of the roof.

23 **Louvers** - A series of slanted slots arranged to keep out rain, yet allow ventilation.

C Walls and Floors

24 **Corner Post** - The vertical member at the corner of the frame, made up to receive inner and outer covering materials.

25 **Studs** - The vertical wood members of the house, usually 2 X 4's generally spaced every 16 inches.

26 **Sill** - The board that is laid first on the foundation, and on which the frame rests.

27 **Plate** - The board laid across the top ends of the studs to hold them even and rigid.

28 **Corner Bracing** - Diagonal strips to keep the frame square and plumb.

29 **Sheathing** - The first layer of outer wall covering nailed to the studs.

30 **Joist** - The structural members or beams that hold up the floor or ceiling, usually 2 X 10's or 2 X 12's spaced 16 inches apart.

31 **Bridging** - Cross bridging or solid. Members at the middle or third points of joist spans to brace one to the next and to prevent their twisting.

32 **Subflooring** - The rough boards that are laid over the joist. Usually laid diagonally.

33 **Flooring Paper** - A felt paper laid on the rough floor to stop air infiltration and, to some extent, noise.

34 **Finish Flooring** - Usually hardwood, of tongued and grooved strips.

35 **Building Paper** - Paper placed outside the sheathing, not as a vapor barrier, but to prevent water and air from leaking in. Building paper is also used as a tarred felt under shingles or siding to keep out moisture or wind.

36 **Beveled Siding** - Sometimes called clapboards, with a thick butt and a thin upper edge lapped to shed water.

37 **Wall Insulation** - A blanket of wool or reflective foil placed inside the walls.

38 **Metal Lath** - A mesh made from sheet metal onto which plaster is applied.

D **Foundation and Basement**

39 **Finished Grade Line** - The top of the ground at the foundation.

40 **Foundation Wall** - The wall of poured concrete (shown) or concrete blocks that rests on the footing and supports the remainder of the house.

41 **Termite Shield** - A metal baffle to prevent termites from entering the frame.

42 **Footing** - The concrete pad that carries the entire weight of the house upon the earth.

43 **Footing Drain Tile** - A pipe with cracks at the joints to allow underground water to drain in and away before it gets into the basement.

44 **Basement Floor Slab** - The 4- or 5-inch layer of concrete that forms the basement floor.

45 **Gravel Fill** - Placed under the slab to allow drainage and to guard against a damp floor.

46 **Girder** - A main beam upon which floor joists rest. Usually of steel, but also of wood.

47 **Backfill** - Earth, once dug out, that has been replaced and tamped down around the foundation.

48 **Areaway** - An open space to allow light and air to a window. Also called a light well.

49 **Area Wall** - The wall, of metal or concrete, that forms the open area.

E **Windows and Doors**

50 **Window** - An opening in a building for admitting light and air. It usually has a pane or panes of glass and is set in a frame or sash that is generally movable for opening and shutting.

51 **Window Frame** - The lining of the window opening.

52 **Window Sash** - The inner frame, usually movable, that holds the glass.

53 **Lintel** - The structural beam over a window or door opening.

54 **Window Casing** - The decorative strips surrounding a window opening on the inside.

F   Stairs and Entry

55 **Entrance Canopy** - A roof extending over the entrance door.

56 **Furring** - Falsework or framework necessary to bring the outer surface to where we want it.

57 **Stair Tread** - The horizontal strip where we put our foot when we climb up or down the stairs.

58 **Stair Riser** - The vertical board connecting one tread to the next.

59 **Stair Stringer** - The sloping board that supports the ends of the steps.

60 **Newel** - The post that terminates the railing.

61 **Stair Rail** - The bar used for a handhold when we use the stairs.

62 **Balusters** - Vertical rods or spindles supporting a rail.

III. Structure

A   Foundation

The word **foundation** is used to mean:
1. Construction below grade such as footings, cellar or basement walls.
2. The composition of the earth on which the building rests.
3. Special construction such as pilings and piers used to support the building.

The foundation bed may be composed of solid rock, sand, gravel, or unconsolidated sand or clay. Rock, sand, or gravel are the most reliable foundation materials. Unconsolidated sand and clay, though found in many sections of the country, are not as desirable, because they are subject to sliding and settling.

The footing (see Figure 2) distributes the weight of the building over a sufficient area of ground so as to ensure that the foundation walls will stand properly. Footings are usually constructed of a masonry-type material such as concrete; however, in the past wood and stone have been used. Some older houses have been constructed without footings.

Although it is usually difficult to determine the condition of a footing without excavating the foundation, a footing in a state of disrepair or lack of a footing will usually be indicated either by large

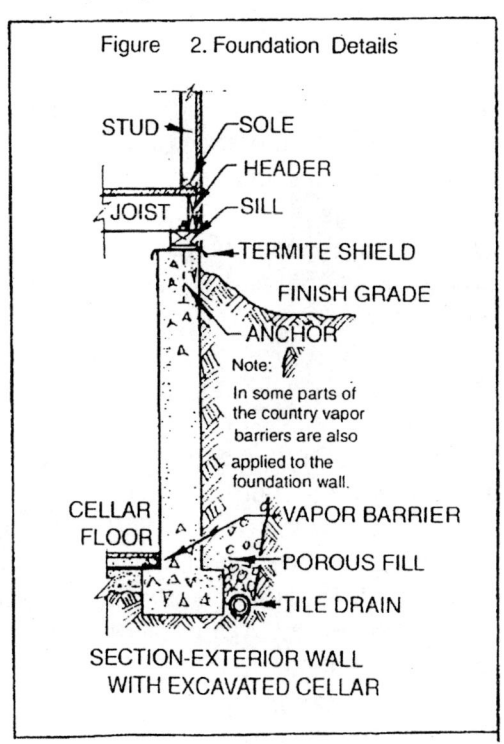

Figure 2. Foundation Details

SECTION-EXTERIOR WALL WITH EXCAVATED CELLAR

SECTION-EXTERIOR WALL WITH CRAWL SPACE

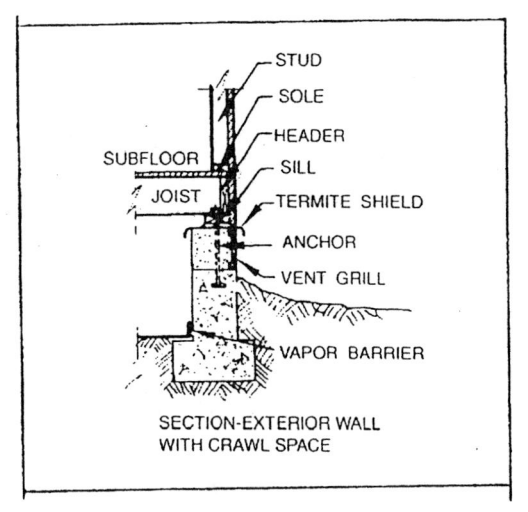

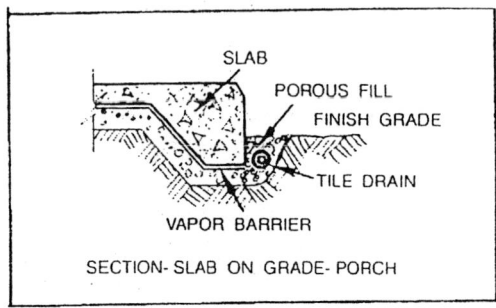

SECTION- SLAB ON GRADE- PORCH

cracks or by settlement in the foundation walls (see Figure 3).

Foundation wall cracks are usually diagonal, starting from the top, the bottom; or the end of the wall. Cracks that do not extend to at least one edge of the wall may not be caused by foundation problems. Such wall cracks may be due to other structural problems and should also be reported.

The foundation walls support the weight of the structure and transfer this weight to the footings. The foundation walls may be made of stone, brick, concrete, or concrete blocks and should be moisture proofed with either a membrane of water-proof material or a coating of portland cement mortar. The membrane may consist of plastic sheeting or a sandwich of standard roofing felt joined and covered with tar or asphalt. The purpose of waterproofing the foundation walls is to prevent water from penetrating the wall material and leaving the basement or cellar walls damp.

Holes in the foundation walls are a common finding in many old houses. These holes may be caused by missing bricks or blocks. Holes and cracks in a foundation wall are undesirable because they make a convenient entry for rats and other rodents and also indicate the possibility of further structural deterioration. These holes should not be confused with adequately installed vents in the foundation wall that permit ventilation and prevent moisture entrapment.

The basement or cellar floor should be made of concrete placed on at least 6 inches of gravel. The purpose of a concrete floor is to protect the basement or cellar from invasion by rodents or from flooding. The gravel distributes ground water movements under the concrete floor, reducing the possibility of the water's penetrating the floor. A waterproof membrane, such as plastic sheeting, should be laid before the concrete is placed for additional protection against flooding.

The basement or cellar floor should be gradually but uniformly sloped towards a drain or a series of drains from all directions. These drains permit the basement or cellar floor to be drained if it becomes flooded.

Evidence of ineffective waterproofing or moisture proofing will be indicated by water or moisture marks on the floor and walls.

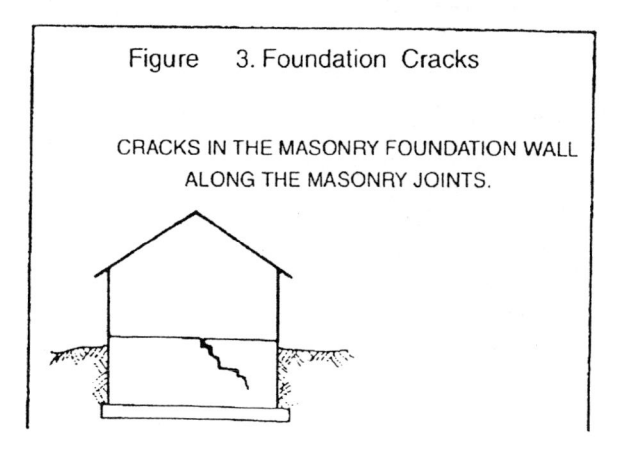

Figure 3. Foundation Cracks

CRACKS IN THE MASONRY FOUNDATION WALL ALONG THE MASONRY JOINTS.

DIFFERENTIAL SETTLEMENT OF THE END OF THE WALL.

DIFFERENTIAL SETTLEMENT OF THE END OF THE WALL.

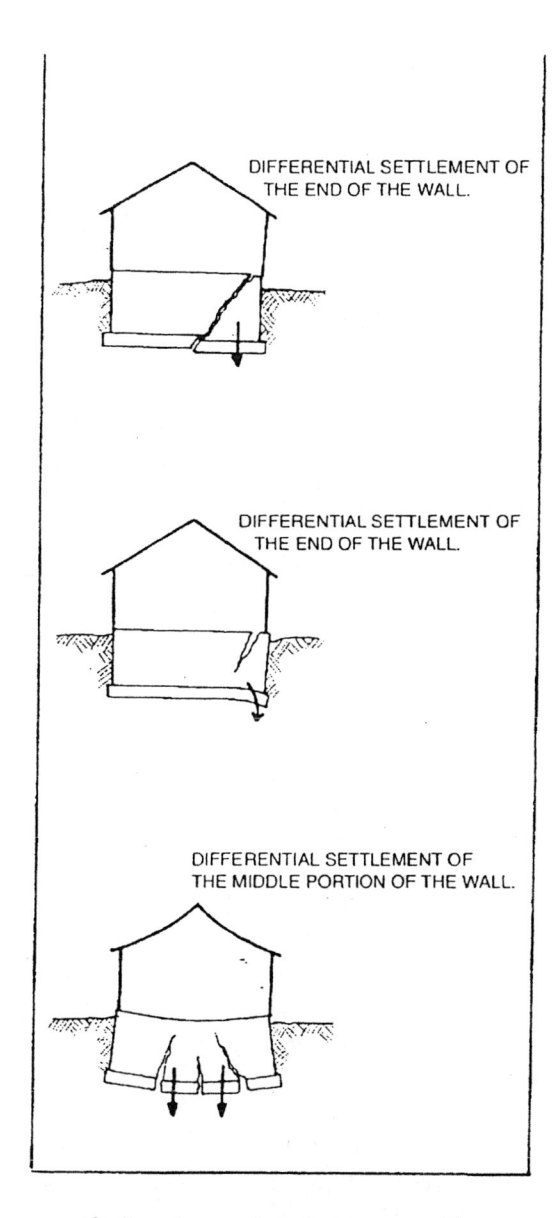

DIFFERENTIAL SETTLEMENT OF THE MIDDLE PORTION OF THE WALL.

Cellar doors, hatchways, and basement windows should be weathertight and rodent proof. A hatchway can be inspected by standing at the lower portion with the doors closed; if daylight can be seen, the door probably needs repair.

B **Framing**
Many different types of house-framing systems are found in various sections of the country; however, the majority of the members in each framing system are the same. They include:
1. **Foundation Sills:** (see Figure 4 and 5). The purpose of the sill is to provide support or a bearing surface for the outside walls of the building. The sill is the first part of the frame to be placed and rests directly on the foundation wall. It is bolted to the foundation wall by sill anchors. It is good practice to protect the sill against termites by extending the foundation wall to at least 18 inches above the ground and using a non-corroding metal shield continuously around the outside top of the foundation wall.

2. **Flooring Systems:** (see Figure 5). The flooring system is composed of a combination of girders, joists, sub-flooring, and finished flooring that may be made up of concrete, steel, or wood. Joists are laid perpendicular to the girders, at about 16 inches on centers, and are the members to which the sub-flooring is attached. When the subfloor is wood, it may be nailed at either right angles or diagonally to the joists.

   As shown in Figure 5, a girder is a member that in certain framing systems supports the joists and is usually a larger section than the joists it supports. Girders are found in framing systems where there are no interior bearing walls or where the span between bearing walls is greater than the joists are capable of spanning. The most common application of a girder is to support the first floor in residences. Often a board known as a ledger is applied to the side of a wood girder or beam to form a ledge for the joists to rest upon. The girder, in turn, is supported by wood posts or steel "lally columns" which extend from the cellar or basement floor to the girder.

3. **Studs:** (see Figure 4 and 5). Wall studs are almost always 2 by 4

inches; studs 2 by 6 inches are occasionally used to provide a wall thick enough to permit the passage of waste pipes. There are two types of walls or partitions: bearing and nonbearing. A bearing wall is constructed at right angles to and supports the joists. A nonbearing wall or partition acts as a screen or enclosure; hence, the headers in it are often parallel to the joists of the floor above.

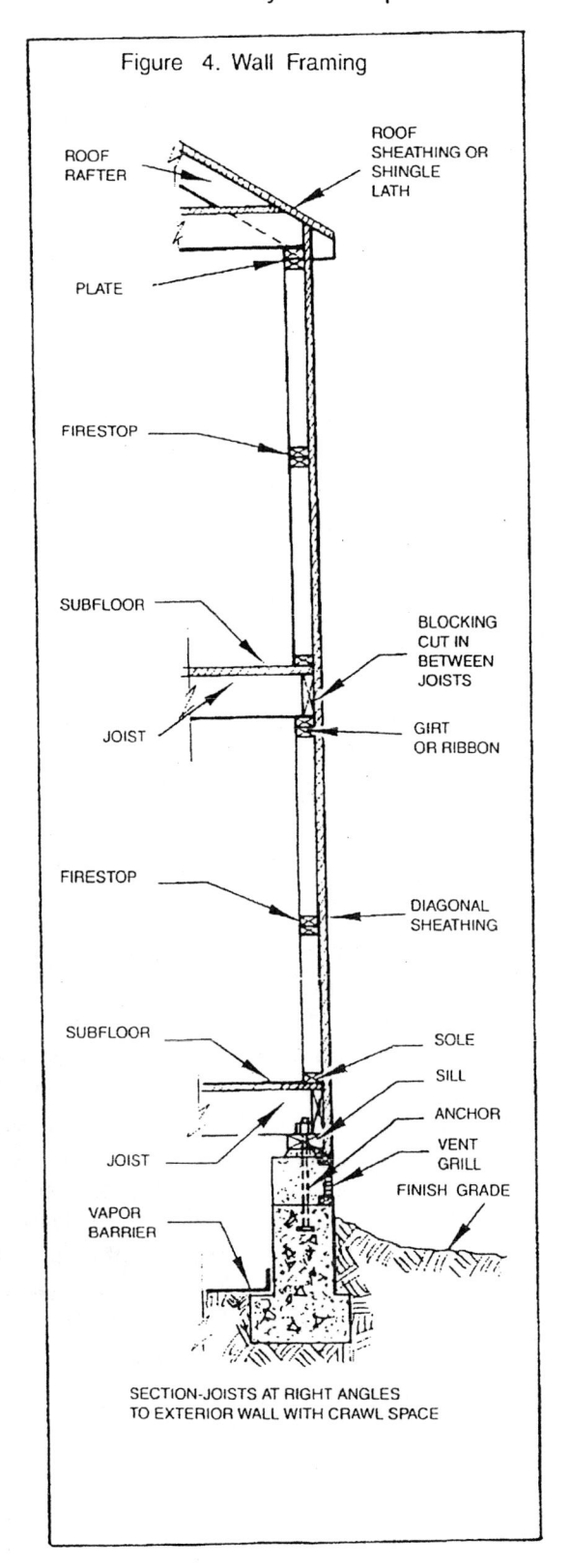

In general, studs like joists are spaced 16 inches on center. In light construction such as garages and summer cottages where plaster is omitted, or some other material is used for a wall finish, wider spacing on studs is common.

Openings for windows or doors must be framed in studs. This framing consists of horizontal members called "headers," and vertical members called "trimmers" (see Figure 1).

Since the vertical spaces between studs can act as flues to transmit flames in the event of a fire, "fire stops" are important in preventing or retarding fire from spreading through a building by way of air passages in walls, floors, and partitions. Fire stops are wood obstructions placed between studs or floor joists to prevent fire from spreading in these natural fluespaces.

Figure 4. Wall Framing

SECTION-JOISTS AT RIGHT ANGLES TO EXTERIOR WALL WITH CRAWL SPACE

4   **Interior Wall Finish:** Many types of materials are used for covering interior walls and ceilings, but the principal types are plaster and dry-wall construction. Plaster is a mixture, usually lime, sand, and water, applied in two or three coats to lath to form a hard-wall surface. Dry-wall finish is a material that requires little, if any, water for application. More specifically, dry-wall finish may be gypsum board, plywood, fiberboard, or wood in various sizes and forms.

Figure 5. Floor Construction

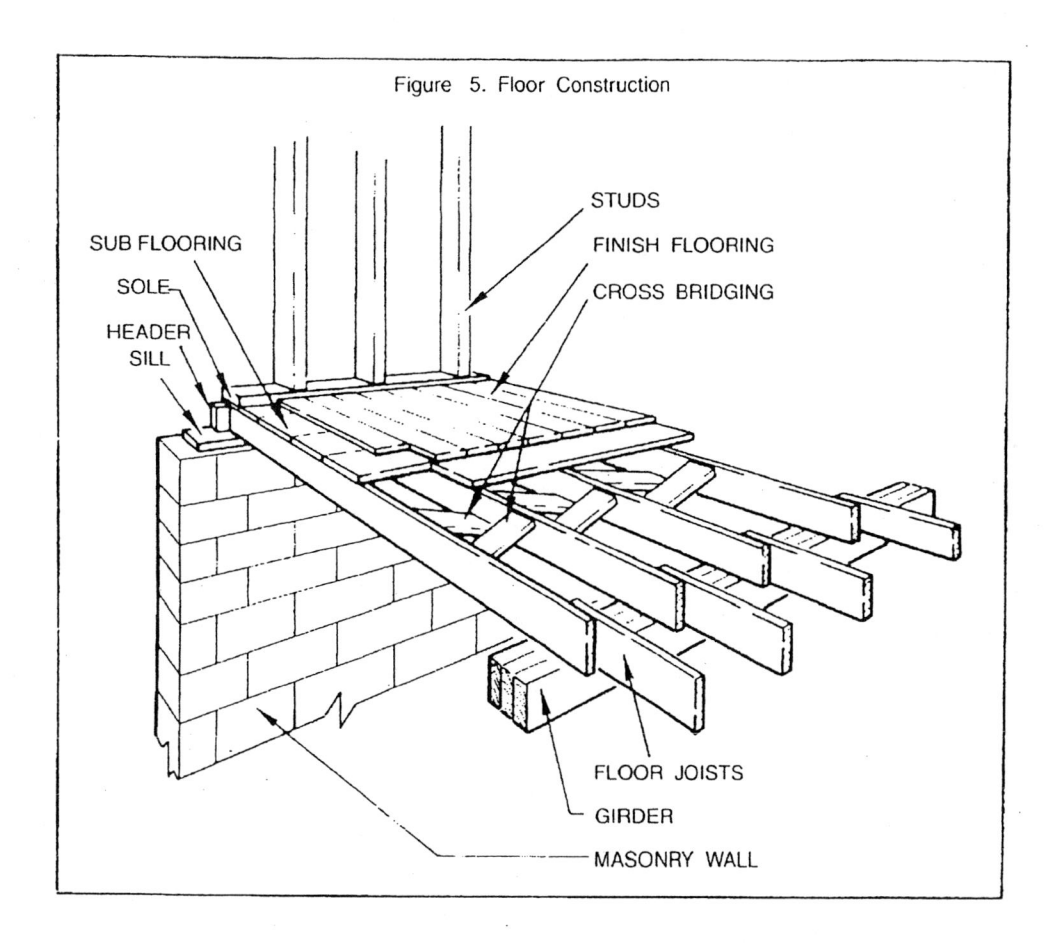

Gypsum board is a sheet material composed of a gypsum filler faced with paper. Sheets are usually 4 feet wide and can be obtained in lengths up to 12 feet. In dry-wall construction, gypsum boards are fastened to the studs either vertically or horizontally and then painted. The edges along the length of the sheet are recessed to receive joint cement and tape.

A plaster finish requires a base upon which plaster can be spread. Wood lath at one time was the plaster base most commonly used, but today gypsum-board lath is more popular. It has paper faces with a gypsum filler. Such lath is 16 by 48 inches and 1/2 or 3/8 inches thick.

It is applied horizontally across the studs. Gypsum lath may be perforated to improve the bond and thus lengthen the time the plaster can remain intact when exposed to fire. The building codes in some cities require that gypsum lath be perforated. Expanded-metal lath may also be used as a plaster base. Expanded-metal lath consists of sheet metal slit and expanded to form openings to hold the plaster. Metal lath is usually 27 by 96 inches and is fastened to the studs.

Plaster is applied over the base to a minimum thickness of 1/2 inch. Because some drying may take place in wood-framing members after the house is completed, some shrinkage can be expected, which, in turn, may cause plaster cracks to develop around openings and in corners. Strips of lath imbedded in the plaster at these locations prevent cracks.

On the inside face of studs that form an exterior wall, vapor barriers are used to prevent condensation on the wall. The vapor barrier is an asphalted paper or metal foil through which moisture-laden air cannot travel.

5 **Stairways:** (see Figure 6). The general purpose of the standards for stairway dimensions is to ensure that there is adequate headroom, width, and uniformity in riser and tread size of every step to accommodate the expected traffic on each stairway safely.

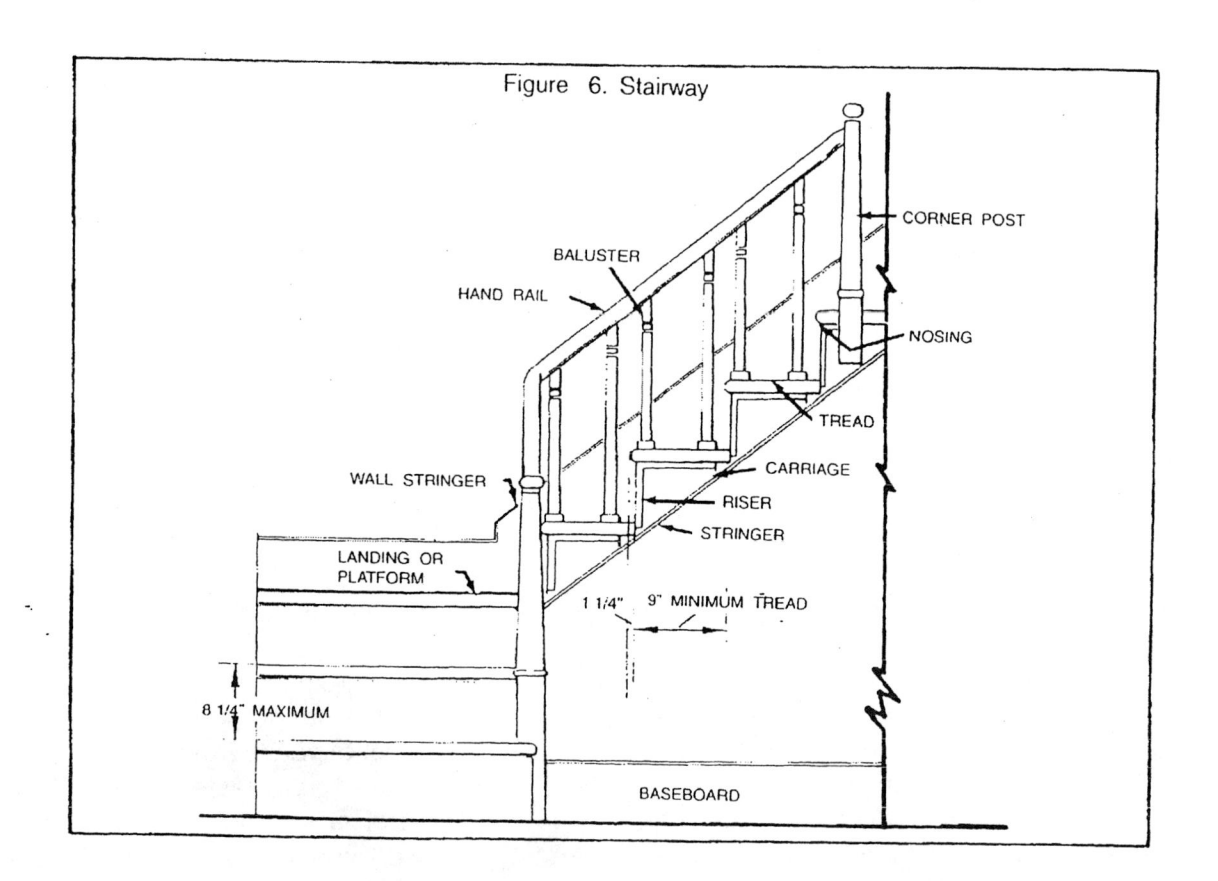

Figure 6. Stairway

Interior stairways should be not less than 44 inches in width. The width of a stairway may be reduced to 36 inches in one- and two-family dwellings. Stairs with closed risers should have maximum risers of 8 1/4 inches and a minimum tread of 9 inches plus 1 1/4-inch nosing. Basement stairs are often constructed with open risers. These stairs should have maximum risers of 8 1/4 inches and minimum treads of 9 inches plus 1/2-inch nosing. The headroom in all parts of the stair enclosure should be no less than 80 inches.

Exterior stairway dimensions should be the same as those called for in interior stairways, except that the headroom requirement does not apply.

6 **Windows:** The four general classifications of windows for residences are:

a Double-hung sash window that moves up or down, balanced by weights hung on chains or ropes, or springs on each side.

b Casement window sash is hinged at the side and can be hung so that it will swing outward or inward.

c Awning window - usually has two or more glass panes that are hinged at the top and swing about a horizontal axis.

d Sliding window - usually has two or more glass panes that slide past one another on a horizontal track.

The principal parts of a double-hung window (see Figure 4-7) are the lights, the top rail-framing members, bars or muntins that separate the lights, stiles - side-framing members, bottom rail, sash weights, and sash cords or chains. (All rails are horizontal, all stiles vertical.) The casement window's principal parts include: top and bottom rails, muntins, butt hinges, and jamb. All types of windows should open freely and close securely.

The exterior sill is the bottom projection of a window. The drip cap is a separate piece of wood projecting over the top of the window and is a component of the window casing.

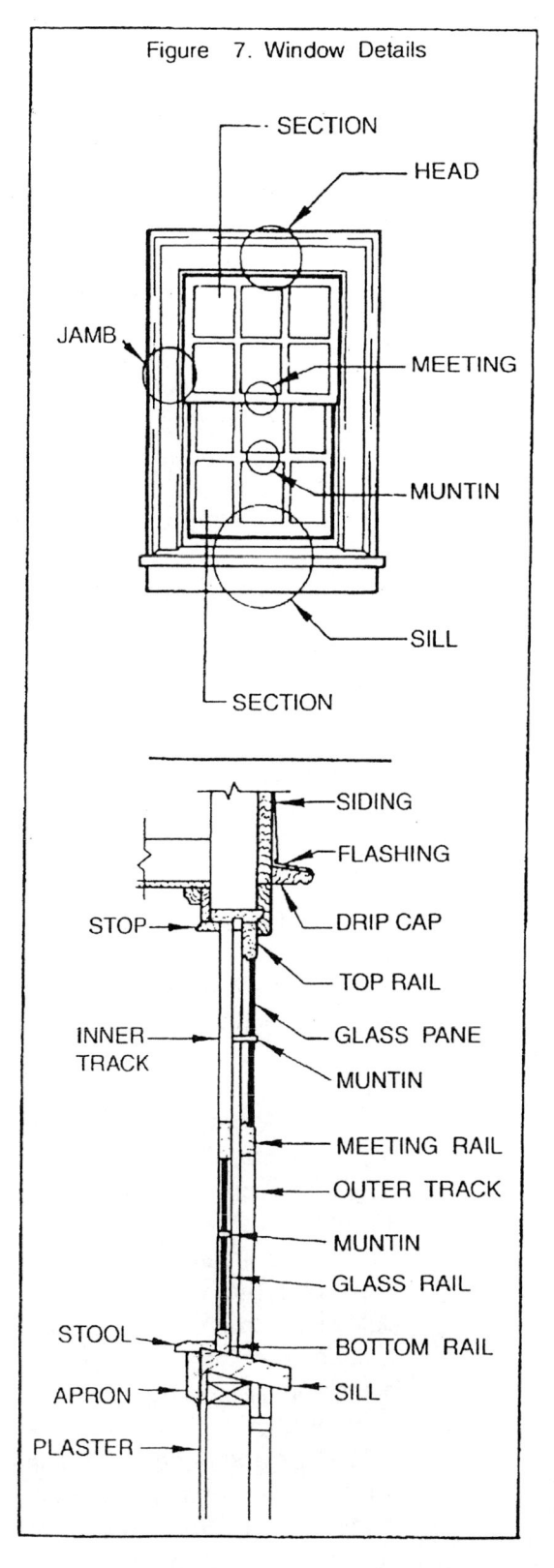

Figure 7. Window Details

7 **Doors:** There are many styles of doors both for exterior and interior use. Interior doors should offer a rea-

sonable degree of privacy. Exterior doors must, in addition to offering privacy, protect the interior of the structure from the elements. The various parts of a door have the same definitions as the corresponding parts of a window.

The most common types of doors are:

a **Batten door**: This consists of boards nailed together in various ways. The simplest is two layers nailed to each other at right angles, usually with each layer at 45 degrees to the vertical.

Another type of batten door consists of vertical boards nailed at right angles to several (two to four) cross strips called ledgers, with diagonal bracing members nailed between ledgers. If vertical members corresponding to ledgers are added at the sides, the verticals are called frames.

Batten doors are often found in cellars and other places where appearance is not a factor and economy is desired.

b **Flush doors**: Solid flush doors are perfectly flat, usually on both sides, although occasionally they are made flush on one side and paneled on the other. Flush doors sometimes are solid planking, but they are commonly veneered and possess a core of small pieces of white pine or other wood. These pieces are glued together with staggered end joints. Along the sides, top, and bottom are glued 3/4-inch edge strips of the same wood, used to create a smooth surface that can be cut or planed. The front and back faces are then covered with a 1/8-to 1/4-inch layer of veneer.

Solid flush doors may be used on both the interior and exterior.

c **Hollow-core doors**: These, like solid flush doors, are perfectly flat, but unlike solid doors, the core consists mainly of a grid of crossed wooden slats or some other type of grid construction. Faces are 3-ply plywood instead of one or two plies of veneer, and the surface veneer may be any species of wood, usually hardwood. The edges of the core are solid wood and are made wide enough at the appropriate places to accommodate locks and butts. Doors of this kind are considerably lighter than solid flush doors.

Hollow-core doors are usually used as interior doors.

d **Paneled doors**: Most doors are paneled, with most panels consisting of solid wood or plywood, either "raised" or "flat," although exterior doors frequently have one or more panels of glass, in which case they are called "lights." One or more panels may be employed although the number seldom exceeds eight. Paneled doors may be used both on the interior or exterior.

In addition to the various types of wood doors, metal is often used as a veneer or for the frame.

In general, the horizontal members are called rails and the vertical members are called stiles. Every door has a top and bottom rail, and some may have intermediate rails. There are always at least two stiles, one on each side of the door. The frame of a doorway is the portion to which the door is hinged. It consists of two side jambs and a head jamb, with an integral or attached stop against which the door closes.

Exterior door frames are ordinarily of softwood plank, with side rabbitted to receive the door in the same way as casement windows. At the foot is a sill, made of hardwood to withstand the wear of traffic, and sloped down and out to shed water.

Interior door frames are similar to exterior, except that they are often set directly on the hardwood flooring without a sill.

Building codes throughout the country call for doors in various locations within the structure to be fire resistant. These doors are often covered with metal or some other fire-resistant materials, and some are completely constructed of metal. Fire-resistant doors are usually located between a garage and a house, stairwells and hallways, all boiler rooms. The fire resistance rating required for various doors differs with local fire codes

C **Roof Framing** (see Figures 1, 4, 8, and 9)

Rafters serve the same purpose for the roof as joists do for floors, i.e., providing support for sheathing and roofing material. Rafters are usually spaced 20 inches on center.

1 **Collar Beam:** Collar beams are ties between rafters on opposite sides of the roof. If the attic is to be used for rooms, the collar beam may double as the ceiling joist.

2 **Purlin:** A purlin is the horizontal member that forms the support for the rafters at the intersection of the two slopes of a gambrel roof.

3 **Ridge Board:** A ridge board is a horizontal member against which the rafters rest at their upper ends; it forms a lateral tie to make them secure.

4 **Hip:** Like a ridge except that it slopes. The intersection of two adjacent, rather than two opposite, roof planes.

5 **Roof Boards:** The manner in which roof boards are applied depends upon the type of roofing material. Roof boards may vary from tongue-and-groove lumber to plywood panels.

6 **Dormer:** The term dormer window is applied to all windows in the roof of a building, whatever their size and shape.

D **Exterior Walls and Trim** (see Figure 4 and 9)

Exterior walls are enclosure walls whose purpose is to make the building weathertight. In most one- to three-story buildings they also serve as bearing walls. These walls may be made of many different materials.

Frequently used framed exterior walls appear to be of brick construction. In this situation, the brick is only one course thick and is called a brick veneer. It supports nothing but itself and is kept from toppling by ties connected to the frame wall.

In frame construction the base material of the exterior walls is called "sheathing." The sheathing material may be square-edge, shiplap, or tongue-and-groove boards.

In recent construction there has been a strong trend toward the use of plywood or composition panels.

Figure 8. Cornice Construction

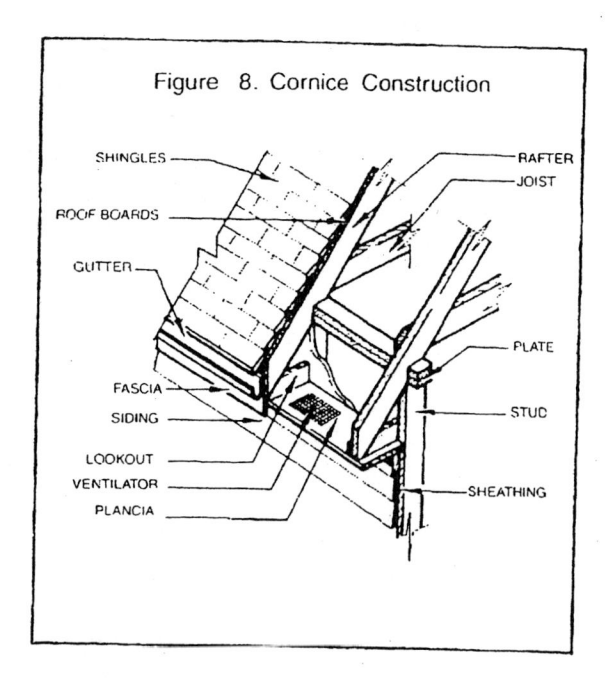

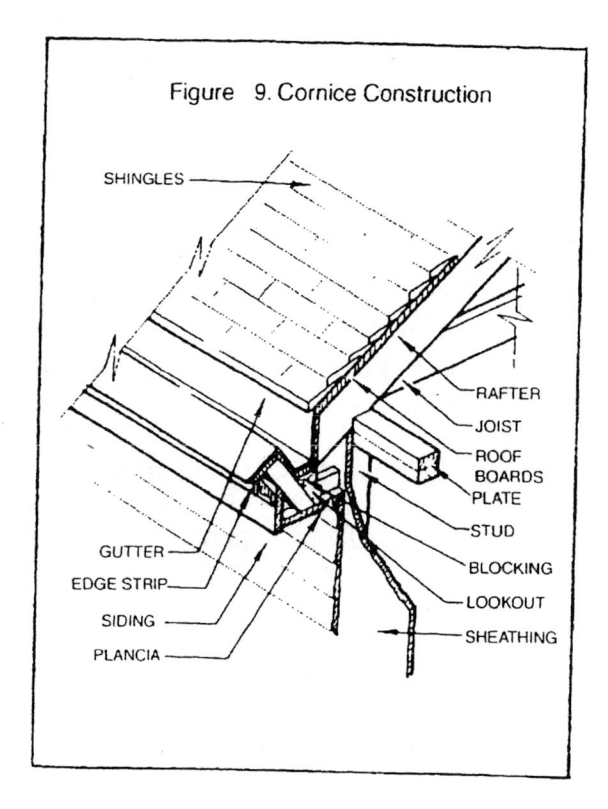

Labels: SHINGLES, RAFTER, JOIST, ROOF BOARDS, GUTTER, PLATE, FASCIA, SIDING, STUD, LOOKOUT, VENTILATOR, SHEATHING, PLANCIA

Figure 9. Cornice Construction

Labels: SHINGLES, RAFTER, JOIST, ROOF BOARDS, PLATE, STUD, GUTTER, BLOCKING, EDGE STRIP, LOOKOUT, SIDING, SHEATHING, PLANCIA

Sheathing, in addition to serving as a base course for the finished siding material, stiffens the frame to resist sway caused by wind. It is for this reason that sheathing has been applied diagonally on frame buildings.

The finished siding may be clapboard, shingles, aluminum, brick asphalt, wood, and so forth, or a combination thereof. Good aluminum siding has a backer board that serves as added insulation and affords rigidity to the siding. Projecting cornices are a decorative trim found at the top of the building's roofline. A parapet wall is that part of the masonry wall that extends up and beyond the roofline and is capped with a noncombustible material. It helps prevent spread of fire, provides a rest for fire department ladders, and helps prevent people on the roof from falling off.

Many types of siding, shingles, and other exterior coverings are applied over the sheathing. Wood siding, cedar, and other wood shingles or shakes, clapboard, common siding (called bevel siding), composition siding, asbestos, cement shingles, asbestos-cement siding, and the aforementioned aluminum siding are commonly used for exterior coverings. Clapboards and common siding differ only in the length of the pieces. Clapboards are 4 feet long while panel siding comes in lengths from 6 to 16 feet. Composition siding is made of felt and asphalt, which are often shaped to look like brick. Asbestos and cement shingles are rigid and produce a covering that is fire resistant. Cedar wood shingles are also manufactured with a backer board that gives insulation and fire-resistant qualities. Asbestos cement siding made of asbestos fiber and portland cement has good fire-resistant qualities and is a rigid covering.

E   Roof Coverings (Flexible Material Class)

   1   **Asphalt Shingle:** The principal damage to asphalt shingle roofs is caused by the action of strong winds on shingles nailed too high. Usually the shingles affected by winds are those in the four or five courses nearest the ridge and in the area

extending about 5 feet down from the edge or rake of the roof.

2. **Asphalt Built-up Roofs:** These may be un-surfaced, the coating of bitumen being exposed directly to the weather, or they may be surfaced having slag or gravel imbedded in the bituminous coating. The use of surfacing material is desirable as a protection against wind damage and the elements. This type of roof should have enough pitch to drain water readily.

3. **Coal Tar Pitch Built-up Roofs:** This type roof must be surfaced with slag or gravel. Coal tar pitch built-up roof should always be used on deck pitched less than 1/2 inch per foot; that is, where waler may collect and stand. This type roof should be inspected on completion, 6 months later, and then at least once a year, preferably in the fall. When the top coating of bitumen shows damage or has become badly weathered, it should be renewed (rigid material class).

4. **Slate Roofs:** The most common problem with slate roofs is the replacement of broken slates. Roofs of this type normally render long service with little or no repair.

5. **Tile Roofs:** Replacement of broken shingle tiles is the main maintenance problem. This is one of the most expensive roofing materials. It requires very little maintenance and gives long service.

6. **Copper Roofs:** Usually are of 16-ounce copper sheeting and applied to permanent structures. When properly installed, they require practically no maintenance or repair. Proper installation allows for expansion and contraction with changes in temperature.

7. **Galvanized Iron Roofs:** Maintenance is done principally by removing rust and keeping roof well painted. Leaks can be corrected by re-nailing, caulking, or replacing all or part of the sheet or sheets in disrepair.

8. **Wood Shingle Roofs:** The most important factors of this type roof are its pitch and exposure, the character of wood, kind of nails used, and preservative treatment given shingles. Creosote and coal tar preservative are satisfactory for both treated and untreated shingles.

9. **Flashing:** Valleys in roofs that are formed by the junction of two downward slopes may be finished, open, or closed. In a closed valley the slates, tiles, or shingles of one side meet those of the other, and the flashing below them may be comparatively narrow. In an open valley, the flashing, which may be made of zinc, copper, or aluminum, is laid in a continuous strip, extending 12 to 18 inches on each side of the valley, while the tiles or slates do not come within 4 to 6 inches of it.

   The ridges built up on a sloping roof where it runs down against a vertical projection, like a chimney or a skylight, should be weather-proofed with flashing.

   Metal flashings are generally used with slate, tile, metal, and wood shingles. Failure of roof flashing is usually due to exposed nails that have come loose. The loose nails allow the flashing to lift with leakage resulting.

10. **Gutters and Leaders:** Gutters and leaders should be of noncombustible materials. They should be securely fastened to the structure and spill into a storm sewer if the neighborhood is so provided. When there is no storm sewer, a concrete or stone block placed on the ground beneath the leader prevents water from eroding the lawn. This store

block is called a splash block. Gutters will not become plugged if protected against clogging of leaves and twigs. Gutters should be checked every spring and fall and then cleaned out when necessary.

IV. Discussion of Inspection Techniques

A serious building defect may often be observed during a housing inspector's routine examination. In many cases it is beyond the scope of the housing inspector's background to analyze the underlying causes and to recommend a course of action that will facilitate repair in an efficient and economical manner. In situations such as this, it is important that the inspector realize his limitations and refer the matter to the proper expert.

A prime example of a technically complex situation that a housing inspector might observe is a leaning, buckling, or bulging foundation or bearing wall. This problem may be the result of a number of hidden or interacting problems. For example, it may be the result of differential building settlement or failure of a structural beam or girder. It is beyond the scope of the housing inspector's responsibilities to discover the cause of the defect, but it is his responsibility to note the problem and refer it to the proper authority. In this case the proper authority would be a building inspector.

In the aforementioned situation where a bulging foundation wall was discovered, this would obviously constitute a violation of the housing ordinance and should be written up as such by the housing inspector. Since the housing inspector is generally not qualified to determine whether the house should be evacuated because it is in danger of imminent collapse, he should seek the advice of a building inspector.

A question that frequently arises is *which violations should be referred to an expert?* Needless to say, circumstances that obviously fall within the jurisdiction of another department should be referred to the department. The housing inspector should discuss with his supervisor any situation in which he feels inadequate to make a decision. In all cases the inspector should inform his supervisor before referring a problem to another agency or expert.

Another reason for referral to other departments is that when a remedial action is completed the other department will be in a better position to determine whether the job is satisfactory.

This principle of referral should be applied to every portion of the inspection, whether it deals with health, heating, plumbing, gas, or electrical as well as structural defects.

Certain structural items should be recognized as unsafe by the housing inspector. For example, a beam that has sagged or slanted may cause a portion of or an entire floor to sag or slope. Where a sagging or sloping floor is found, examine the ceiling of the room below or the basement for a broken or dropped girder or joist.

Doors and windows that are out of level will not close completely. It may be possible to see outside light through openings around window rails and door jambs. If an inspector detects such a situation, the condition of the supporting girders, girts, posts, and studs should be questioned, since this condition is evidence that some of these members may be termite infested or rotted and may be causing the outside wall to sag. Glass panes in doors and windows should be replaced if found to be broken or missing. Windows should also be checked for proper operation, and items such as broken sash cords or chains noted.

If the roof of the structure appears to be sagging, the inspector should make a special effort to examine the rafters, purlin, collar beams, and ridge boards if these members are exposed as in unfinished attics. The condition of the roof boards may be examined while he is in the attic. If light can be seen between these boards the roof is unsound. Evidence of a leaking roof will be indicated by loose plaster or peeling or stained paint and wall paper. Areas of the roof where flashing occurs, such as around the chimney, are frequent origins of roof leaks. It is essential that the leak be found and repaired, not only to prevent the entrance of moisture into the building, but also to prevent the loosening of the plaster, rotting of timbers, and extension of damage to the remainder of the house.

Gutters and rain leaders should be placed around the entire building to insure proper drainage of water. This will lessen the possibility of seepage of water through siding and window frames, and entrance of water into the cellar or basement. Lack of or leaking gutters may result in rotting of the siding or erosion of the exposed portion of the cellar or basement walls. This situation commonly exists where the mortar between bricks or concrete blocks in foundation walls is found to be heavily eroded. Gutters should be free from dirt and leaves.

The exterior siding should be in sound, weathertight condition. Peeled or worn paint on wood siding will expose the bare wood to the elements and result in splitting and warping of siding. This condition will eventually lead to the entrance of rain water with resultant rotting of the sheathing and studs as well as inside dampness and falling plaster. Sound and painted siding will prevent major repairs and expenses in the future. This condition will often be particularly prevalent on the north face of the structure.

Roof and chimneys should be inspected for tilting, missing bricks, deterioration of flashing, and pointing of chimney bricks. In addition, roof covering should be checked for broken spots and missing shingles or tiles. Roof doors should be metal clad, self-closing, tight fitting, and unlockable. The roof should also be examined for weather-tightness and broken TV antennas.

Porches should be carefully examined for weakened treads, missing or cracked boards, holes, and holes covered with tin plates, railing rigidity, missing posts, handrail rigidity, condition of the columns that support the porch roof, and the condition of the porch roof itself. The open section beneath the porch should be inspected for broken lattice-work. Check under the porch for accumulation of dirt and debris that can offer a harborage for vermin and rodents.

Loose plaster and missing or peeling wallpaper or paint should be noted. Bugs and cockroaches eat the paste from the wallpaper while leaving behind loose paper.

The basic parts of a stairway that a housing inspector should be able to identify correctly are the following:

A   Riser

B   Tread

C   Nosing

D   Handrail

E   Balustrade and Balusters, the Vertical Members that Support the Handrail, and

F   The Soffit, Underpart of the Stairway.

In the examination of a stairway (be careful to turn the light on) initially check the underside, if visible, to see if it is intact. Then proceed slowly up the stairs placing full weight on each tread and checking for loose, wobbling, or uneven treads and risers. Regardless of the size of the treads or risers they should all be of uniform size. For all stairs that rise 3 or more feet, a handrail should be present and in a sound and rigid condition.

Any fireplace should conform to the requirements of the local code. An unused fireplace that has its opening covered with wallpaper or other material should have a solid seal behind the paper. Operable fireplaces should have a workable damper and a fire screen, and should be clean.

Garages and accessory structures should be inspected in the same manner as the main building.

Sidewalks and driveways, whether constructed of flagstone, concrete, or asphalt, should be checked for creaking, buckling, and other conditions dangerous to pedestrian travel.

Stone, brick, or concrete steps should be inspected for cracks, deterioration, and pointing.

Fences should be in a sound condition and painted. Fire escapes should be checked for paint condition, loose or broken treads and rails, proper operating condition, and proper connection to the house.

V. Noise as an Environmental Stress

People feel comfortable in an environment with a low-level, soothing, steady, unobstrusive level of sound, typical of the natural undisturbed environment. All of us have experienced the anguish that noise can cause, whether it be noise from a neighbor's television, the grinding of truck gears while asleep, the persistent whine of a fan motor, or the sound of children racing down the halls. These annoyances experienced in the home are producing public demands for noise control legislation.

Not only is noise disturbing, but studies also indicate that extreme noise can cause deafness and perhaps interfere with other bodily functions.

While few existing housing ordinances contain enforceable noise provisions, noise problems must be considered by the building inspector because they intimately affect and are affected by his decisions. As a housing inspector, you can help residents by suggesting corrective noise measures that can be taken; you can refer them to agencies, if needed, for corrective action; you can help them to understand that their noisy environment can place limitations on their behavior, capabilities, and satisfaction with their home.

Noise is unwanted sound. Noise can travel through air or through the building structure. The first stage of noise control is the control of sound at its source. If attempts to quiet the source are not completely successful, then other, more expensive corrective measures will be required.

Although a visual examination of a dwelling may detect some sources of noise leaks (see Figure 10) such as wide gaps or cracks at ceiling, floor, or adjoining wall edges, it is usually inadequate since it fails to detect sources of noise leaks hidden from the eye. A far more effective test is to be alert for the operation of some noisy device like a vacuum cleaner in a closed room and listen near the other side of the wall for any noise leakage. The ear is a reasonably good sensing device. If a noise leak is noticed, the partition may be surveyed at critical points with a bright flashlight while an observer looks for light leakage in a darkened room on the other side. Detection of any light leakage in the darkened room will signify a noise leak.

Noise carried as vibration by a building structure is called structure-borne noise. Detecting structure-borne noise caused by the operation of mechanical equipment is somewhat more difficult (see Figure 11). With noisy equipment in operation, the inspector can sometimes locate noise leaks or structure-borne noise paths by conducting similar hearing tests along with pressing the ear against various room surfaces or using fingertips to sense the vibration of these surfaces.

A Airborne Noise

The sources of airborne noise that cause the most frequent disturbances in the home are audio instruments such as televisions, radios, phonographs, or pianos; adults and children speaking loudly, singing, crying and shouting; household appliances such as garbage disposals, dishwashers, vacuum cleaners, clothes washers, and dryers; plumbing noises such as pipes knocking, toilets flushing, and water running.

The disturbing influences of airborne noise are generally limited to the areas near the noise source. For example, a phonograph may cause annoyance in rooms of a neighbor's apartment adjacent to the phonograph but rarely in rooms farther removed unless doors or passageways are left open. Sound absorption materials such as carpeting, acoustical tile, drapery, and upholstered furniture in the intervening rooms may often provide a significant reduction in the disturbing noise before it reaches rooms where quiet is desired.

Under no conditions should sound-absorptive materials be used on the surfaces of walls and ceilings for the sole purpose of preventing the transmission of sound as structure-borne noise. To do so would be a complete waste of effort. To illustrate, imagine the noise conducted by a wall constructed solely of drapery or acoustical tile attached to studs. The noise level in the room would be reduced, but sound produced in the room would pass through the wall to adjoining rooms with little, if any, reduction in noise level. Sound absorptive materials should be used in and near areas of high noise levels to limit airborne noise at the source of the noise and reduce the effects of noise along corridors.

The transmission of noise from one completely enclosed room to an adjoining room separated by a partition wall may be either direct transmission through the wall, indirect transmission through other walls, ceilings, and floors common to both rooms, or through corridors adjacent to such rooms.

In some older wood frame houses, the open troughs between studs and joists are efficient sound transmission paths. This noise transmission by indirect paths is known as "flanking transmission" (see Figure 10 and 11). In addition to the flanking paths, there may be noise leaks particularly along the ceiling, floor, and sidewall edges of the wall. In order to obtain the highest sound insulation performance, a partition wall must be of airtight construction. Care must be exercised to seal all openings, gaps, holes, joints, and penetrations of piping and conduits with a nonsetting caulking compound. Even hairline cracks, particularly at adjoining wall, floor, and ceiling edges, transmit a substantially greater amount of noise than would normally be expected on the basis of the size of the crack.

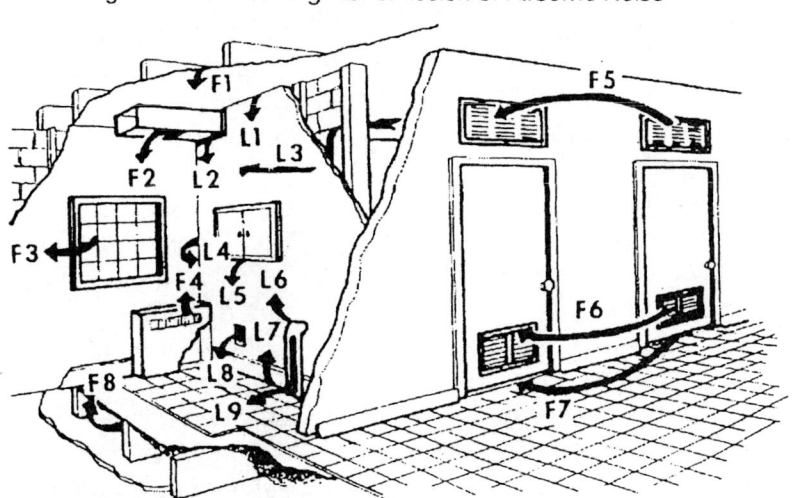

Figure 10. Flanking Transmission of Airborne Noise

FLANKING NOISE PATHS	**NOISE LEAKS**
F1 Open plenums over walls, false ceilings	L1 Poor seal at ceiling edges
F2 Unbaffled duct runs	L2 Poor seal around duct penetrations
F3 Outdoor path, window to window	L3 Poor mortar joints, porous masonry block
F4 Continuous unbaffled inductor Units	L4 Poor seal at sidewall, filler panel, etc.
F5 Hall path, open vents	L5 Back-to-back cabinets, poor workmanship
F6 Hall path, louvered doors	L6 Holes, gaps at wall penetrations
F7 Hall path, openings under doors	L7 Poor seal at floor edges
F8 Open troughs in floor-ceiling structure	L8 Back-to-back electrical outlets
	L9 Holes, gaps at floor penetrations

Other points to consider are these: leaks are (a) batten strip A/O post connections of prefabricated walls, (b) under-floor pipe or service chases, (c) recessed, spanning light fixtures, (d) ceiling and floor cover plates of movable walls, (e) unsupported A/O unbacked wall-board joints (f) edges and backing of built-in cabinets and appliances, (g) prefabricated, hollow metal, exterior curtain walls.

It is often helpful to use one sound to drown out another disturbing noise; for example, music on the radio can be used to drown out the noise of traffic. The use of sound to drown out noise is particularly useful in masking noises that occur infrequently, such as accelerating or braking vehicles, periodic mechanical equipment noise, barking dogs, laughter, or shouting.

B **Structure-Borne Noise**

Structure-borne noise occurs when wall, floor, or other building elements are set into vibration by direct contact with vibrating sources such as mechanical equipment or domestic appliances. A small, vibrating pipe firmly attached to a plywood or gypsum wall panel will amplify the vibration noise. An illustration of this amplification of structure-borne noise is provided by the sound board of a piano. The major sources of structure-borne noise are the impact of walking on wood floors or of slamming doors, plumbing system noises, heating and air-conditioning system noises, noise from mechanical equipment or appliances, and vibration from sources outside the building. If the vibration is severe enough, it may have adverse effects not only on the occupants of a building but also on the building structure. Household appliances such as refrigerators, washing machines, sewing machines, clothes dryers, televisions, and pianos should be vibration isolated from the floor by means of rubber mounts placed under them if disturbing structure-borne noise is to be avoided. Residents should also be cautioned against locating these noise sources along party walls and in particular against mounting these appliances and kitchen cabinets directly on party walls so that the walls act as sounding boards in adjoining apartments. Window air-conditioners should be completely vibration isolated from the surrounding window frame by rubber gaskets and padding. The importance of isolating a vibrating source from the structure in the control of equipment noise cannot be overemphasized.

Another source of disturbing structure-borne noise is squeaking of wood floors. Some squeaks can be eliminated by lubricating the tongues of wood floor boards with mineral oil applied sparingly to the openings between adjacent boards. Loose finish flooring may be securely fastened to subflooring by surface nailing into the

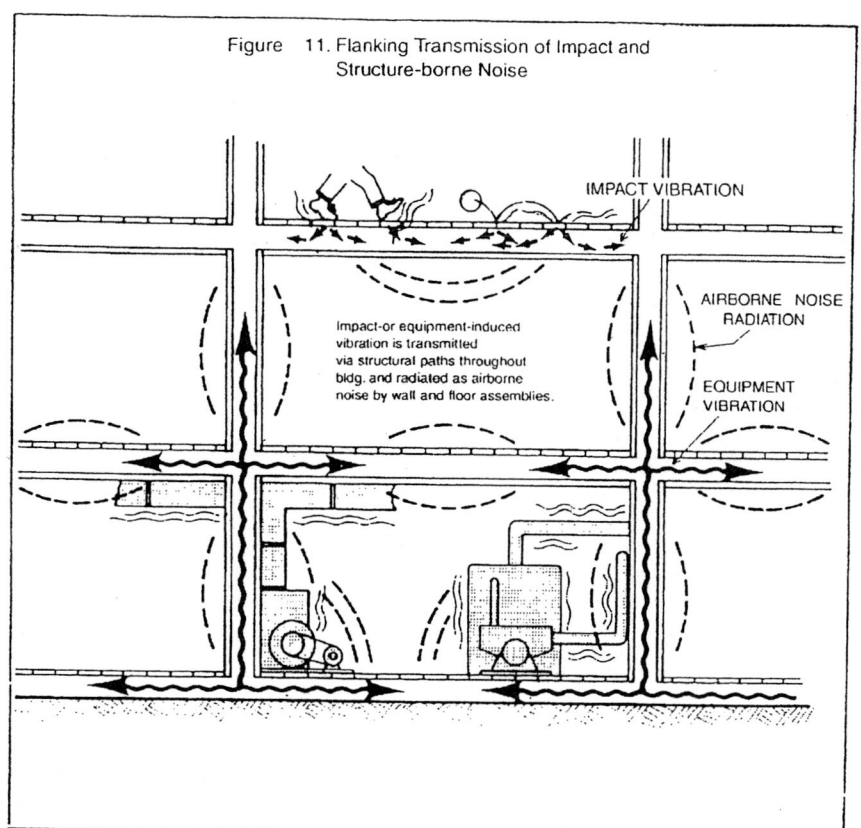

Figure 11. Flanking Transmission of Impact and Structure-borne Noise

subfloor and preferably the joists. Ring-type nails or sawtooth staples properly spaced should be used in nailing finish flooring to subflooring. In an exposed joist structure, where finish flooring is warped, driving screws up through the subfloor and into the finish floor will be effective in drawing the layers of flooring tightly together to reduce noise.

Of course, noise caused by the impact of walking or scraping can be substantially reduced by the use of carpets. In the case of door slams, the impact noise may be eliminated by the use of door closers or rubber bumpers.

The noisy hammering of a plumbing system is usually caused by the sudden interruption of water-flow, for example, by a quick closing or opening of a tap.

Air chambers can be built into the plumbing system to reduce water hammer. The air pockets, rubber inserts, or spring elements in air chambers act to reduce noise. Air chambers are explained in Chapter 6.

Defective, loose, or worn valve stems create intense chattering of the plumbing system. The defective device can frequently be found without difficulty, since immediate use of the device causes the vibration, which generally occurs at some low-flow-velocity setting and diminishes or disappears at a higher flow setting. For example, if a chattering noise occurs when a particular faucet or tap is opened partially and diminishes when fully opened, the faucet more than likely has some loose or defective parts and should be repaired.

Noise can be a very complex problem. The housing inspector is not expected to be an acoustics expert. Nor is he expected to be able to analyze and solve the noise problems that an acoustics consultant would normally handle. He can, however, help teach the public that the annoyances and stress caused by noise can be partially alleviated by a simple awareness of common noise problems found in many residences.

Although the housing inspector is not an expert in the fields of zoning, plumbing, building, and electrical systems, he should be familiar with the applicable code in each of the respective fields. Familiarization with these codes will better enable him to recognize violations.

BASIC FUNDAMENTALS OF DRAWINGS AND SPECIFICATIONS

CONTENTS

	Page
I. STRUCTURES	1
II. CONSTRUCTION DRAWINGS	4
III. SPECIFICATIONS	9
IV. BUILDER'S MATHEMATICS	10

BASIC FUNDAMENTALS OF DRAWINGS AND SPECIFICATIONS

A building project may be broadly divided into two major phases: (1) the DESIGN phase, and (2) the CONSTRUCTION phase. In accordance with a number of considerations, of which the function and desired appearance of the building are perhaps the most important, the architect first conceives the building in his mind's eye, as it were, and then sets his concept down on paper in the form of PRESENTATION drawings. Presentation drawings are usually done in PERSPECTIVE, by employing the PICTORIAL drawing techniques.

Next the architect and the engineer, working together, decide upon the materials to be used in the structure and the construction methods which are to be followed. The engineer determines the loads which supporting members will carry and the strength qualities the members must have to bear the loads. He also designs the mechanical systems of the structure, such as the lighting, heating, and plumbing systems. The end-result of all this is the preparation of architectural and engineering DESIGN SKETCHES. The purpose of these sketches is to guide draftsmen in the preparation of CONSTRUCTION DRAWINGS.

The construction drawings, plus the SPECIFICATIONS to be described later, are the chief sources of information for the supervisors and craftsman responsible for the actual work of construction. Construction drawings consist mostly of ORTHOGRAPHIC views, prepared by draftsmen who employ the standard technical drawing techniques, and who use the symbols and other designations

You should make a thorough study of symbols before proceeding further with this chapter. Figure 1 illustrates the conventional symbols for the more common types of material used on structures. Figure 2 shows the more common symbols used for doors and windows.

Before you can interpret construction drawings correctly, you must also have some knowledge of the structure and of the terminology for common structural members.

I. STRUCTURES

The main parts of a structure are the LOAD-BEARING STRUCTURAL MEMBERS, which support and transfer the loads on the structure while remaining in equilibrium with each other. The places where members are connected to other members are called JOINTS. The sum total of the load supported by the structural members at a particular instant is equal to the total DEAD LOAD plus the total LIVE LOAD.

The total dead load is the total weight of the structure, which gradually increases, of course, as the structure rises, and remains constant once it is completed. The total live load is the total weight of movable objects (such as people, furniture, bridge traffic or the like) which the structure happens to be supporting at a particular instant.

The live loads in a structure are transmitted through the various load-bearing structural members to the ultimate support of the earth as follows. Immediate or direct support for the live loads is provided by HORIZTONAL members; these are in turn supported by VERTICAL members; which in turn are supported by FOUNDATIONS and/or FOOTINGS; and these are, finally, supported by the earth.

The ability of the earth to support a load is called the SOIL BEARING CAPACITY; it is determined by test and measured in pounds per square foot. Soil bearing capacity varies considerably with different types of soil, and a soil of given bearing capacity will bear a heavier load on a wide foundation or footing than it will on a narrow one.

VERTICAL STRUCTURAL MEMBERS

Vertical structural members are high-strength columns; they are sometimes called PILLARS in buildings. Outside wall columns and inside bottom-floor columns, usually rest directly on footings. Outside-wall columns usually extend from the footing or foundation to the roof line. Inside bottom-floor columns extend upward from footings or foundations to horizontal members which in turn support the

DRAWINGS AND SPECIFICATIONS

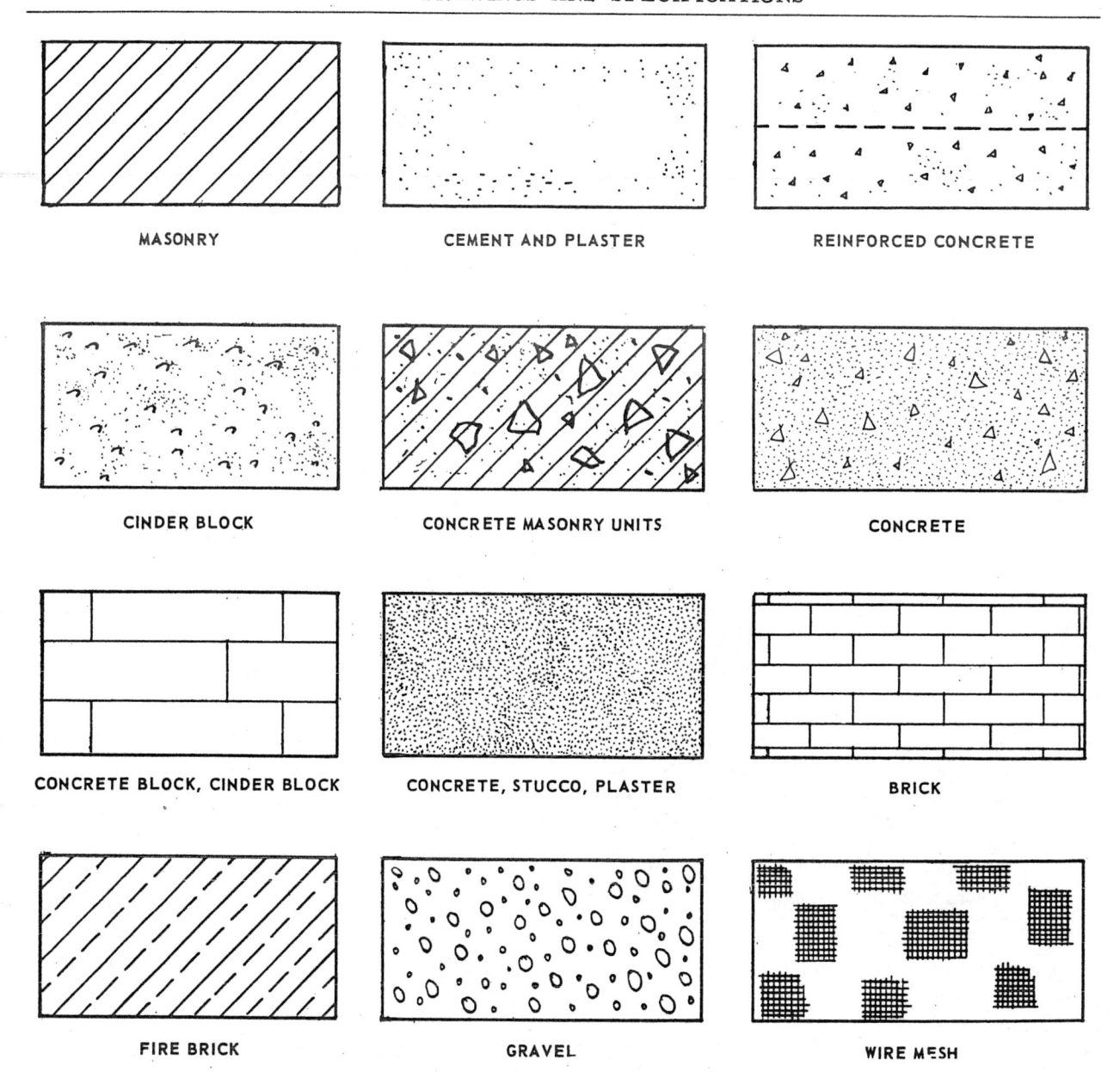

MASONRY	CEMENT AND PLASTER	REINFORCED CONCRETE
CINDER BLOCK	CONCRETE MASONRY UNITS	CONCRETE
CONCRETE BLOCK, CINDER BLOCK	CONCRETE, STUCCO, PLASTER	BRICK
FIRE BRICK	GRAVEL	WIRE MESH

Figure 1.—Material symbols.

first floor. Upper floor columns usually are located directly over lower floor columns.

A PIER in building construction might be called a short column. It may rest directly on a footing, or it may be simply set or driven in the ground. Building piers usually support the lowermost horizontal structural members.

In bridge construction a pier is a vertical member which provides intermediate support for the bridge superstructure.

The chief vertical structural members in light frame construction are called STUDS. They are supported on horizontal members called SILLS or SOLE PLATES, and are topped by horizontal members called TOP PLATES or RAFTER PLATES. CORNER POSTS are enlarged studs, as it were, located at the building corners. In early FULL-FRAME construction a corner post was usually a solid piece of larger timber. In most modern construction BUILT-UP

DOOR SYMBOLS

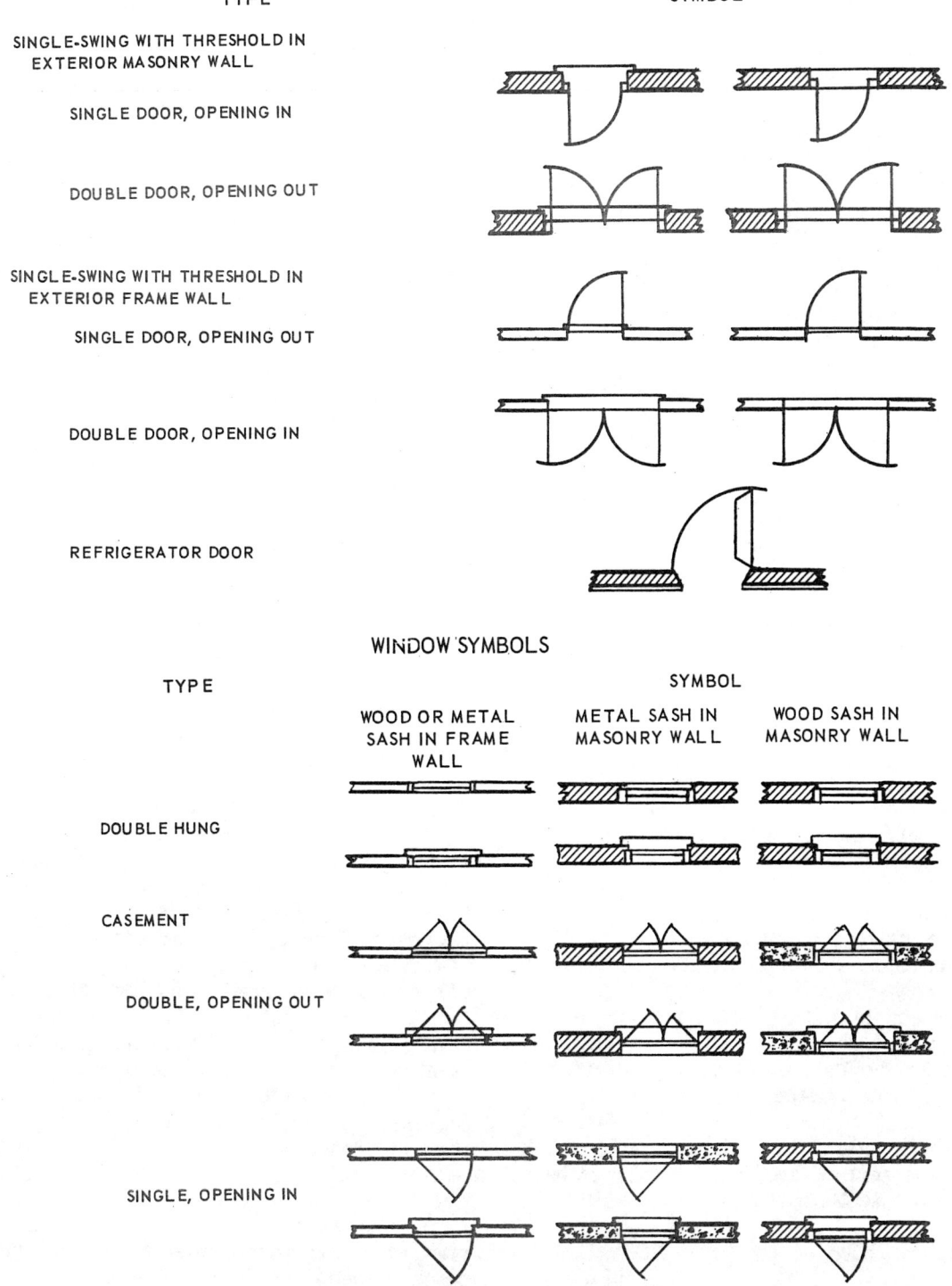

TYPE	SYMBOL
SINGLE-SWING WITH THRESHOLD IN EXTERIOR MASONRY WALL	
SINGLE DOOR, OPENING IN	
DOUBLE DOOR, OPENING OUT	
SINGLE-SWING WITH THRESHOLD IN EXTERIOR FRAME WALL	
SINGLE DOOR, OPENING OUT	
DOUBLE DOOR, OPENING IN	
REFRIGERATOR DOOR	

WINDOW SYMBOLS

TYPE	WOOD OR METAL SASH IN FRAME WALL	METAL SASH IN MASONRY WALL	WOOD SASH IN MASONRY WALL
DOUBLE HUNG			
CASEMENT			
DOUBLE, OPENING OUT			
SINGLE, OPENING IN			

Figure 2 —Architectural symbols (door and windows).

corner posts are used, consisting of various numbers of ordinary studs, nailed together in various ways.

HORIZONTAL STRUCTURAL MEMBERS

In technical terminology, a horizontal load-bearing structural member which spans a space, and which is supported at both ends, is called a BEAM. A member which is FIXED at one end only is called a CANTILEVER. Steel members which consist of solid pieces of the regular structural steel shapes are called beams, but a type of steel member which is actually a light truss is called an OPEN-WEB STEEL JOIST or a BAR STEEL JOIST.

Horizontal structural members which support the ends of floor beams or joists in wood frame construction are called SILLS, GIRTS, or GIRDERS, depending on the type of framing being done and the location of the member in the structure. Horizontal members which support studs are called SILL or SOLE PLATES. Horizontal members which support the wall-ends of rafters are called RAFTER PLATES. Horizontal members which assume the weight of concrete or masonry walls above door and window openings are called LINTELS.

TRUSSES

A beam of given strength, without intermediate supports below, can support a given load over only a certain maximum span. If the span is wider than this maximum, intermediate supports, such as a column must be provided for the beam. Sometimes it is not feasible or possible to install intermediate supports. When such is the case, a TRUSS may be used instead of a beam.

A beam consists of a single horizontal member. A truss, however, is a framework, consisting of two horizontal (or nearly horizontal) members, joined together by a number of vertical and/or inclined members. The horizontal members are called the UPPER and LOWER CHORDS; the vertical and/or inclined members are called the WEB MEMBERS.

ROOF MEMBERS

The horizontal or inclined members which provide support to a roof are called RAFTERS. The lengthwise (right angle to the rafters) member which support the peak ends of the rafters in a roof is called the RIDGE. (The ridge may be called the Ridge board, the Ridge PIECE, or the Ridge pole.) Lengthwise members other than ridges are called PURLINS. In wood frame construction the wall ends of rafters are supported on horizontal members called RAFTER PLATES, which are in turn supported by the outside wall studs. In concrete or masonry wall construction, the wall ends of rafters may be anchored directly on the walls, or on plates bolted to the walls.

II. CONSTRUCTION DRAWINGS

Construction drawings are drawings in which as much construction information as possible is presented GRAPHICALLY, or by means of pictures. Most construction drawings consist of ORTHOGRAPHIC views. GENERAL drawings consist of PLANS AND ELEVATIONS, drawn on a relatively small scale. DETAIL drawings consist of SECTIONS and DETAILS, drawn on a relatively large scale.

PLANS

A PLAN view is, as you know, a view of an object or area as it would appear if projected onto a horizontal plane passed through or held above the object or area. The most common construction plans are PLOT PLANS (also called SITE PLANS), FOUNDATION PLANS, FLOOR PLANS, and FRAMING PLANS.

A PLOT PLAN shows the contours, boundaries, roads, utilities, trees, structures, and any other significant physical features pertaining to or located on the site. The locations of proposed structures are indicated by appropriate outlines or floor plans. By locating the corners of a proposed structure at given distances from a REFERENCE or BASE line (which is shown on the plan and which can be located on the site), the plot plan provides essential data for those who will lay out the building lines. By indicating the elevations of existing and proposed earth surfaces (by means of CONTOUR lines), the plot plan provides essential data for the graders and excavators.

A FOUNDATION PLAN (fig. 3) is a plan view of a structure projected on a horizontal plane passed through (in imagination, of course) at the level of the tops of the foundations. The plan shown in figure 3 tells you that the main foundation of this structure will consist of a rectangular 12-in. concrete block wall, 22 ft

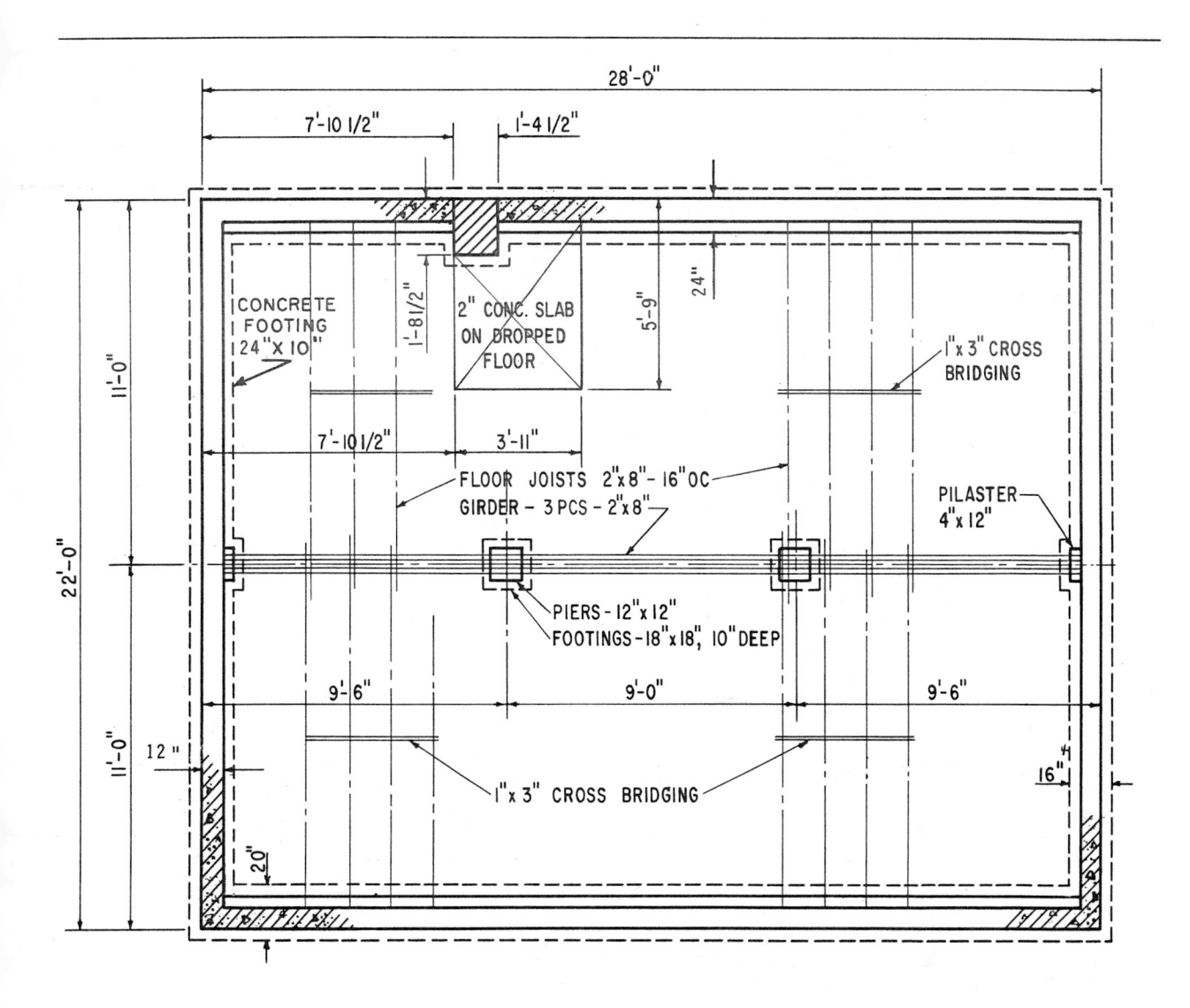

Figure 3.—Foundation plan.

wide by 28 ft long, centered on a concrete footing 24 in. wide. Besides the outside wall and footing, there will be two 12-in. square piers, centered on 18-in. square footings, and located on center 9 ft 6 in. from the end wall building lines. These piers will support a ground floor center-line girder.

A FLOOR PLAN (also called a BUILDING PLAN) is developed as shown in figure 4. Information on a floor plan includes the lengths, thicknesses, and character of the building walls at that particular floor, the widths and locations of door and window openings, the lengths and character of partitions, the number and arrangement of rooms, and the types and locations of utility installations. A typical floor plan is shown in figure 5.

FRAMING PLANS show the dimensions, numbers, and arrangement of structural members in wood frame construction. A simple FLOOR FRAMING PLAN is superimposed on the foundation plan shown in figure 3. From this foundation plan you learn that the ground-floor joists in this structure will consist of 2 x 8's, lapped at the girder, and spaced 16 in. O. C. The plan also shows that each row of joists is to be braced by a row of 1 x 3 cross bridging. For a more complicated floor framing problem, a framing plan like the one shown in figure 2-6 would be required. This plan

PERSPECTIVE VIEW OF A BUILDING SHOWING CUTTING PLANE WXY

PREVIOUS PERSPECTIVE VIEW AT CUTTING PLANE WXYZ, TOP REMOVED

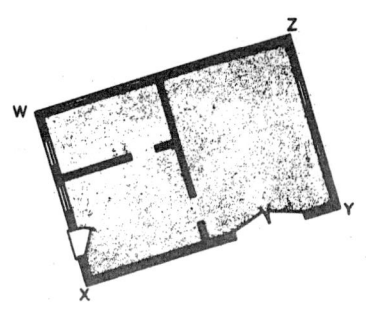

DEVELOPED FLOOR PLAN WXYZ

Figure 4.—Floor plan development.

shows, among other things, the arrangement of joists and other members around stair wells and other floor openings.

A WALL FRAMING PLAN gives similar information with regard to the studs, corner posts, bracing, sills, plates, and other structural members in the walls. Since it is a view on a vertical plane, a wall framing plan is not a plan in the strict technical sense. However, the practice of calling it a plan has become a general custom. A ROOF FRAMING PLAN gives similar information with regard to the rafters, ridge, purlins, and other structural members in the roof.

A UTILITY PLAN is a floor plan which shows the layout of a heating, electrical, plumbing, or other utility system. Utility plans are used primarily by the ratings responsible for the utilities, but they are important to the Builder as well. Most utility installations require the leaving of openings in walls, floors, and roofs for the admission or installation of utility features. The Builder who is placing a concrete foundation wall must study the utility plans to determine the number, sizes, and locations of the openings he must leave for utilities.

Figure 7 shows a heating plan. Figure 8 shows an electrical plan.

ELEVATIONS

ELEVATIONS show the front, rear, and sides of a structure projected on vertical planes parallel to the planes of the sides. Front, rear, right side, and left side elevations of a small building are shown in figure 9.

As you can see, the elevations give you a number of important vertical dimensions, such as the perpendicular distance from the finish floor to the top of the rafter plate and from the finish floor to the tops of door and window finished openings. They also show the locations and characters of doors and windows. Dimensions of window sash and dimensions and character of lintels, however, are usually set forth in a WINDOW SCHEDULE.

A SECTION view is a view of a cross-section, developed as indicated in figure 10. By general custom, the term is confined to views of cross-sections cut by vertical planes. A floor plan or foundation plan, cut by a horizontal plane, is, technically speaking, a section view as well as a plan view, but it is seldom called a section.

The most important sections are the WALL sections. Figure 11 shows three wall sections for three alternate types of construction for the building shown in figures 3, 5, 7 and 8. The angled arrows marked "A" in figure 5 indicate the location of the cutting plane for the sections.

The wall sections are of primary importance to the supervisors of construction and to the craftsmen who will do the actual building. Take the first wall section, marked "masonry construction," for example. Starting at the bottom, you learn that the footing will be concrete, 2 ft wide and 10 in. high. The vertical distance of the bottom of the footing below FINISHED GRADE (level of the finished earth surface around the house) "varies"—meaning that it will depend on the soil-bearing capacity at the particular site. The foundation wall will consist of

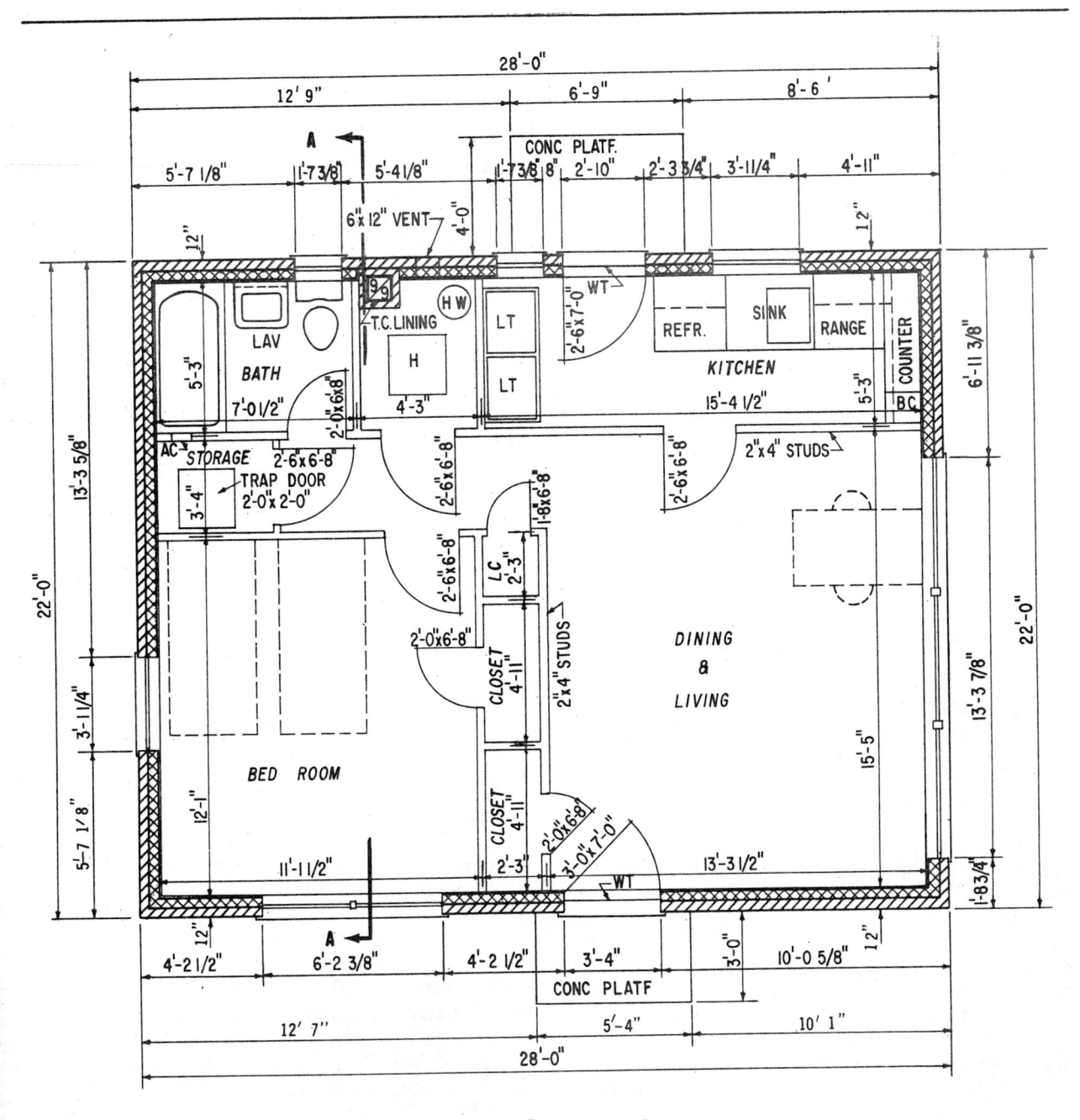

Figure 5.—Floor plan.

12-in. CMU, centered on the footing. Twelve-inch blocks will extend up to an unspecified distance below grade, where a 4-in. brick FACING (dimension indicated in the middle wall section) begins. Above the line of the bottom of the facing, it is obvious that 8-in. instead of 12-in. blocks will be used in the foundation wall.

The building wall above grade will consist of a 4-in. brick FACING TIER, backed by a BACKING TIER of 4-in. cinder blocks. The floor joists, consisting of 2 x 8's placed 16 in. O.C., will be anchored on 2 x 4 sills bolted to the top of the foundation wall. Every third joist will be additionally secured by a 2 x 1/4 STRAP ANCHOR embedded in the cinder block backing tier of the building wall.

The window (window B in the plan front elevation, fig. 9) will have a finished opening

7

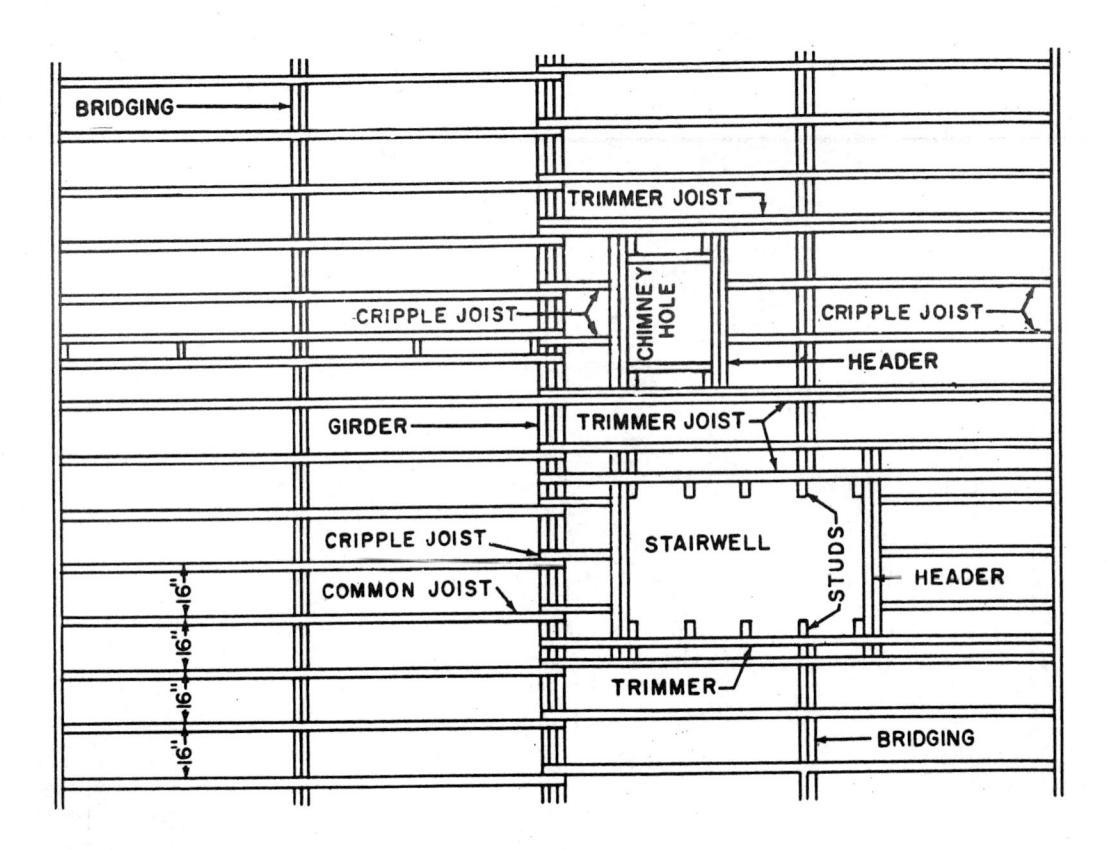

Figure 6.—Floor framing plan.

4 ft 2-5/8 in. high. The bottom of the opening will come 2 ft 11-3/4 in. above the line of the finished floor. As indicated in the wall section, (fig. 11) 13 masonry COURSES (layers of masonry units) above the finished floor line will amount to a vertical distance of 2 ft 11-3/4 in. As also indicated, another 19 courses will amount to the prescribed vertical dimension of the finished window opening.

Window framing details, including the placement and cross-sectional character of the lintel, are shown. The building wall will be carried 10-1/4 in., less the thickness of a 2 x 8 RAFTER PLATE, above the top of the window finished opening. The total vertical distance from the top of the finished floor to the top of the rafter plate will be 8 ft 2-1/4 in. Ceiling joists and rafters will consist of 2 x 6's, and the roof covering will consist of composition shingles laid on wood sheathing.

Flooring will consist of a wood finisher floor laid on a wood subfloor. Inside walls will be finished with plaster on lath (except on masonry wall which would be with or without lath as directed). A minimum of 2 vertical feet of crawl space will extend below the bottoms of the floor joists.

The middle wall section in figure 2-11 gives you similar information for a similar building constructed with wood frame walls and a DOUBLE-HUNG window. The third wall section shown in the figure gives you similar information for a similar building constructed with a steel frame, a casement window, and a concrete floor finished with asphalt tile.

DETAILS

DETAIL drawings are drawings which are done on a larger scale than that of the general drawings, and which show features not appearing at all, or appearing on too small a scale, on the general drawings. The wall sections just described are details as well as sections, since

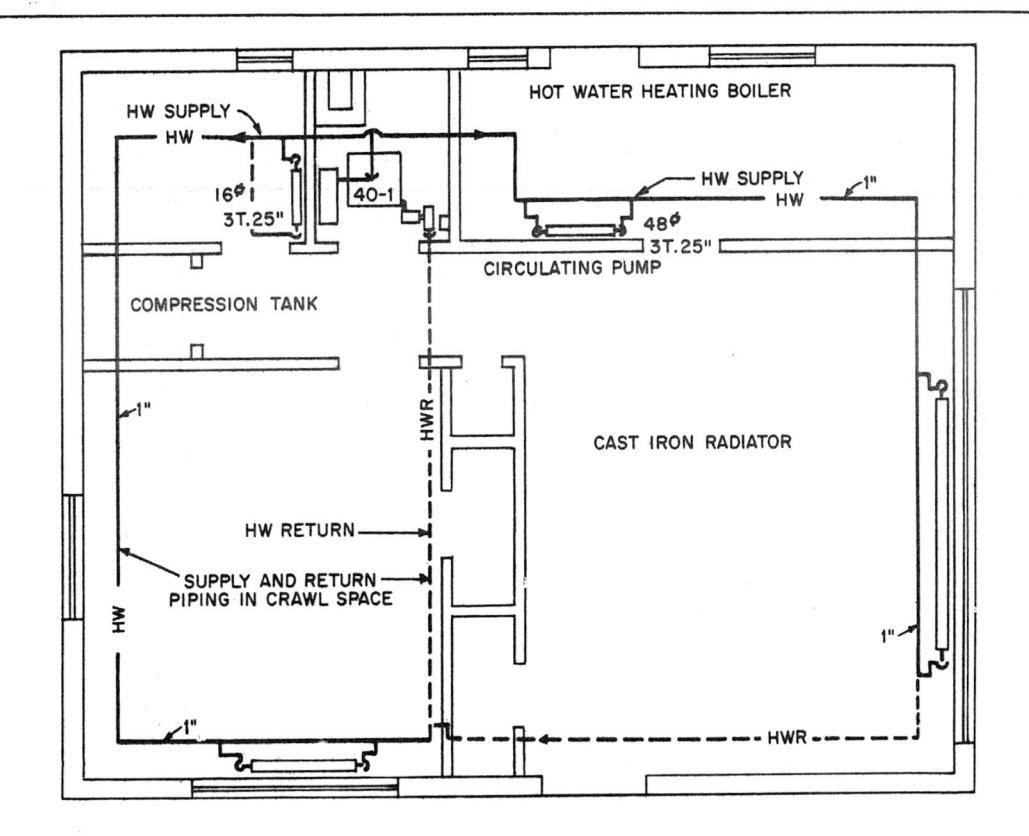

Figure 7.—Heating plan.

they are drawn on a considerable larger scale than the plans and elevations. Framing details at doors, windows, and cornices, which are the most common types of details, are practically always sections.

Details are included whenever the information given in the plans, elevations, and wall sections is not sufficiently "detailed" to guide the craftsmen on the job. Figure 12 shows some typical door and window wood framing details, and an eave detail for a very simple type of CORNICE. You should study these details closely to learn the terminology of framing members.

III. SPECIFICATIONS

The construction drawings contain much of the information about a structure which can be presented GRAPHICALLY (that is, in drawings). A very considerable amount of information can be presented this way, but there is more information which the construction supervisors and artisans must have and which is not adaptable to the graphic form of presentation. Information of this kind includes quality criteria for materials (maximum amounts of aggregate per sack of cement, for example), specified standards of workmanship, prescribed construction methods, and the like.

Information of this kind is presented in a list of written SPECIFICATIONS, familiarly known as the "SPECS." A list of specifications usually begins with a section on GENERAL CONDITIONS. This section starts with a GENERAL DESCRIPTION of the building, including the type of foundation, type or types of windows, character of framing, utilities to be installed, and the like. Next comes a list of DEFINITIONS of terms used in the specs, and next certain routine declarations of responsibility and certain conditions to be maintained on the job.

SPECIFIC CONDITIONS are grouped in sections under headings which describe each of the major construction phases of the job. Separate specifications are written for each phase, and the phases are then combined to more or less follow the usual order of construction sequences on the job. A typical list of sections under "Specific Conditions" follows:

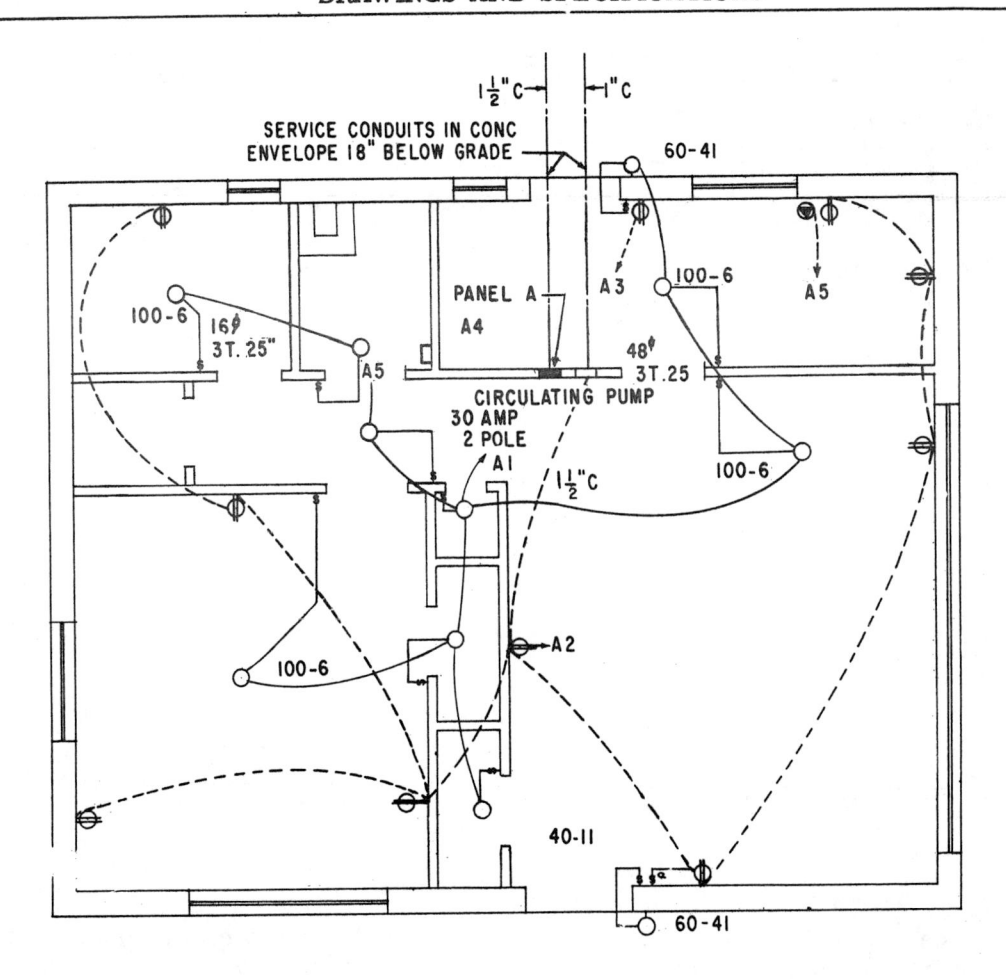

Figure 8.—Electrical plan.

2.—EARTHWORK 3.—CONCRETE 4.—MASONRY 5.—MISCELLANEOUS STEEL AND IRON 6.—CARPENTRY AND JOINERY 7.—LATHING AND PLASTERING 8.—TILE WORK 9.—FINISH FLOORING 10.—GLAZING 11.—FINISHING HARDWARE 12.—PLUMBING 13.—HEATING 14.—ELECTRICAL WORK 15.—FIELD PAINTING.

A section under "Specific Conditions" usually begins with a subsection of GENERAL REQUIREMENTS which apply to the phase of construction being considered. Under Section 6, CARPENTRY AND JOINERY, for example, the first section might go as follows:

6-01. GENERAL REQUIREMENTS. All framing, rough carpentry, and finishing woodwork required for the proper completion of the building shall be provided. All woodwork shall be protected from the weather, and the building shall be thoroughly dry before the finish is placed. All finish shall be dressed, smoothed, and sandpapered at the mill, and in addition shall be hand smoothed and sandpapered at the building where necessary to produce proper finish. Nailing shall be done, as far as practicable, in concealed places, and all nails in finishing work shall be set. All lumber shall be S4S (meaning, "surfaced on 4 sides"); all materials for millwork and finish shall be kiln-dried; all rough and framing lumber shall be air- or kiln-dried. Any cutting, fitting, framing, and blocking necessary for the accommodation of other work shall be provided. All nails, spikes, screws, bolts, plates, clips, and other fastenings and rough hardware necessary for the proper completion of the building shall be provided.

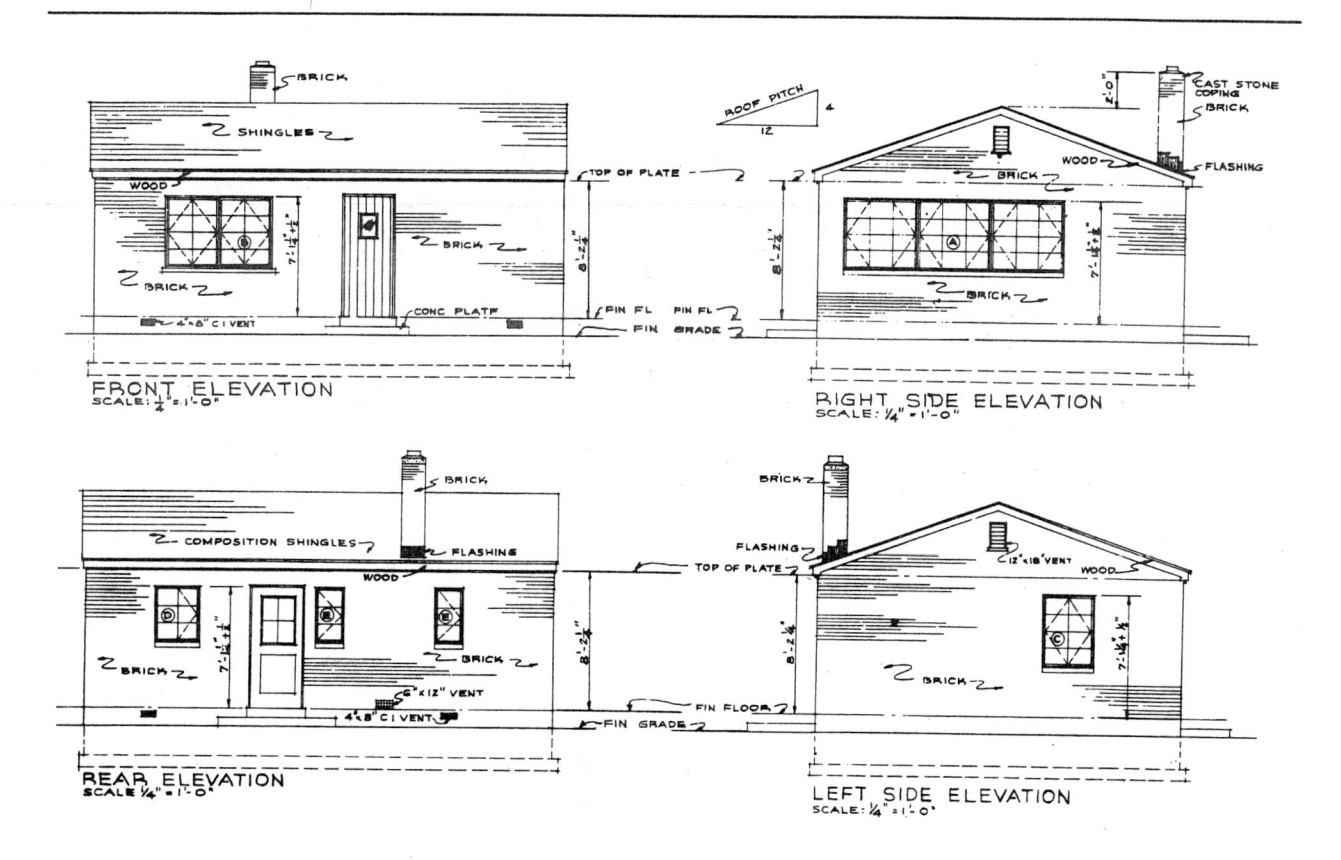

Figure 2-9.—Elevations.

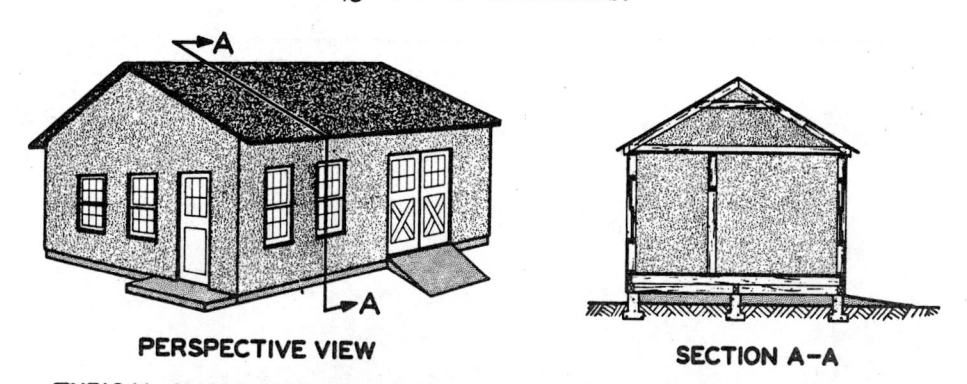

Figure 10.—Development of a section view.

All finishing hardware shall be installed in accordance with the manufacturers' directions. Calking and flashing shall be provided where indicated, or where necessary to provide weathertight construction.

Next after the General Requirements for Carpentry and Joinery, there is generally a subsection on "Grading," in which the kinds and grades of the various woods to be used in the structure are specified. Subsequent subsections

DRAWINGS AND SPECIFICATIONS

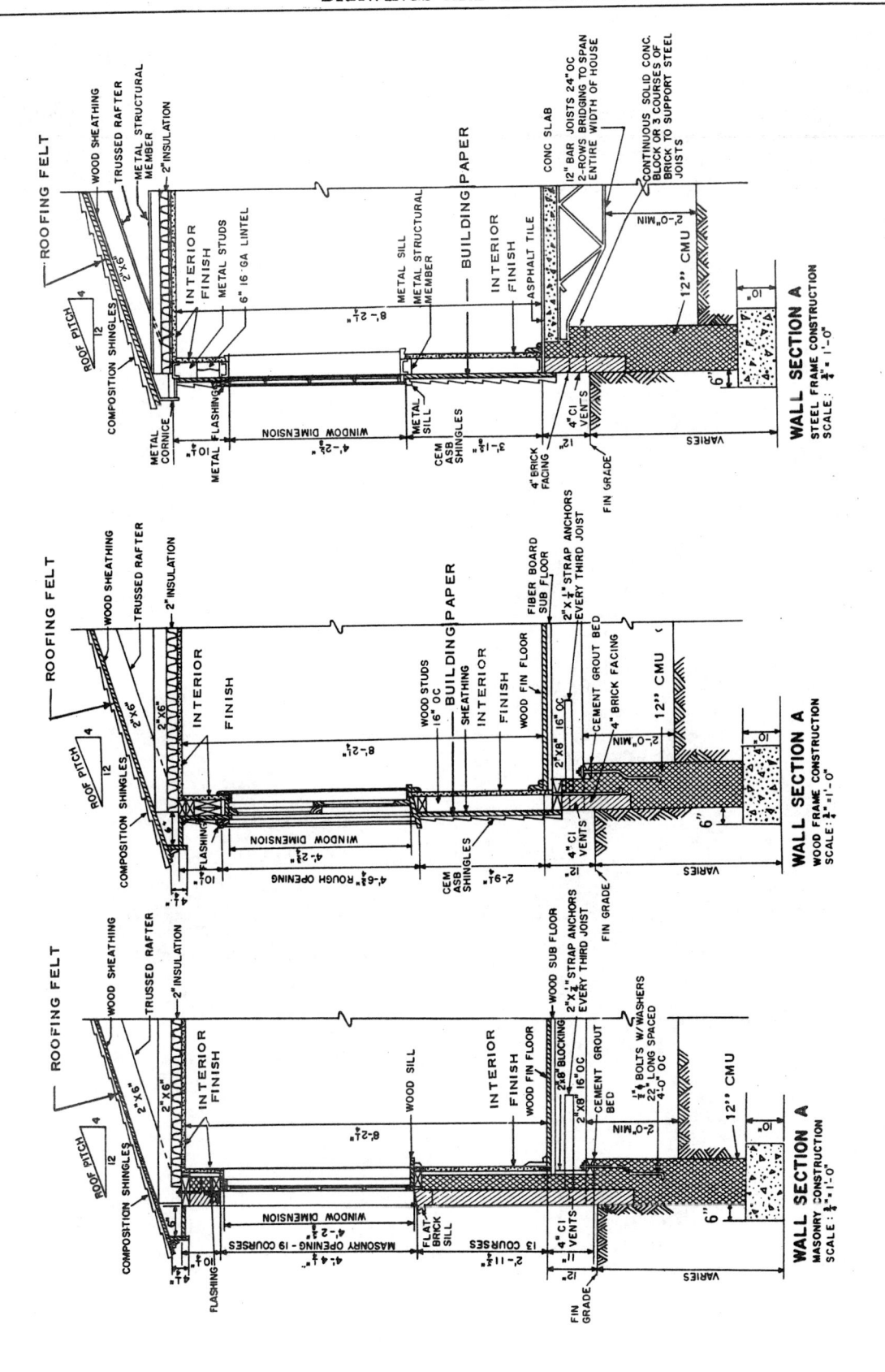

Figure 11.—Wall sections

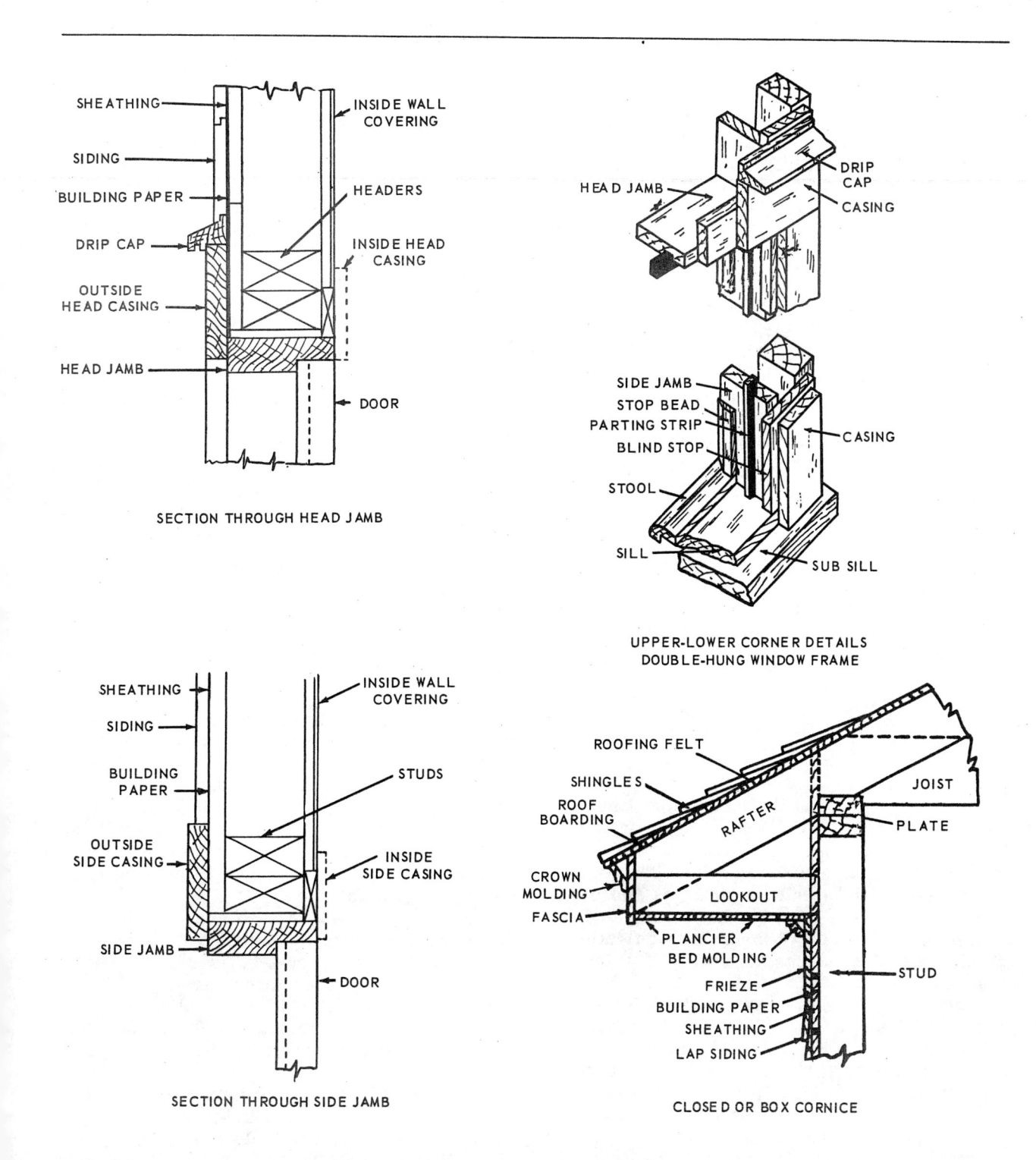

Figure 12.—Door, window and eave details.

DRAWINGS AND SPECIFICATIONS

specify various quality criteria and standards of workmanship for the various aspects of the rough and finish carpentry work, under such headings as FRAMING; SILLS, PLATES, AND GIRDERS; FLOOR JOISTS AND ROOF RAFTERS; STUDDING; and so on. An example of one of these subsections follows:

STUDDING for walls and partitions shall have doubled plates and doubled stud caps. Studs shall be set plumb and not to exceed 16-in. centers and in true alignment; they shall be bridged with one row of 2 x 4 pieces, set flatwise, fitted tightly, and nailed securely to each stud. Studding shall be doubled around openings and the heads of openings shall rest on the inner studs. Openings in partitions having widths of 4 ft and over shall be trussed. In wood frame construction, studs shall be trebled at corners to form posts.

From the above samples, you can see that a knowledge of the relevant specifications is as essential to the construction supervisor and the construction artisan as a knowledge of the construction drawings.

It is very important that the proper spec be used to cover the material requested. In cases in which the material is not covered by a Government spec, the ASTM (American Society for Testing Materials) spec or some other approved commercial spec may be used. It is EXTREMELY IMPORTANT in using specifications to cite all amendments, including the latest changes.

As a rule, the specs are provided for each project by the A/E (ARCHITECT-ENGINEERS). These are the OFFICIAL guidelines approved by the chief engineer or his representative for use during construction. These requirements should NOT be deviated from without prior approval from proper authority. This approval is usually obtained by means of a change order. When there is disagreement between the specifications and drawings, the specifications should normally be followed; however, check with higher authority in each case.

IV. BUILDER'S MATHEMATICS

The Builder has many occasions for the employment of the processes of ordinary arithmetic, and he must be thoroughly familiar with the methods of determining the areas and volumes of the various plane and solid geometrical figures. Only a few practical applications and a few practical suggestions, will be given here.

RATIO AND PROPORTION

There are a great many practical applications of ratio and proportion in the construction field. A few examples are as follows:

Some dimensions on construction drawings (such as, for example, distances from base lines and elevations of surfaces) are given in ENGINEER'S instead of CARPENTER's measure. Engineer's measure is measure in feet and decimal parts of a foot, or in inches and decimal parts of an inch, such as 100.15 ft or 11.14 in. Carpenter's measure is measure in yards, feet, inches, and even-denominator fractions of an inch, such as 1/2 in., 1/4 in., 1/16 in., 1/32 in., and 1/64 in.

You must know how to convert an engineer's measure given on a construction drawing to a carpenter's measure. Besides this, it will often happen that calculations you make yourself may produce a result in feet and decimal parts of a foot, which result you will have to convert to carpenter's measure. To convert engineer's to carpenter's measure you can use ratio and proportion as follows:

Let's say that you want to convert 100.14 ft to feet and inches to the nearest 1/16 in. The 100 you don't need to convert, since it is already in feet. What you need to do, first, is to find out how many twelfths of a foot (that is, how many inches) there are in 14/100 ft. Set this up as a proportional equation as follows: x:12::14:100.

You know that in a proportional equation the product of the means equals the product of the extremes. Consequently, 100x = (12 x 14), or 168. Then x = 168/100, or 1.68 in. Next question is, how many 16ths of an in. are there in 68/100 in.? Set this up, too, as a proportional equation, thus: x:16::68:100. Then 100x = 1088, and x = 10 88/100 sixteenths. Since 88/100 of a sixteenth is more than one-half of a sixteenth,

14

you ROUND OFF by calling it 11/16. In 100.14 ft, then, there are 100 ft 1 11/16 in. For example:

A. $\underbrace{x:12::\overbrace{14:100}^{\text{means}}}_{\text{Extremes}}$

Product of extremes = product of means:

$$100x = 168$$
$$x = 1.68 \text{ IN.}$$

B. $x:16::68:100$

$$100x = 1088$$
$$x = 10.88$$
$$x = 10\frac{88}{100} \text{ sixteenths}$$

Rounded off to 11/16

Another way to convert engineer's measurements to carpenter's measurements is to multiply the decimal portion of a foot by 12 to get inches; multiply the decimal by 16 to get the fraction of an inch.

There are many other practical applications of ratio and proportion in the construction field. Suppose, for example, that a table tells you that, for the size and type of brick wall you happen to be laying, 12,321 bricks and 195 cu ft of mortar are required per every 1000 sq ft of wall. How many bricks and how much mortar will be needed for 750 sq ft of the same wall? You simply set up equations as follows; for example:

Brick: $x:750::12,321:1000$
Mortar: $x:750::195:1000$

Brick: $\frac{X}{750} = \frac{12,321}{1000}$ Cross multiply

$$1000X = 9,240,750 \quad \text{Divide}$$
$$X = 9,240.75 = 9241 \text{ Brick.}$$

Mortar: $\frac{X}{750} = \frac{195}{1000}$ Cross multiply

$$1000X = 146,250 \quad \text{Divide}$$
$$X = 146.25 = 146\ 1/4 \text{ cu ft}$$

Suppose, for another example, that the ingredient proportions by volume for the type of concrete you are making are 1 cu ft cement to 1.7 cu ft sand to 2.8 cu ft coarse aggregate. Suppose you know as well, by reference to a table, that ingredients combined in the amounts indicated will produce 4.07 cu ft of concrete. How much of each ingredient will be required to make a cu yd of concrete?

Remember here, first, that there are not 9, but 27 (3 ft x 3 ft x 3 ft) cu ft in a cu yd. Your proportional equations will be as follows:

Cement: $x:27::1:4.07$

Sand: $x:27::1.7:4.07$

Coarse aggregate: $x:27::2.8:4.07$

Cement: $x:27::1:4.07$

$$\frac{x}{27} = \frac{1}{4.07}$$
$$4.07x = 27$$
$$x = 6.63 \text{ cu ft Cement}$$

Sand: $x:27::1.7:4.07$

$$\frac{x}{27} = \frac{1.7}{4.07}$$
$$4.07x = 45.9$$
$$x = 11.28 \text{ cu ft Sand}$$

Coarse aggregate: $x:27::2.8:407$

$$\frac{x}{27} = \frac{2.8}{4.07}$$
$$4.07x = 75.6$$
$$x = 18.57 \text{ cu ft Coarse aggregate}$$

ARITHMETICAL OPERATIONS

The formulas for finding the area and volume of geometric figures are expressed in algebraic equations which are called formulas. A few of the more important formulas and their mathematical solutions will be discussed in this section.

DRAWINGS AND SPECIFICATIONS

To get an area, you multiply 2 linear measures together, and to get a volume you multiply 3 linear measures together. The linear measures you multiply together must all be expressed in the SAME UNITS; you cannot, for example, multiply a length in feet by a width in inches to get a result in square feet or in square inches.

Dimensions of a feature on a construction drawing are not always given in the same units. For a concrete wall, for example, the length and height are usually given in feet and the thickness in inches. Furthermore, you may want to get a result in units which are different from any shown on the drawing. Concrete volume, for example, is usually expressed in cubic yards, while the dimensions of concrete work are given on the drawings in feet and inches.

You can save yourself a good many steps in calculating by using fractions to convert the original dimension units into the desired end-result units. Take 1 in., for example. To express 1 in. in feet, you simply put it over 12, thus: 1/12 ft. To express 1 in. in yards, you simply put it over 36, thus: 1/36 yd. In the same manner, to express 1 ft in yards you simply put it over 3, thus 1/3 yd.

Suppose now that you want to calculate the number of cu yd of concrete in a wall 32 ft long by 14 ft high by 8 in. thick. You can express all these in yards and set up your problem thus:

$$\frac{32}{3} \times \frac{14}{3} \times \frac{8}{36}$$

Next you can cancel out, thus:

$$\frac{32}{3} \times \frac{14}{3} \times \frac{8}{36} = \frac{896}{81}$$

Dividing 896 by 81, you get 11.06 cu yds of concrete in the wall.

The right triangle is a triangle which contains one right (90°) angle. The following letters will denote the parts of the triangle indicated in figure 2-13—a = altitude, b = base, c = hypotenuse.

In solving a right triangle, the length of any side may be found if the lengths of the other two sides are given. The combinations of 3-4-5 (lengths of sides) or any multiple of these combinations will come out to a whole number. The following examples show the formula for finding

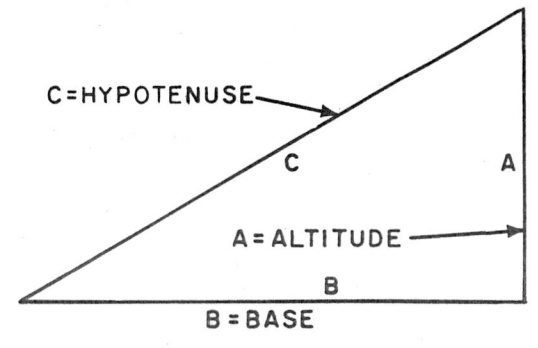

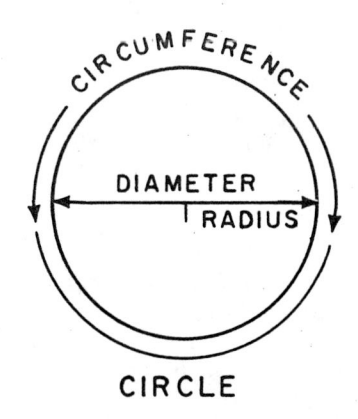

Figure 13.—Right triangle and circle.

each side. Each of these formulas is derived from the master formula $c^2 = a^2 + b^2$.

(1) Find c when a = 3, and b = 4.

$$c = \sqrt{a^2 + b^2} = \sqrt{3^2 + 4^2} = \sqrt{9 + 16} = \sqrt{25} = 5$$

(2) Find a when b = 8, and c = 10.

$$a = \sqrt{c^2 - b^2} = \sqrt{10^2 - 8^2} = \sqrt{100 - 64} = \sqrt{36} = 6$$

(3) Find b when a = 9, and c = 15.

$$b = \sqrt{c^2 - a^2} = \sqrt{15^2 - 9^2} = \sqrt{225 - 81} = \sqrt{144} = 12.$$

There are tables from which the square roots of numbers may be found; otherwise, they may be found arithmetically as explained later in this chapter.

Areas And Volumes Of
Geometric Figures

This section on areas and volumes of geometric figures will be limited to the most commonly used geometric figures. Reference books, such as Mathematics, Vol. 1, are available for additional information if needed. Areas are expressed in square units and volumes in cubic units.

1. A circle is a plane figure bounded by a curved line every point of which is the same distance from the center.
   a. The curved line is called the circumference.
   b. A straight line drawn from the center to any point on the circumference is called a radius. (r = 1/2 the diameter.)
   c. A straight line drawn from one point of the circumference through the center and terminating on the opposite point of the circumference is called a diameter. (d = 2 times the radius.) See figure 2-13.
   d. The area of a circle is found by the following formulas: $A = \pi r^2$ or $A = .7854 d^2$. (π is pronounced pie = 3.1416 or 3 1/7, .7854 is 1/4 of π.) Example: Find the area of a circle whose radius is 7". $A = \pi r^2 = 3\ 1/7 \times 7^2 = 22/7 \times 49 = 154$ sq in. If you use the second formula you obtain the same results.
   e. The circumference of a circle is found by multiplying π times the diameter or 2 times π times the radius. Example: Find the circumference of a circle whose diameter is 56 inches. $C = \pi d = 3.1415 \times 56 = 175.9296$ inches.

2. The area of a right triangle is equal to one-half the product of the base by the altitude. (Area = 1/2 base x altitude.) Example: Find the area of a triangle whose base is 16" and altitude 6". Solution:

$$A = 1/2\ bh = 1/2 \times 16 \times 6 = 48 \text{ sq in.}$$

3. The volume of a cylinder is found by multiplying the area of the base times the height. ($V = 3.1416 \times r^2 \times h$). Example: Find the volume of a cylinder which has a radius of 8 in. and a height of 4 ft. Solution:

$$8 \text{ in} = \frac{2}{3} \text{ ft and } \left(\frac{2}{3}\right)^2 = \frac{4}{9} \text{ sq ft.}$$

$$V = 3.1416 \times \frac{4}{9} \times 4 = \frac{50.2656}{9} = 5.59 \text{ cu ft.}$$

4. The volume of a rectangular solid equals the length x width x height. (V = lwh.) Example: Find the volume of a rectangular solid which has a length of 6 ft, a width of 3 ft, and a height of 2 ft. Solution:

$$V = lwh = 6 \times 3 \times 2 = 36 \text{ cu ft.}$$

5. The volume of a cone may be found by multiplying one-third times the area of the base times the height.

$$\left(V = \frac{1}{3} \pi r^2 h\right)$$

Example: Find the volume of a cone when the radius of its base is 2 ft and its height is 9 ft. Solution:

$$\pi = 3.1416,\ r = 2,\ 2^2 = 4$$
$$V = \frac{1}{3} r^2 h = \frac{1}{3} \times 3.1416 \times 4 \times 9 = 37.70 \text{ cu ft.}$$

Powers And Roots

1. Powers—When we multiply several numbers together, as 2 x 3 x 4 = 24, the numbers 2, 3, and 4 are factors and 24 the product. The operation of raising a number to a power is a special case of multiplication in which the factors are all equal. The power of a number is the number of times the number itself is to be taken as a factor. Example: 2^4 is 16. The second power is called the square of the number, as 3^2. The third power of a number is called the cube of the number, as 5^3. The exponent of a number is a number placed to the right and above a base to show how many times the base is used as a factor. Example:

4^3 ← exponent =
← base

$$4 \times 4 \times 4 = 64.$$

2. Roots—To indicate a root, use the sign $\sqrt{\ }$, which is called the radical sign. A small figure, called the index of the root, is placed in the opening of the sign to show which root is to be taken. The square root of a number is one of the two equal factors into which a number is

DRAWINGS AND SPECIFICATIONS

divided. Example: $\sqrt{81} = \sqrt{9 \times 9} = 9$. The cube root is one of the three equal factors into which a number is divided. Example: $\sqrt[3]{125} = \sqrt[3]{5 \times 5 \times 5} = 5$.

Square Root

1. The square root of any number is that number which, when multiplied by itself, will produce the first number. For example; the square root of 121 is 11 because 11 times 11 equals 121.

2. How to extract the square root arithmetically:

$$\sqrt{9025} \quad \sqrt{90'25.} = 95.$$

$$: -81$$

$$180 : 925$$
$$+5 : -925$$

$$185 : 000$$

a. Begin at the decimal point and divide the given number into groups of 2 digits each (as far as possible), going from right to left and/or left to right.
b. Find the greatest number (9) whose square is contained in the first or left hand group (90). Square this number (9) and place it under the first pair of digits (90), then subtract.
c. Bring down the next pair of digits (25) and add it to the remainder (9).
d. Multiply the first digit in the root by 20 and use it as a trial divisor (180). This trial divisor (180) will go into the new dividend (925) five times. This number, 5 (second digit in the root), is added back to the trial divisor, obtaining the true divisor (185).
e. The true divisor (185) is multiplied by the second digit (5) and placed under the remainder (925). Subtract and the problem is solved.
f. If there is still a remainder and you want to carry the problem further, add zeros (in pairs) and continue the above process.

Coverage Calculations

You will frequently have occasion to estimate the number of linear feet of boards of a given size, or the number of tiles, asbestos shingles, and the like, required to cover a given area. Let's take the matter of linear feet of boards first.

What you do here is calculate, first, the number of linear feet of board required to cover 1 sq ft. For boards laid edge-to-edge, you base your calculations on the total width of a board. For boards which will lap each other, you base your calculations on the width laid TO THE WEATHER, meaning the total width minus the width of the lap.

Since there are 144 sq in. in a sq ft, linear footage to cover a given area can be calculated as follows. Suppose your boards are to be laid 8 in. to the weather. If you divide 8 in. into 144 sq in., the result (which is 18 in., or 1.5 ft) will be the linear footage required to cover a sq ft. If you have, say, 100 sq ft to cover, the linear footage required will be 100 x 1.5, or 150 ft.

To estimate the number of tiles, asbestos shingles, and the like required to cover a given area, you first calculate the number of units required to cover a sq ft. Suppose, for example, you are dealing with 9 in. x 9 in. asphalt tiles. The area of one of these is 9 in. x 9 in. or 81 sq in. In a sq ft there are 144 sq in. If it takes 1 to cover 81 sq in., how many will it take to cover 144 sq in.? Just set up a proportional equation, as follows.

$$1:81::x:144$$

When you work this out, you will find that it takes 1.77 tiles to cover a sq ft. To find the number of tiles required to cover 100 sq ft, simply multiply by 100. How do you multiply anything by 100? Just move the decimal point 2 places to the right. Consequently, it takes 177 9 x 9 asphalt tiles to cover 100 sq ft of area.

Board Measure

BOARD MEASURE is a method of measuring lumber in which the basic unit is an abstract volume 1 ft long by 1 ft wide by 1 in. thick. This abstract volume or unit is called a BOARD FOOT.

There are several formulas for calculating the number of board feet in a piece of given dimensions. Since lumber dimensions are most frequently indicated by width and thickness in inches and length in feet, the following formula is probably the most practical.

$$\frac{\text{Thickness in in.} \times \text{width in in.} \times \text{length in ft}}{12}$$

= board feet

Suppose you are calculating the number of board feet in a 14-ft length of 2 x 4. Applying the formula, you get:

$$\frac{\overset{1}{\cancel{2}} \times \overset{2}{\cancel{4}} \times 14}{\underset{\underset{3}{\cancel{6}}}{\cancel{12}}} = \frac{28}{3} = 9\ 1/3\ \text{bd ft}$$

The chief practical use of board measure is in cost calculations, since lumber is bought and sold by the board foot. Any lumber less than 1 in. thick is presumed to be 1 in. thick for board measure purposes. Board measure is calculated on the basis of the NOMINAL, not the ACTUAL, dimensions of lumber.

The actual size of a piece of dimension lumber (such as a 2 x 4, for example) is usually less than the nominal size.

ANSWER SHEET   JUL - - 2017

TEST NO. _____ PART ____ TITLE OF POSITION _____
(AS GIVEN IN EXAMINATION ANNOUNCEMENT - INCLUDE OPTION, IF ANY)

PLACE OF EXAMINATION _____ DATE _____
(CITY OR TOWN)   (STATE)

RATING

USE THE SPECIAL PENCIL. MAKE GLOSSY BLACK MARKS.

Make only ONE mark for each answer. Additional and stray marks may be counted as mistakes. In making corrections, erase errors COMPLETELY.